ADVANCE PRAISE FOR
FREAKS, GLEEKS, AND DAWSON'S CREEK

"As addicting as an afternoon bingeing your favorite TV show. In this book, Thea Glassman has written the definitive text on the teen shows that defined our popular culture. Insightful, smart, delightful. A must-read for all pop culture devotees."

—DANA SCHWARTZ, NEW YORK TIMES BESTSELLING AUTHOR OF ANATOMY: A LOVE STORY

"*Freaks, Gleeks, and Dawson's Creek* is as sharp, clever, and full of heart as the seven iconic TV shows Thea Glassman so eloquently writes about within these pages. Thea takes us on a lovely behind-the-scenes tour of a glorious bygone era, when TV was a slow, seasonal burn, characters were old familiar friends, and their relationships something to live and die for."

—TOM KAPINOS, SHOWRUNNER AND EXECUTIVE PRODUCER OF DAWSON'S CREEK

"Thea Glassman has done her homework—I'm happy to be included in this fun and informative book."

—WINNIE HOLZMAN, CREATOR OF MY SO-CALLED LIFE

"Clear your schedule and cancel your evening plans: I stayed up all night reading Thea Glassman's smart, insightful, funny book like it was the notes for tomorrow's trig test I had forgotten to study for. This book is the perfect read for anyone who ever fell in love with a TV show about adolescence that felt like it spoke just to you, be it *My So-Called Life* or *Freaks and Geeks* or *Friday Night Lights*. *Freaks, Gleeks, and Dawson's Creek* is a book to savor, whether you are in high school, remember high school fondly, or wish you didn't remember it at all."

—SAUL AUSTERLITZ, AUTHOR OF GENERATION FRIENDS

"Thea Glassman has served up a lively inside look at the making of the shows that spoke to the modern teenage experience in groundbreaking ways. Full of heart, drama, and delicious insight, *Freaks, Gleeks, and Dawson's Creek* is a must-read for anyone who swooned over Riggins, who identified with Angela Chase or Seth Cohen or the New Directions, and who laughed and cried watching The Fresh Prince of Bel-Air. Reading this book felt like watching my favorites all over again—I shed nostalgic tears!"

—ERIN CARLSON, AUTHOR OF I'LL HAVE WHAT SHE'S HAVING AND QUEEN MERYL

"*Freaks, Gleeks, and Dawson's Creek* is compulsively readable, teeming with insights into what made our favorite teen shows some of television's most influential series. Reading this book is like dishing with a good friend who loves TV as much as you do—except that Thea Glassman has taken the extra step of speaking to the creatives who made these shows so impactful. A delightful and informative read from beginning to end, it deserves a spot on every TV fan's bookshelf."

—KIRTHANA RAMISETTI, AUTHOR OF *GOOD MORNING AMERICA'S* PICK
DAVA SHASTRI'S LAST DAY

"If you're someone who pauses TV shows to say 'Did you know that . . . ' then this book is definitely for you, with some of the best behind-the-scenes stories for your trivia arsenal. *Freaks, Gleeks, and Dawson's Creek* is an insightful history of how today's television came to be and is chock-full of interviews with the people who were actually there. I'd say I couldn't put this book down, but it's so nostalgic that I had to pause after every chapter to watch the shows again!"

—EM SCHULZ, *NEW YORK TIMES* BESTSELLING AUTHOR OF *A HAUNTED ROAD ATLAS*
AND HOST OF THE PODCAST *AND THAT'S WHY WE DRINK*

Freaks, Gleeks, and Dawson's Creek

How Seven Teen Shows Transformed Television

Thea Glassman

RUNNING PRESS

PHILADELPHIA

Running Press
Hachette Book Group
1290 Avenue of the Americas, New York, NY 10104
www.runningpress.com
@Running_Press

Printed in the United States of America

First Edition: June 2023

Published by Running Press, an imprint of Perseus Books, LLC, a subsidiary of Hachette Book Group, Inc. The Running Press name and logo are trademarks of the Hachette Book Group.

The Hachette Speakers Bureau provides a wide range of authors for speaking events. To find out more, go to www.hachettespeakersbureau.com or email HachetteSpeakers@hbgusa.com.

Running Press books may be purchased in bulk for business, educational, or promotional use. For more information, please contact your local bookseller or the Hachette Book Group Special Markets Department at Special.Markets@hbgusa.com.

The publisher is not responsible for websites (or their content) that are not owned by the publisher.

Print book cover and interior design by Tanvi Baghele.

Library of Congress Cataloging-in-Publication Data has been applied for.
Library of Congress Control Number: 2023930514

ISBNs: 978-0-7624-8076-0 (hardcover), 978-0-7624-8077-7 (ebook)

LSC-C

Printing 1, 2023

To Mom, Dad, and Kira with love

A Note on
REPORTING

This book features original interviews with the cast, crew, writers, and creatives behind each of the seven shows featured. I've listed every person who spoke to me in the Acknowledgments. When I didn't have interview access to individuals, I supplemented with archival sourcing, which can be found in the References section in the back of the book.

CONTENTS

FOREWORD

Jennifer Keishin Armstrong

When Thea Glassman told me she was writing a book about teen television, I was jealous. As jealous as Dawson finding out Joey slept with Pacey.

Okay, I take it back, it wasn't that dramatic—*what could possibly be?*—but the fact is that I have always loved teen shows. What a delicious subject to immerse yourself in! I am a TV historian who's written several books on sitcoms like *Seinfeld* and *Sex and the City,* but nothing stirs my heart like a great teen drama. Ever since Brandon and Brenda Walsh moved to Beverly Hills, back when I was still a teenager, too, I've been smitten. There is no drama like a teenage drama, in life and in fiction. There is nothing more relatable and satisfying than watching young people flail through young adulthood, where the stakes are as emotionally high as possible but come with, for the most part, a built-in safety net. As adults, we know: these kinds of moments *feel* like everything, but they're almost always a mere blip in the grand scheme of life. That doesn't make them any less emotional in the moment.

Teen television is at once escapist and quite serious. They have always pushed boundaries, able to take risks because of their young audiences when bigger, more stodgy programs couldn't. *Dawson's Creek* gave us the first "passionate," as we say, kiss between two male characters on television in 2000, while *Modern Family* took flak a decade-plus later for the hands-off nature of its central married gay couple. Young audiences have always demanded progressiveness in their programming, pushing television further earlier in terms of diversity and sensitivity; look at ABC Family's shows in the 2000s or the immortal *Degrassi* franchise, and you'll see a remarkable variety of races and sexualities depicted far earlier than mainstream, grown-up TV got with the program.

More recently, teen shows like *Never Have I Ever* and *Sex Education* have gone sex-positive, LGBTQ-affirming, and gender-respecting in ways that would blow Brandon and Brenda's '90s minds. There's a remarkable level of sweetness and comfort present in both these shows alongside plotlines about girls with voracious sexual desire, for instance, or a choir performance of Peaches' "Fuck the Pain Away" that gives a person hope that we have a real shot at a less-repressed, more-accepting future.

Yet teen TV is routinely dismissed in conversations about serious television. They've rarely gotten serious awards consideration until recently (and even that goes mostly to HBO's awards-baiting *Euphoria*). Granted, not every one of the teen shows of the past, riveting as they were, could compete with *The Sopranos* and *Mad Men*, or *ER* and *NYPD Blue* back in the day. But that singular, beautiful season of *Freaks and Geeks* is absolutely a work of art, the result of a clear vision, excellent writing, superb dialogue, and a precarious balance between comedy and poignancy. Furthermore, it's my contention that there should be a special Emmy for spectacular pilot episodes, and I'd give a legacy award to *The O.C.*, so well-acted and perfectly constructed that I personally watched it a good ten times—when I was twenty-eight. In fact, the first half of its first season actually was Emmy material in the most traditional way, an innovative blend of drama and comedy with a heavy dose of self-awareness that broke ground in its time. (Alas, the arrival of the show-hijacking character of Oliver shattered the perfection. If you were there, you remember the sheer pain of Oliver and his wretched gun, which tipped into melodramatic territory in the worst way. I will never forgive Oliver.)

Friday Night Lights did snag some Emmy nominations, and even a win, as well as plenty of critical love—though I would argue that its focus on the coach helped it be seen as "more" than a teen drama. White, middle-aged men with problems equal prestige! But that's just the point: young people's problems should be taken seriously on their face. Yet it's always a struggle to gain respect for anything for and about those with less power—women, people of color, and teens. Like boy bands, these shows are for teen girls, and therefore they'll always have to fight to be taken seriously, even if they come up with something as transcendent as "I Want It That Way."

This book will, of course, tug on your nostalgia strings, and there's nothing wrong with that. But it will also help you see these youthful loves anew, the way reading an old diary might give you a new appreciation of that sweet, smart boy in English class whom you really should have given more of a chance.

You will learn how an overdue tax bill led to the creation of *The Fresh Prince of Bel-Air,* how *My So-Called Life* proved the power of teen girls (with a serious assist from the phenomenon that was *thirtysomething*), and what Jim Belushi has to do with Pacey Witter. *Freaks, Gleeks, and Dawson's Creek* takes readers on an intimate journey behind the dreams, hopes, coincidences, loves, and losses that led to some of the greatest teen dramas of our time. Thank goodness *Freaks and Geeks* creator Paul Feig got written out of *Sabrina the Teenage Witch* and watched *Felicity* to soothe his weary soul. And thank goodness for Steven Spielberg, such a gravitational force for aspiring young filmmakers growing up in the '80s that he could get a co-creator credit on, at minimum, *Dawson's Creek* and *The O.C.* Like your favorite teen dramas, you'll want to binge the entire book as fast as possible—and yet you'll be very sad when it's over. And you'll be better equipped than ever to argue the timeless importance of the teen drama with the next guy at a party who tries to tell you *The Wire* is the only good thing to come out of television.

Even Shakespeare understood the fundamental power of teen drama. Ask anyone to name his most memorable work, and there's a good chance you'll hear the names of two tragic teenagers. Perhaps he'd appreciate Ryan and Marissa as much as we do.

—Jennifer Keishin Armstrong
New York Times bestselling author of *Seinfeldia* and *Sex and the City and Us*
New Paltz, New York
JenniferKArmstrong.com

INTRODUCTION

D o you remember the first TV show you really, truly loved as a teen? Mine was *Dawson's Creek*. I rented DVD after DVD and spent my whole summer break after freshman year of high school watching every season, long after my eyes were alarmingly sore, transported into the fictional world of cozy, small-town Capeside, Massachusetts. It was the perfect escape from all the discomforts of adolescence, filled with romance, magical moments, and Pacey Witter, a wise-cracking yet deeply poetic dreamboat who really knew how to wear a long-sleeve tee. *Dawson's Creek* was the chicken soup for my teenage soul.

And that's exactly what makes the shows we fall for when we're young so special, even years after they've gone off the air. As *Dawson* actor Michelle Williams put it during the show's twenty-year reunion, "When something affects you while you were growing up, it kind of stays in there forever. When you're so permeable and open and trying to figure out who you are . . . whatever reaches you in those moments really becomes part of you."

Today's teen shows are leading the charge when it comes to progressive, diverse, and creative storytelling. They're tackling serious, complex issues and finding footing in everything from cringe comedy to noir drama. After years of disregard from critics, networks, and broader audiences, teen television is finally starting to get the credit it deserves. Zendaya has snagged two Emmys for her portrayal of Rue, a high school student on *Euphoria*, making history as the youngest woman to win the Emmy for Outstanding Lead Actress in a Drama Series. *Sex Education* has landed multiple BAFTA nominations. *Pen15* nabbed an Emmy nomination for Outstanding Writing in a Comedy Series.

So, how did we get here? On the hardworking backs of teen shows of years past that defined generations and shaped the landscape of TV as we know it.

Many critics say that *The Sopranos* and *Mad Men* paved the way to prestige television. But some of the most important work was happening inside the fictional hallways of high schools across America. There, revolutionary queer romance scenes took place, genre boundaries were pushed, and comedy was redefined. Some of these shows would get canceled almost immediately. Others were constantly on the bubble. And for a long time, networks struggled with how to possibly market to this mysterious new demographic of young people.

In these pages, I go behind the scenes of seven teen shows that pushed the limits of what television could be: *The Fresh Prince of Bel-Air*, *My So-Called Life*, *Dawson's Creek*, *Freaks and Geeks*, *The O.C.*, *Friday Night Lights*, and *Glee*. Not only did these shows help catapult the careers of future acting heavyweights like Michael B. Jordan, Claire Danes, and Seth Rogen, but they also took young people seriously, proving that teen TV could be just as smart and groundbreaking as its adult contemporaries and remain firmly entrenched in pop culture's hall of fame long after wrapping.

These shows and other teen series like them gave us, the fans, a shared language. Years and years later, we can still whip out renditions of the theme songs, have *lengthy* discussions about who Joey was more compatible with, Pacey or Dawson (controversial take: neither), and debate which *Glee* story line was the most delightfully unhinged.

Offscreen, the casts and creative teams went through a raw, experimental filmmaking boot camp. Paul Feig learned how to direct comedy. Adam Brody mastered the art of improvisation. Josh Schwartz and Stephanie Savage figured out how to tell juicy tales of misbehaving teens. Just off camera, people fell in love and people fought. There were insecurities and bad behavior. Some actors were eager to break free and never look back. Others hold the memories of those times tightly to this day.

The bedrock of work was happening inside the writers' rooms, where closeknit groups maneuvered through the unique challenges of writing teen TV, from crafting iconic love triangles to walking the tightrope of will they/won't they story lines. They'd pull from their own high school experiences to tell truthful stories of adolescence, digging back into their most painful and awkward memories, many of which, quite understandably, happened during gym class. In these writers' rooms, they got another shot to live out high school—only this time on their terms.

This is a coming-of-age story about coming-of-age stories, told by the people who lived it. So, grab your necessary accessories—a baby-blue puffer jacket, Panthers jersey, that Jem song from the Season 1 finale of *The O.C.*—and let's head to the wonderful, chaotic, hormone-filled worlds of Dillon, Capeside, and more.

Class is back in session.

The Fresh Prince of Bel-Air

(1990–1996)

It's the story known around the world (or, at the very least, a story people can hum the tune to).

A West Philadelphia teen, born and raised, spent most of his days on the playground outside of school. He got in one little fight, and his mom got scared . . . so she decided to ship him off to live with her sister, her sister's husband, and their three children in the wealthy Los Angeles neighborhood of Bel-Air. The sixteen-year-old would turn their world topsy-turvy, delivering laugh-a-minute quips, a plethora of antics, and too many brightly colored hats to count.

And he'd turn network TV on its head, too, giving a much-needed shakeup to the landscape of regularly scheduled programming. In the land of Fresh Prince, *well-worn comedy tropes were torn up, a rapper was turned—for the first time—into a massive sitcom star, and America was offered a brand-new portal into the Black experience.*

Time to head home to Bel-Air.

W ill Smith was in trouble. In 1988, the Philadelphia native hit the jackpot with the release of his rap single "Parents Just Don't Understand" alongside collaborator and pal DJ Jazzy Jeff. It was a sunny, catchy tune for kids and an instant win, nabbing a Grammy while the duo's album, *He's the DJ, I'm the Rapper* went triple platinum.

Nineteen-year-old Smith, who went by the moniker "The Fresh Prince," came from a middle-class home; his mom was a school board employee, and his dad was a refrigerator engineer. Suddenly, he was experiencing a new, unimaginable kind of wealth and, cash burning a hole in his wallet, he was excited to spend, spend, spend.

Smith bought motorcycles and nice cars. He called the Gucci store in Atlanta one day and asked them to shut it down so he and his friends could go shopping. Tax season came and went, and the rapper didn't pay a dime. "I didn't forget," he would later say. "I wasn't, like, trying to avoid paying taxes." Still, he made a risky choice that would alter the course of his life and livelihood.

The IRS took everything. His cars, his motorcycles, all the goodies he had piled up while he was flush with success. There wasn't much of a chance to recoup the losses; the next album he released with Jazzy Jeff, *And in This Corner*, flopped. If the previous album had gone triple platinum, he said, this one went "double plastic."

It was a weird thing, being famous without any money. Carless, he would ride the bus and get noticed by excited fans, one of whom thrust a Sharpie and a baby at him, asking for his autograph (after some uncomfortable back-and-forth, he defeatedly signed the child). Smith spent most of his time moping around, feeling lost, until his girlfriend got fed up. Their conversation, he later recounted, went something like this:

"We're not doing this," she told him. "You're not just going to be laying around this house all day. You've got to do something."

"What?" Smith asked, agitated. "*What* am I supposed to do?"

She suggested that he head to a taping of *The Arsenio Hall Show*, a popular late-night talk show on Fox.

"Just stand around at *The Arsenio Hall Show*?" he asked.

"Yes!"

"That's stupid."

But really, what else was he doing that night? Smith begrudgingly took her advice and peeled himself away from the house.

It was at the talk show that a twist of fate happened. Smith met record executive and talent manager Benny Medina, whose glittery roster of clients would include Jennifer Lopez, Tyra Banks, and P. Diddy. As the two got to talking, Medina told Smith he was in the process of developing a television series loosely based on his own life, alongside legendary record producer Quincy Jones. Maybe, he suggested, Smith could play the lead character.

The rapper had never acted before, but the idea was certainly a tantalizing one, especially if it meant a paycheck that would dig him out of debt.

Medina's early life, it would turn out, was a sad, troubling one. He grew up in the low-income Los Angeles district of Watts, where he suffered two early tragedies as a child: his mom died of cancer and his father walked out on him. Medina bounced from foster home to foster home and, at age twelve, was selling joints and amphetamine pills. He and a group of friends rented a house together and threw rum-punch parties.

It was around that time that he found his unexpected ticket out. While hanging out at a community arts center, he met nine-year-old Alan Elliott, a wealthy kid from Beverly Hills whose father, Jack Elliott, was a film and TV composer. Medina would end up moving in with the family, making a home for himself in their refurbished garage and enrolling in Beverly Hills High, which, he was excited to learn, had a swimming pool, a photography class with Nikon cameras, and a football team with uniforms.

All that to say, the television version of his life would be a highly sanitized one, set to a cheery laugh track. NBC executives were interested in the idea, and they were sold on Smith after hearing him read some script pages. Not *quite* sold enough to offer him a pilot, though—instead, they ordered a presentation, which is a shorter, low-budget version of a pilot. NBC called for nineteen minutes' worth of content and, to save money, decided to reuse old sets from a soap opera called *Generations*.

Now they just needed somebody to write the presentation.

That spring, TV writers and then-married couple Andy and Susan Borowitz sat down with NBC television executive Brandon Tartikoff.

"Have you heard of Fresh Prince?" Tartikoff asked the two.

"Well," Andy responded quizzically, "I've heard of Prince."

Nope. Not that Prince, Tartikoff explained. The Fresh Prince was a rapper they were about to make into a TV star.

"OK," Andy said. "What's the concept?"

"Well, it's going to be fish-out-of-water. Think *Beverly Hills Cop*," Tartikoff replied, referencing the hit buddy-cop comedy starring Eddie Murphy.

You know you're talking to a network executive, Andy later told me, when they reference another show or movie with no compunction about lifting the idea. *If it's not broken, don't fix it* was the attitude. He got the sense that Tartikoff was trying to make Smith into the next Murphy largely because they were both young Black men.

The vague idea took clearer shape when Andy and Susan went to Jones's Bel-Air mansion for dinner. The producer was between marriages at the time, and his grand home had all the trappings of a bachelor pad. As the three ate, Jones told them about his life. He may have lived in one of the wealthiest zip codes in Los Angeles, but there was an intriguing duality about him. Jones was born on the south side of Chicago during the Depression, where he saw dead bodies littering the streets every day. His dad, a carpenter, worked for one of the city's biggest gangsters, and young Jones was privy to back rooms with cigars, bottles of liquor, and stacks of money. The producer had one foot in two very different worlds, a fish out of water in his own right who had lived life at both ends of the social spectrum. The core of the show's protagonist, Uncle Phil, began to form that evening—a successful lawyer with a Harvard degree whom we would later learn grew up with humble beginnings, on a farm in Yamacraw, North Carolina, and was an activist during the civil rights movement.

Jones also spoke, much to Andy's amusement, about his kids growing up with great wealth and excess in Los Angeles. One of them once called home from summer camp and left a message on the answering machine saying, "Dad, the water here sucks, please FedEx Evian."

In that moment, the seedling of Hilary Banks, Uncle Phil's ultra-spoiled daughter, was born.

The rest of the fictional family came together fairly quickly after that meeting with Jones. Aunt Vivian would be Uncle Phil's wife and the heart of the show, a professor of English literature at a university and, for a period of time, the teacher of Black history at Bel-Air Academy. Carlton, named after Andy's friend from college, was the second oldest child, a preppy teen with an affinity for Tom Jones and the unironic use of the word "darn."

Ashley would be the youngest child, a charming combination of sunshine and rebellion, who forges a quick connection with Will. Completing the Banks family was Geoffrey, the household's butler, a prim, proper Brit with a deadpan sense of humor whom Will calls "G." The character was originally written as white until Jones intervened—he didn't think that Uncle Phil would have a white butler.

There had never been a Black family on TV as monied as Uncle Phil and Aunt Viv. We had the Huxtables, who lived comfortably as upper-middle-class characters, but the goal was to give the Bankses a totally different level of wealth, one that afforded them a butler, an enviable mansion flanked by elegant pillars, and a place firmly within the upper echelons of society.

With a deal freshly signed, the Borowitzes still needed to meet their star. They sat down with Smith for the first time at a TGI Fridays in his hometown of Philadelphia. Smith sipped on a fruit-laden tropical concoction called the Gold Medalist as Andy quietly observed him. He was so funny, in such an effortless way. But underneath, the writer noticed, was a serious young man who was at a turning point in his life. Here was a Grammy Award–winning artist who, at age twenty, was suddenly feeling obsolete. This sitcom, Andy remembers thinking, could be a life raft for him.

The young man came into clearer focus when the three attended a party at Jones's house, packed with television executives. As Andy milled around, watching everybody schmoozing in the mogul's living room, he spotted Smith off by himself. The young man wandered over to the baby grand piano, slid into the seat, and began playing the opening bars to Beethoven's "Für Elise."

"That's kind of interesting," Andy remembers thinking.

He decided to stitch that moment into the end of the pilot, following a particularly emotionally charged scene. Uncle Phil and Will have gotten into a big argument at home in the living room. They are not seeing eye to eye. Uncle Phil thinks Will is running a wrecking ball through his home. Will tells Uncle Phil he must feel threatened by having his nephew there, that seeing him reminds him of where he came from. Somewhere between his fancy education and his fancy job, Will says, Uncle Phil got soft. The scene rolls on tensely with no joke in sight, just the two men going back and forth fiercely. It was a bold move to write all that dialogue without a single crack—particularly in the first episode of a sitcom whose fate hung narrowly in the balance.

"You forgot who you are and where you came from," Will tells his uncle dismissively.

"You think you're so wise. *Look* at me when I'm talking to you," Uncle Phil fires back. "Let me tell you, son. I grew up on the streets just like you. I encountered bigotry you could not imagine. Now, you have a nice poster of Malcolm X on your wall. I heard the brother speak. I read every word he wrote. Believe me, I know where I come from."

In that moment, something switches inside Will. "You heard Malcom speak, man?" he asks, his voice softening.

"That's right. So before you criticize someone, you find out what he's all about."

Uncle Phil leaves the room. Will, alone, makes his way to the piano. He slouches down and begins to gently play the beginning notes of "Für Elise." Uncle Phil reemerges in the doorway, then, and watches his nephew. He smiles quietly to himself. Maybe he had gotten Will a little wrong too.

Writers usually get roughly ten days to two weeks to create a pilot. The Borowitzes had five days. They wrote quickly, cast quickly, and shot quickly, all on a slim budget. "Let's not get bogged down in the paralysis of analysis," Jones would tell them.

When it came time to cast the show's stalwart leader, Uncle Phil, James Avery, a seasoned actor who earned his BA in drama and literature from UC San Diego, was offered the role. Avery had a storied career; he was a Navy veteran who served in Vietnam, wrote scripts and poetry for PBS, and landed roles on shows like *L.A. Law*. He wasn't expected to audition, but he was asked to read with Smith on the understanding that, unless something went terribly wrong, the part was his. The duo tackled that weighty last scene of the episode, where Will and Uncle Phil go head-to-head. At one point, Smith broke eye contact, and Avery ad-libbed: "You *look at me* when I'm talking to you." That moment rocked Andy to his core. It was parental authority at its finest. Avery was so intimidating in that exchange, but there was a softness to the man too. The actor's commanding presence was balanced with a warm, fantastic laugh. He was their Uncle Phil. And he already had all the early makings of a beloved TV dad.

Susan had a very specific idea when it came to Aunt Viv. She was going to be a tough woman who had lived a life and was her husband's equal. When Janet Hubert walked in to read for the part, Susan was immediately struck by just how much Hubert embodied her vision of who Aunt Viv was. "She had this innate toughness and you knew she had been through hell. Nothing got her down, nothing would cow her, and you just got a sense this is a person who fought, this is a person who really, really fought."

Precious time slipped by as they raced to fill out the rest of the cast. Casting director Allison Jones, meanwhile, was busy butting heads with the network. She put her foot down when executives wanted to cast a non-British actor to play the role of the Banks family's butler. Jones was not in the business of hiring somebody who faked an accent. Instead, she set her sights on Joseph Marcell, an English performer who had trained at the Royal Central School of Speech and Drama in London and spent time in the world of British theatre, with roles in the likes of *Endgame* and *Hamlet*. Marcell's friend Sir Patrick Stewart put him up for the part. Stewart had been talking to a television executive when he learned that they were casting a butler for an upcoming NBC sitcom.

"Know anyone who might be up for it?" the executive asked.

"Matter of fact," Stewart said, "I do."

Aspiring actor Karyn Parsons was juggling hostessing duties at a seafood restaurant and cat-sitting when she got called to read for the part of a "model type" named Hilary Banks. The sitcom's whole concept sounded silly to her. "A rapper on a TV show?" she recalled thinking.

Parsons didn't immediately take to Hilary, who, on paper, sounded like a too-cool-for-school beauty queen. She *did*, however, flash back to some of the girls she grew up with. They were from Malibu, had loads of family money, and drove fancy cars. She decided to channel those young women for her audition and leaned firmly into their unabashed love of materialism. Parsons still has the day planner where she excitedly scribbled the time and date she would get to stand in front of Quincy Jones to read for the role. Much to her delight, he made for such an expressive, interactive audience, slapping the table and throwing his head back when she read her jokes. Parsons popped her hip, script in hand, as she said, dripping with boredom, "Dad, I need $300." She landed the role but didn't quit her job hostessing at that seafood restaurant. Just to be safe.

When Alfonso Ribeiro first read the script pages for the role of Hilary's brother, Carlton, the character immediately spoke to him. He just *knew* this kid. Ribeiro already had a recurring role on *Silver Spoons* under his belt when he came in for the audition, decked out in a black-and-blue Adidas sweatsuit. Ribeiro had the young man down pat, whipping out that slow, signature know-it-all smile and deeply patronizing tone that, as episodes went on, would go from annoying to endearing.

Rounding out the cast was Tatyana Ali, who was eleven when she came in to audition for the role of Ashley, the youngest of the Bankses. Her mom and aunts were so excited that she was going to read for *the* Quincy Jones. Ali was less than thrilled because, much to her dismay, she was instructed to come up with her own rap and perform it in front of a roomful of strangers. Ali didn't know how to rap, let alone how to write her own rap verse. She gritted her teeth and did her best, later concluding that the lyrics probably had just the right amount of corniness to help win her the role.

Andy was just as lost as Ali when it came to the world of hip-hop. The writer didn't want to make a pilot where kids who actually loved rap would write *Fresh Prince* off as the corniest show ever. "Obviously, [I was] some white guy who has no understanding of any of this, and so . . . I had to learn things quickly."

If this sitcom were being made now, he added, there's no way two white writers would have been hired to tell the Bankses' story. But it was a different time in the TV industry and a prime example of just how far network television had to go. Yes, they were making a show about a Black family, but hiring Black writers to helm the series either didn't occur to the network or was something they just weren't interested in.

Andy decided to weave his lack of knowledge into the script, using Uncle Phil as a mouthpiece. The patriarch of the family would need to learn about the world of hip-hop through Smith, who was tasked with bringing him into the fold, teaching him the slang, and simplifying the culture for both the character and the less-informed segment of the audience at home.

The release of the pilot landed at a pivotal moment in hip-hop history. The same year that *Fresh Prince* premiered, the rap group 2 Live Crew were standing trial for obscenity, which the prosecution described as "graphic descriptions of sexual intercourse, anal intercourse, [and] oral intercourse," along with "deviant sexual acts" that were degrading to women. Two weeks earlier, Charles Freeman, the owner of a Florida record store that was selling the 2 Live Crew album, had been convicted of obscenity charges.

Warren Littlefield, a top executive at NBC, was quick to differentiate the *Fresh Prince* from the likes of 2 Live Crew while talking to the *L.A. Times* ahead of the show's premiere. "In no way is this an effort to put a rap show on the air," he insisted. "This is an effort to put Will Smith on the air. That's who we're banking on."

Smith, for his part, emphasized in the same article that there was a knowledge gap when it came to rap. "Rap music—which a lot of white America doesn't understand—rap music is not just music. Rap music is a subculture: hip-hop. It's a style of dress, an attitude, a look, a language. It's more than just music."

As he worked on the presentation, Andy felt the pressure of bringing the very concept of rap to a potentially wary audience. To lower the learning curve, he came up with a clever gimmick. Instead of having Will rap on-screen, he would get Ashley to take the mic first. "She's so sweet and everybody's all worried about Will and what kind of chaos he's going to create, actually it's the little girl that starts rapping at the dinner table and wreaks havoc," Andy said. Later, Will and Ashley rap together, and Andy was pretty pleased when he learned that Smith didn't think the lyrics he had written were half bad.

The whole production was a scrappy affair. Their makeshift set was so flimsy that in the beginning of the second act, the wall jiggles when Will hangs a picture of Malcolm X. Both Andy and Susan were well aware that they weren't writing for a trained actor, so they tried to quickly build the character of Will around Will Smith himself. They didn't want him to feel like he had to play someone who was too much of a departure from his own reality.

As they crafted Smith's alter-ego, Andy found himself relating to the sixteen-year-old kid developing on the page. While he contends that he wasn't as cool or smooth as Will in high school (he self-described as "more of a nerd"), he was the class clown. Andy was the editor of his school newspaper, largely because on April 1, he got to be in charge of the April Fools issue, where all the stories were entirely made-up and satirical. (Andy Borowitz, by the way, is *the* Andy Borowitz, who currently writes *The Borowitz Report*, an entirely made-up and satirical column for *The New Yorker*.)

The show felt like a closer fit than the previous teen sitcom he worked on, *The Facts of Life*. A spin-off of *Diff'rent Strokes*, the series ran for nine seasons and featured a group of young women at the fictional Eastland School who learned about the ups and downs of puberty from their housemother. It just wasn't Andy's thing. He wasn't quite sure how to write for its protagonists, Tootie, Natalie, Jo, and Blair. As a twenty-five-year-old man, he found that their dramas weren't his dramas.

The Facts of Life leaned heavily into the "Very Special Episode" format, popularized in the '70s and '80s, which featured young characters learning a lesson about serious topics like drugs and drunk driving, and settled comfortably into the saccharine. Andy wasn't interested in making that kind of content. Neither was Susan, who had her own run-in with the network TV constraints when she was working as writer on the sitcom *Family Ties*. After writing a big, realistic family argument into an episode, the pages came back with a large X drawn across them.

"People don't want to see real life, they want to see the fantasy," she was told.

This time around, finally at the helm, she was set on eliminating any kind of family-hug stuff. "It just had to go!" she emphatically told me.

Fresh Prince was scheduled to air at eight on Monday nights. The Bankses would be replacing the much-loved science-fiction show *Alf*, about an alien who moves into a suburban family's home after his spaceship crashes into their garage. *Alf* had cracked the top ten in the Nielsen ratings and churned out hundreds of millions of dollars' worth of licensed merchandise, from backpacks to toothbrushes. So now the big question remained: Would *Fresh Prince*, a world away from this furry, wisecracking alien, be able to generate the same kind of enthusiasm?

On the night of the taping, Susan and Andy sat adjacent to the stage and watched as the Banks family took the stage for their first live performance. There was just *something* about Smith when he got in front of an audience. It was like a faucet of charisma turned on. Susan noticed that Brandon Tartikoff began inching closer and closer to the stage, until he was right there, pulling up a chair beside the Borowitzes, in plain view of everyone. That sealed the deal. He wanted to be associated with this show. Later that evening, he told Susan that he hadn't seen a breakout star like that since Eddie Murphy.

The presentation tested at record-breaking levels. *Fresh Prince* was picked up for twelve episodes, and the Borowitzes were told to go back and shoot three extra minutes so that the episode could go from presentation to pilot. Viewers had quickly fallen for the Banks family. Reviewers, however, felt tepid at best. I'm not sure exactly what I expected when I went back in the archives to read the reviews (enthusiasm about this up-and-coming star? Interest in a new kind of sitcom?), but the consensus was altogether lukewarm.

The *Hollywood Reporter* called *Fresh Prince* "tolerable television," equating the show to "bubble gum rap."

Entertainment Weekly gave the pilot a "B." "The punch lines are predictable, but the kid and his stern uncle generate a great deal of comic energy. Avery does excellent slow burns while the fresh young prince mouths off," reviewer Ken Tucker wrote. "Given all the bad publicity that rap has received lately, *The Fresh Prince* might help convince lots of viewers that rap can be good, clean fun."

The *New York Times*, though, demonstrated some promising interest in this new sitcom. It ran a feature on the show shortly after the premiere in which writer Larry Rohter interviewed Smith and the *Fresh Prince*'s creative team. The group reinforced that they were hoping to add some realism into the sitcom landscape and offer "another view of the Black experience."

"Will is not threatening," Benny Medina said. "As the show develops, we will start to deal with some of the same things as N.W.A., Public Enemy, Ice Cube and artists with a much more radical way of communicating their lifestyle. But we'll do it Will's way, rather than in their language."

Susan, meanwhile, told Rohter that she suspected NBC wanted something like *Crocodile Dundee*, a squeaky-clean romp without a hint of edge. Executives were "freaked out" when they read the pilot script and discovered that Smith would showcase a photo of Malcolm X in his bedroom.

But the Borowitzes were trying to do something different with the sitcom format. They weren't interested in writing the typically rigid six-scene structure, which was popular in the '70s and '80s. Instead, they liked what *Seinfeld* was doing, which was embedding smaller scenes and moments within the usual structure. "Let's mix it up," they said. "Let's tell the story, and the story will decide how many scenes we need."

Fresh Prince was a live-action cartoon of sorts, she contended. But there was room for serious content, sandwiched between laughs and farce. In the show's sixth episode, "Mistaken Identity," Will and Carlton are pulled over by a police officer (played by an early-in-his-career Hank Azaria) when they're spotted driving a Mercedes, which they had borrowed from a friend of Uncle Phil's. Carlton attempts a jovial exchange, thinking nothing of it at first, while Will, who has clearly been in this situation before, anticipates every word the officer is going to say, from instructing Carlton to keep his hand on the wheel to being forced to get out of the car. And then, without even being told to do so, Will slams himself down on the hood of the vehicle. As the episode unfolds, we see Carlton slowly come to terms with the idea that his wealth and social class can't protect him from racism. Even by the end of the episode, he's continuing to struggle with that reality.

The episode was inspired by a conversation the Borowitzes overheard between Smith and some of the show's Black writers. They were talking about "DWB" and how Smith had been pulled over while driving his Mercedes-Benz. "What happened?" Susan asked, not quite getting it. They looked at her, she told me, like, *Oh, you poor sheltered woman.* DWB, it turned out, meant "driving while Black," and they had all experienced the same phenomenon, getting pulled over for no justifiable reason. Later, Smith would go into more detail about those incidents, sharing that he had been stopped frequently by cops in Philadelphia and called the N-word on more than ten occasions.

Andy and Susan began discussing the idea of writing an episode around these lived experiences. The caveat, though, was that it couldn't tread into "Very Special Episode" territory. The duo tried to pack in enough comedy set pieces that it didn't feel preachy, bringing an opera singer into the prison to add extra humor and penning bits like one character misunderstanding when Carlton calls to say that he's in jail ("You got into Yale?!" they screech on the other line).

"You can communicate serious messages so much more successfully if you're not being messagey, if you're making people laugh," Andy told me. "If someone's laughing, there's almost a physiological difference. They're on the edge of their chair, they're really taking in all the information because they don't want to miss the next joke and the next laugh. And if you're preaching at somebody, then they're kind of sitting back in their chair with their arms folded."

As a new actor, Smith was being given meatier material than expected. He was hard on himself about becoming a better performer and would stay late to watch tapes of the show like an athlete going back and studying replays. When Don Cheadle had a guest spot as Ice Tray, Will's old friend from Philly, the rapper studied Cheadle so intently that he unknowingly began mouthing his lines. Susan eventually had to intervene and give him a heads-up on what he was doing.

Smith was already having an issue with mouthing other people's lines. He was so nervous about failing on-screen that he would diligently learn the whole script ahead of time and then perform everyone's part alongside them. The editors tried to cut around it, but you can easily spot some of those moments in early episodes. As a viewer, it's endearing to catch quick glimpses of Smith playing the roles of several other characters, openly and unknowingly reciting their words. It was far *less* endearing for his costars. Finally, Parsons had to call him out during a rehearsal. "Stop!" she begged. He was making her too nervous.

Andy and Susan were set on finding the layered specificity of each of the family members, in the hopes of giving the action-packed sitcom a more realistic edge. Susan liked the idea of Uncle Phil growing up on a farm, owning a pet pig named Melvin, splashing around in the swimming pools, and going by the childhood nickname of Zeke. It added a little bit of vulnerability to this powerful patriarch of a character. It was important to Susan that their characters have strengths that were balanced by foibles and frailties. She felt those contradictions would create the kind of three-dimensional people whom audiences want to invite into their homes every week, and maybe even start to view as friends.

Susan had a firm grip on Aunt Viv's backstory. She loved that this character was a professor and her career was tied up in the academic world. So when Janet Hubert, an accomplished dancer, wanted Vivian to pursue her passion for dance, Susan resisted. "That's not what your character is about," she would reply.

"We thought it was so important to show a strong, intelligent, beautiful Black woman as something other than an entertainer," Susan later explained. "Because especially at that time, those were the images that were being sent out, not just to Black kids but to white kids."

Hubert disagreed. She had a different idea of who Aunt Viv could be and, when the Borowitzes left after the first season, the actor got her wish. In one memorable episode, Vivian enrolls in a dance class where a group of younger, snarky women look down on her. She performs a complex number in front of the whole room, wearing a blush-pink unitard. When she's done, she snaps a finger in front of the faces of the women who had rolled their eyes at her.

For Hubert, Vivian's talent felt important and unexpected. "When people say to me, 'To see a Black woman your age who was playing a mom do that role and dance like that'—they were shocked," she told *The Root*.

Carlton, meanwhile, was a preppy, sheltered teen who burst out of his one-dimensional framework thanks to an off-handed comment from Smith. "Carlton is cool to his friends," the actor told Andy one day. That stuck with the writer. He liked the idea that this character, who could so easily be dismissed as a nerd, was actually considered the leader of his high school group and a tremendously confident guy to boot. It gave him depth while also making him an even more worthy adversary of his cousin Will.

That realization prompted an episode called "72 Hours," where Will bets Carlton that he can't last a weekend in Jazz's rough neighborhood of Compton. Not only does Carlton last those two days, he *flourishes*. He learns the slang, knows how to hang, and everybody absolutely loves him. The guys call him "C Note" and one of them is so excited that Carlton is going to help him set up an investment account.

A third of the way through the first season, Susan turned to Andy and declared, "I think we have a hit on our hands." She didn't have the nerve to look at the ratings, but Andy, who was a far more data-driven person, would read the trades and report back to her. From 1990 to 1991, *Fresh Prince* ranked as the twelfth most popular show on NBC—not too shabby, considering that it shared a network with hits like *The Cosby Show* (3rd place), *60 Minutes*

(2nd place), and *Cheers* (1st place). By the show's second season, it had shot all the way up to number 2.

David Steven Simon, whose writing credits included *Full House* and *Charles in Charge*, came aboard in that sophomore year, as *Fresh Prince* mania ramped up. There was no better indication of the audience's love of the show, he remembers, than taping nights. Those frenetic, exciting affairs would kick off fifteen minutes before shooting as the cast, the writer, and the director of the episode gathered in Smith's dressing room for a weekly ritual called "The Dance." Smith would start by giving a speech that felt akin to a pregame pep talk, telling everyone to have fun out there and bring the energy. Then he'd cue somebody to blast one of Smith's own rap songs from a speaker, and he began performing. His energy would reverberate through the room. Everybody started dancing just as the clock ticked down to showtime.

Then they'd rush to the Bankses' kitchen and grab random items—cymbals, maracas, pots, pans, wooden spoons—and head to the living-room set, where heaps of plywood painted black hid the set from the audience's view. The actors began banging their instruments of choice on those slabs of wood as the audience got more and more excited, screaming and clapping in their seats.

The announcer would say, "Ladies and gentlemen, *The Fresh Prince*." The sliders opened, the cast was introduced one by one to monstrous applause, and the show began.

Simon would sit on the floor of that studio, furiously hoping for big laughs to his punch lines. Sometimes, a joke would fall flat. Those were the moments of his job he hated the most. "It's your responsibility, right then and there, to come up with something funnier. It was like, *Dance, monkey*."

Smith was usually the first person to come over when a joke wasn't clicking. "This could be funnier," he'd say.

Then he'd go back onstage and "just do shit off the top of his head," Simon recalled. That's hardly common behavior for sitcoms—scripts are tightly written to fit the time frame allotted, and improvisation just isn't baked into that formula. None of that mattered to Smith. He seemed hyperfocused on the live-audience experience. The cast would do several takes of a scene, which meant that the joke everybody laughed at the first time would be a lot less funny the third time.

With each take, Smith would change up the punch line, hoping to keep the audience laughing. At first, David Pitlik, a writer who joined in the show's fifth season, was confused. "Where's that coming from?" he wondered as he camped out in a back office, watching the show in real time. But soon enough he caught on. Things were done differently on the *Fresh Prince* set.

Smith had a group of friends just offstage, a mix of childhood buddies and musicians, who operated like a shadow writers' room, brainstorming comedy bits with him between takes. In the beginning, Pitlik wondered where he, as a writer, fit into all this. "You finally start to figure out, OK, this is the way it's done," he told me. "And we will contribute what we can, where we're needed. If the boss says, 'Hey, this joke is falling flat, come up with something else,' we contribute, and then Will and his people were sort of doing their own thing." Still, he remembers having some fear around the idea that Smith and his friends might come up with better material than the actual writers. That wasn't good for job security.

Watching your jokes get rewritten or thrown out altogether comes with the territory of being a sitcom writer. You move on quickly if something gets cut, no matter how much you loved what you had written. Still, there *were* ways to strategically campaign for material. Rehearsals took place at four o'clock onstage, and the episode's writer would be there to watch the actors run through the show with their scripts in hand.

As they walked from set to set, Simon would trail them, laughing heartily at each punch line as if it were the funniest thing he had ever heard. "If the actors hear laughter, they feel secure. If they don't hear laughter or feel like we're faking it, those lines go bye-bye real fast," he explained. Being a writer on *Fresh Prince* meant a complex equation of being very quick and very funny, having zero ego, making the actors feel confident, and, above all else, keeping Will Smith happy.

Shelley Jensen, a director whose credits included *Caroline in the City*, *Friends*, and *The Wayans Bros.*, joined in the show's second season and tapped right into that formula. He would go on to direct eighty-seven episodes of the series, something he attributes to the gentle way he approached the cast of young actors.

Early on, Jensen was tasked with directing a landmark coming-of-age scene: Ashley's first kiss. This would be Ali's first kiss as well, and Jensen wanted to be sensitive in the way he handled a significant life moment. He decided to rehearse it with just Ali and her young costar before they tried it in front of a live audience. They sat on the couch in the Bankses' living room and talked through what the two actors were feeling at the time. Then, he built them slowly up to the moment, starting with a hug, then a cheek kiss, and then the peck on the lips.

That first kiss ended up being perfect, he remembers. "It was just kind of magical. It was very sensitive, very sweet."

Little did he know, Smith was watching from the wings. He liked Jensen's style and decided to make him a permanent member of the *Fresh Prince* family.

There was a line that Jensen always liked to say to the cast during his multi-year tenure on the series. "I'm out there with you, in front of the audience," he'd tell them. They were on a "comedy ledge," he called it, and if they got that laugh, he was sharing that triumph with them. If they bombed, he bombed. They were never alone.

Even if the actors weren't crazy about a joke, he encouraged them to commit to it. If nothing else, it would show the writers that, despite their best efforts, the bit wasn't landing and they should rethink the dialogue. The actors always committed 100 percent, Jensen remembers. Only once did Parsons push back. It was after a scene involving a heart-to-heart with Will in the backyard. True to form, the poignant moment needed to be bookended with a big laugh. So, Simon, who wrote the episode, added that Hilary would walk smack into a clear glass door following her conversation with Will. Parsons approached him.

"I think you're making her too dumb," she said. "I don't believe she'd walk into a door."

"I'll make you a deal," Simon told her. "You do it once. If the audience laughs their heads off, we keep it. If they are uncomfortable, we get no laugh at all, or a groan, we'll cut it."

Jensen remembers the story differently. The way he tells it, he was the one who instructed Parsons to walk into that door. Still, by both accounts, the audience screamed with laughter. "It was one of the longest laughs we got on the series," Jensen said. "After an emotional scene the audience needed that laugh relief." The show was continuing to find its balance between the light and dark, using comedy as a clever buffer that allowed for more honest moments. And they were learning that, sometimes, it paid to be really, really silly.

Working for the *Fresh Prince* felt like being in a "foxhole," Simon remembers, but a very high-end foxhole with unique perks. After each taping, the writers would pick up a bouquet of flowers to bring home from the arrangements brought daily to the Bankses' living room (and worth nearly $500). Once the season was done, they could snag items from any of the characters' wardrobes, including Smith's, which were bought at high-end L.A. boutiques where sports jackets could go for as much as $1,500. While Carlton's polos often went untouched, Uncle Phil's cozy sweaters were a hit.

Then came the foxhole part. The schedule went something like this: during the course of a week, they'd work on three shows at the same time. Last week's show was being edited, this week's show is in rehearsal, and next week's show is being written. Every story needed Smith's approval.

Smith didn't often reject ideas, but he did when Simon pitched a cameo from RuPaul, a drag queen who was making a name for himself with dance tracks like "Supermodel (You Better Work)."

"I remember him saying that would be a really bad idea. And I said, 'No, listen, hear my story—'"

Smith, as Simon remembers it, refused. He just kept repeating that it was a bad idea.

"OK, OK. We don't need to do it," Simon demurred.

From Simon's perspective, "The reason he would say no is because of his image. Period. The End," he told me.

An episode would be written within hours. The writers knew the characters so well that they'd sit around a table together, lines flowing out of them. To this day, Simon will find himself at a stoplight, internally pitching jokes about Carlton's height. The bits are that ingrained in him.

When Simon worked on *Roseanne*, he was required to come up with ten backup jokes per page. ("That's insane. You do it, but that's insane.") *Fresh Prince* wasn't like that. The writers weren't given a quota of jokes, but there was a rhythm to every scene they had to stick to, which went like: setup, joke; setup, joke; setup, joke; setup, joke; setup, setup, setup, joke. Each week, the writers sat down with network executives to listen to their notes. Sometimes, Simon remembers, they gave bad notes—"unbelievably stupid notes." "You would have to be kind about it, and gently say something like 'Are you aware that if we do that note, we have to put the whole script in the garbage because it negates everything else?'"

That would make the network execs think twice.

The actors needed their scripts by Tuesday morning. Between five p.m. on Monday and five the next morning, the writers would divvy up the pages and write scenes on their own. They'd hope to God that when each of those scenes came together, it was a lucid episode. Ninety-eight percent of the time, it wasn't. Then, their brains officially mush, they'd have to start over from page one to make it work. They didn't have email then, so *Fresh Prince* hired assistants who would sit around until five a.m. waiting for the script to be done and then quickly hop in their cars to hand-deliver the material to each actor before six.

The writers worked out of NBC's offices on Bob Hope Drive in Burbank, a sleepy city in Los Angeles County dotted with television studios. Their windows were soundproof but in the mornings they would start to rattle as Smith pulled up in his white Bronco, blasting music.

He'd come hang out in the writers' room, put his feet up on the desk, and shoot the breeze. The absurdity of hanging out so casually with someone so famous wasn't lost on the writers. Sometimes, as a prank, Simon would pick up the phone and say to the actor, "OK, Will, I'm gonna just dial someone at random, and hand you the phone and tell them you're calling." Smith would amiably agree, and Simon punched in a number. "Hold for Will Smith, please," he'd say.

People would either assume it was a joke and promptly hang up or frantically scream into the phone.

The writers' room, I discovered, wasn't all fun and silly phone calls. It could also be a dark place packed with toxic, inappropriate behavior. Jenji Kohan, who would go on to create hits like *Orange Is the New Black* and *Weeds*, joined the show's staff in 1993, under the helm of showrunner Gary Miller. She was fresh out of Columbia University, and *Fresh Prince* was her first foray into TV writing. She was introduced to this strange new world by way of a group of writers who, she later told *The New Yorker*, fought constantly and kept insane hours. While working in the room, she was given the nickname "White Devil Jew Bitch."

Kohan hasn't spoken much about the year she worked on *Fresh Prince*, but she did tell the story behind that antisemitic nickname during an interview with NPR's Terry Gross.

"Was *Fresh Prince* a fun show to write for?" Gross asked.

"No. It was really . . . it was a really fun set. The cast was lovely. The writers' room was wildly dysfunctional, and I was the only girl. And it was a time in L.A., you know, around the riots . . . Farrakhan rallies, I got my nickname, you know, 'White Devil Jew Bitch,' which you know I hold dear."

Pranks, she said, included one writer peeing in another's bottle of tequila. It was, Kohan would later tell *The Guardian*, "a rough and fascinating entrance into the business."

There was trouble on-set too. For a long time, Janet Hubert's tumultuous experience on the show has been something of a mystery; a piece of *Fresh Prince* lore that hung over a seemingly scandal-free sitcom. One season, Hubert was there, playing Aunt Vivian. Then, the next season, she was gone. Following her departure, news would trickle out that there was some sort of clash between Smith and Hubert, with bits and pieces of insight coming out in interviews over the years. But it wasn't until more than two decades later, when the cast reunited for an HBOMax special, that Hubert shared the whole story.

At the time of filming *Fresh Prince*, the actor was pregnant and in an abusive relationship.

"Something I would like to clarify is during that third season when I got pregnant, there were a lot of things going on in my life and in Will's life as well," she said, facing the camera. "There was some friction because I was pregnant. Home life was not good at all. I was no longer laughing, smiling, joking, because there were things that were going on that nobody knew about."

That turn in mood ramped up Smith's own insecurities. "On my 'little boy in me' level, I needed Mommy to think I was great. And then once I realized that she didn't, my dragon woke up," Smith explained during an interview with his now-wife Jada on *Red Table Talk*.

Off-camera tensions were running high when it came time for contract negotiations. Hubert was offered a reduced deal for the fourth season—ten weeks of work, and she was told she couldn't take acting gigs anywhere else. Her agent instructed her not to sign. They'd come back with a better offer, she was reassured. They never did. Hubert was replaced by an actor named Daphne Maxwell Reid, who had appeared on a number of hit shows, like *Murder, She Wrote* and *Hill Street Blues.*

How does a show go about completely swapping out a crucial cast member in the middle of its run? In this case, it all came down to one look. The writers decided to just lean into the weirdness of the whole situation and break the fourth wall. The first scene of the fourth season has Jazzy Jeff walking into the Bankses' living room and eying Aunt Viv, who recently gave birth. He seems a little confused.

"You know Ms. Banks, since you had that baby, there's something different about you," he declares. The camera cuts to Will, who makes direct eye contact with the lens, eyebrows raised. And then, just like that, the show moved on. There was a new Aunt Viv now.

The fourth season would take Will and Carlton out of high school and into the fictional world of the University of Los Angeles. There, Will works at a campus store called the Peacock (a nod to NBC's logo, which, Simon told me eye-rollingly, he always balked at) and dates his childhood friend Jackie (played by Tyra Banks). Smith was always happier when the writers wrote his character into relationships. "I think he felt like that was where he could really shine," Pitlik said. "We tried to have as many of them as we could because he seemed to really like that, and ultimately we needed to make him happy."

With Smith's character now firmly in the throes of adulthood, the actor informed the writers that he was interested in telling challenging, realistic stories that might not fit within the typical framework of a half-hour sitcom. The show had already begun to dip its toe into heavier storytelling in the previous season when, for the first time, members of the cast approached the writers with a unified request.

An uprising was happening in Los Angeles, sparked by the acquittal of four policemen, three of whom were white, who were videotaped brutally beating a Black motorist named Rodney King.

"We have to address it. We have to deal with it," the cast told the writers.

Simon came up with the idea that Will and the Banks family would clean up Uncle Phil and Aunt Viv's old neighborhood, which had been torn apart during the riots. It would be a chance for the couple to reminisce about their lives before Bel-Air, look back on their younger selves, and reunite with friends from their past life. It was a delicate negotiation, once again, of balancing serious matters with a flurry of jokes, all while striking a tone that didn't feel preachy.

"Because our show is about an affluent black family, they should not act like the riots didn't happen," Winifred Hervey, co-executive producer of *Fresh Prince*, told the *L.A. Times* at the time. "But we didn't want to trivialize or editorialize. We tried to take a positive look at the aftermath, and inject some humor into the situation."

As seasons stretched on, Smith was itching to flex his acting muscles outside the sitcom world. He began dipping his toe into film, landing a part in *Six Degrees of Separation*, a dramedy starring Stockard Channing and Donald Sutherland. It was his first serious role, playing a con artist who scams his way into the lives of a wealthy married couple—a far leap from his affable sitcom persona. Early reviews were mixed. Janet Maslin at the *New York Times* expressed doubt about Smith's range. "Mr. Smith recites his lines plausibly without bringing great passion to the role," she wrote. *Variety*'s Leonard Klady, however, offered kudos for "an extremely charismatic presence."

Ironically, Smith would prove that he could turn out a compelling, dramatic performance right back home in the Banks mansion. As Pitlik remembers it, Smith approached the writers about the idea of bringing his character's absent father back into the picture. It would give him a great chance to explore some more emotional material.

The whole thing made Pitlik nervous. His instinct was to find the humor in every scene, and the idea of an absent father's return felt like they'd be treading into some darker territory. Pitlik's job was to give Smith funny lines and put him in crazy situations. He thought of the young man as a comedy genius but not really an actor per se.

The first draft of the script, "Papa's Got a Brand New Excuse," penned by David Zuckerman and Bill Boulware, introduced Smith's father, Lou (played by

Broadway actor Ben Vereen), as a pool shark, who's been gone from Will's life for the past fourteen years. After the first table read, Smith approached the writers. He wasn't happy with the script. Something just didn't feel right. The writers quickly retooled the character of Lou, turning him into a long-haul trucker who was clearly damaged and unprepared to be a father, hiding his troubles behind bravado and cheek.

The episode is startlingly thin on jokes. This time around, Zuckerman, Boulware, and Jensen, who directed the episode, didn't try to bookend the dramatic moments with punch lines. It was a risky choice but well worth it, giving Smith and Avery the opportunity to really demonstrate their dramatic chops. Two moments stand out from that episode, where Smith and Avery particularly shine and the writing feels unapologetically real.

The first happens in the kitchen. Lou has offered to take Will on the road that summer, and the young man is beside himself with excitement. Uncle Phil, however, is suspicious and tries to warn Will not to get too attached to his father, who has let him and his mother down so many times before.

"Wake up, Will," Uncle Phil says. "This is the same guy who didn't think enough of you to pick up the damn phone."

"He made a mistake," Will retorts. "I'm sorry that everybody can't be as perfect as you, Uncle Phil. But if I can forgive him, how come you can't?"

"Because he isn't doing this for you, he's doing this for himself. If you think any differently, then you're a fool."

"I've been waiting for this for a long time, my whole life, and ain't nobody gonna stop me. Come tomorrow, I'm out of here."

"Yeah, I don't think so."

"Who cares what you think? You are not my father!"

That last line hits Uncle Phil hard, and his face crumples. Will storms out of the kitchen, banging the doors as he goes, and silence follows. The episode cuts to commercial break.

Later, Will's father tells him that he's changed his mind. The timing isn't quite right for his son to join him on the road. Will had already packed up all his belongings for the summer, along with the gift he was going to give his dad, which the camera lingers on—a statue of a father cradling his young son. Will is left in the living room with Uncle Phil, his plans crushed. He tries to play it off like he doesn't care, but the veneer begins to wear off.

"How come he don't want me, man?" Will asks, the tears starting to fall. He collapses into Uncle Phil, who holds him tight.

That day, Avery refused to allow Smith anything but an airtight, momentous performance. "James Avery was relentless on me to elevate. He wouldn't give me a damn inch," the actor later said. Smith kept messing up his lines because he was so nervous. His costar offered some words of comfort.

"Relax. It's already in there. Look at me. Use me. Don't act around me, act with me."

Smith finally found his way and, as he fell into Uncle Phil's arms, Avery whispered to him: "That's fucking acting right there."

That moment, in the Banks living room, was a snapshot of who James Avery was. In 2013, the actor passed away at the age of sixty-eight during complications from open-heart surgery. He would leave behind a legacy as a vocal, gentle fixture on the *Fresh Prince* set, who was a father figure and mentor to all. Avery was a large, commanding man with a big heart, Jensen remembers. "A honey bear," Simon affectionately called him. Avery tricked out his dressing room to look like a comfy living room, and he and Joseph Marcell, who became tight with Avery over the course of the series, hung out there every day, listening to jazz.

The actor took great pride in the fact that his character felt like family to the many, many people who tuned in every week. "He strove to present an Uncle Phil that everybody wishes was their uncle," Marcell told CNN after Avery died. Following his passing, J. Cole would name-check Avery in his song "No Role Modelz": "First things first, rest in peace Uncle Phil/For real, you the only father that I ever knew."

By 1995, Will Smith had worked his way up to becoming a full-fledged movie star. He landed the lead in the action blockbuster *Bad Boys*, the feature directorial debut of Michael Bay, who would go on to helm the *Transformers* franchise. *Bad Boys* might not have gotten the strongest reviews (the *Times* said it was "stitched together, like some cinematic Frankenstein's monster, from the body parts of other movies"), but it was a hit at the box office, earning more than $140 million worldwide. Smith had gone from rapper to TV star to movie star in just a few years. And now he was ready to leave his sitcom roots behind.

At the end of the show's fifth season, Smith invited the cast, their significant others, and Shelley Jensen to Hawaii, flying them first class to Maui for a week. There, he told them that there was going to be only one more season of *The Fresh Prince of Bel-Air*. It was a bittersweet moment for Jensen. He knew it was time, but it was hard to say goodbye to the people who had grown to be his family.

In the show's final farewell, we find out that Hilary is moving to New York City to host her talk show. She's gone from a spoiled twentysomething with her parents' credit card to a professional woman with a career she cares about. Ashley joins her sister in New York to attend a performing arts school. Carlton finally gets his dream to go to Princeton. Geoffrey returns to London. Uncle Phil and Aunt Viv head out east, to be with Hilary and Ashley. Will stays behind in California to finish up his education.

As Carlton and Will empty the pool house, they look back on their time in that Bel-Air mansion.

"We've been through a lot together," Carlton says.

"Childhood to manhood," Will replies.

"It's been a good trip."

"It's been a *great* trip."

"Look, wherever, whenever, I've got your back, C."

"Wherever, whenever I've got your back, W," Carlton responds, trying, in earnest, a new nickname on his cousin (this bit of dialogue lands as one of the show's best off-handed jokes).

Then, for the last time, Will puts on "It's Not Unusual," his cousin's favorite song, and the two do the Carlton dance, arms flailing, hips sashaying. To this day, anytime Jensen catches up with Ribeiro, he finds himself doing that dance. The two chat frequently and, all these years later, he still sees the character of Carlton in his friend, "because he is him," he told me. "He is Carlton."

In the show's last scene, Will surveys the now-empty Banks mansion. During rehearsal, Jensen decided that Will should flip the light switch off, leaving everyone in a darkened studio. There would be more of a note of finality that way. "It was a special moment for the audience, too," he said. "This is it, we're done, it's over."

Fresh Prince was gone but far from forgotten. Years later, Susan Borowitz relocated from Los Angeles to Westchester, New York, where she enrolled her kids in a private school. The one other mother she liked there was a Black woman named Gina, who "wasn't full of Westchester bullshit." Susan doesn't usually tell people that she co-created *The Fresh Prince of Bel-Air*. She wants to make sure they're laughing at her jokes because they genuinely think she's funny, not because she's the person who created *Fresh Prince*.

So, Gina didn't know who she was talking to when, one day, she brought up the show.

"I remember when we were watching the NAACP Image Awards and there was Quincy Jones and then there was some skinny white woman next to him, I don't know what she was doing," Gina declared.

"That . . . would be me," Susan responded, guilty as charged.

Gina taught elementary school at the time, and she approached Susan with a proposition. "Want to teach a bunch of fifth graders how to write?" she asked.

"Why not?"

A generation later, these little kids were still watching *The Fresh Prince of Bel-Air*. When Susan walked in, they were in awe. They couldn't believe they were meeting the person who made the show they loved. For eight years, Susan would go to that middle school in Yonkers and play the pilot. The kids would sing along to the theme song, which they knew by heart, and then Susan discussed how to express characters through dialogue and action.

One day, Gina called her out of breath from laughing so hard.

"You have to go to the auditorium," she said. Susan drove over to the school and spotted a display the kids had created to celebrate Women's Appreciation Month. There, they had hung a photo of Susan between Michelle Obama and Harriet Tubman. She really wishes she had taken a picture that day. Just her, Michelle, and Harriet, hanging out together on the wall.

And then there was this.

Morgan Cooper was in second grade when he watched a rerun of the *Fresh Prince* episode that revolved around cops racially profiling Will and Carlton. He was a young Black boy growing up in Kansas City, Missouri, and his father had recently spoken to him about how to react to police if they ever stopped him. That half-hour episode, which the Borowitzes had so carefully constructed to hit all the right notes, spoke volumes to him. Years later, in 2019, he shot his own short film that transformed the comedy into a gritty drama and uploaded it to YouTube. Titled *Bel-Air*, the three-and-a-half-minute trailer presented an alternate version of what Will's life might have looked like without a fizzy laugh track. Several million views later and twenty-four hours after the video was posted, Smith reached out to Cooper to set up a meeting. The two ended up adapting his short into a full-fledged series for Peacock.

And it all started with that rerun. "I feel seen and I feel heard through this family," Cooper later told the *New York Times* as he looked back on that moment as a child. "Though *Fresh Prince* was a 30-minute sitcom, it was still planting seeds. It really used comedy as a Trojan Horse into these ideas."

Fresh Prince offered comedy and heart. It challenged the traditional sitcom format and painted a nuanced picture of the Black experience, presenting us with episodes of network television that remain as painfully relevant now as they were then. It helped birth one of the world's biggest movie stars. It gave us Aunt Viv and Uncle Phil. It gave us the Carlton dance.

There was a comfort to the show, the kind that only the best sitcoms offer. The Bankses were the kind of family you wanted to invite into your home every week. There was joy in being transported to that familiar Bel-Air living room, where Will was most likely in the process of needling Uncle Phil and Jazz was being thrown out the window (again).

On a deeper level, the series proved that a rapper from West Philly not only deserved his own TV show but could absolutely dominate ratings, bringing an audience to their feet every week. "Our show meant Black excellence to people," Ali said during *The Fresh Prince*'s HBOMax Reunion. "The excellence was the way that we loved each other."

Now we head to a very different Philadelphia-adjacent story, which came to the fore during the final years of *Fresh Prince*. This one was set in a fictional suburb called Three Rivers, home to a teenage girl named Angela Chase, who was going to make her own lasting mark on the small screen.

The fifteen-year-old and her classmates would redefine what teen TV could be, delivering messy, complicated young characters and a new kind of cinematic, stripped-down version of filmmaking. *My So-Called Life* was about to fling the door open for shows about teenage girls, proving to skeptical networks that theirs were stories that needed to be told. And, of course, it would introduce the world to Jordan Catalano, who lives on in the minds, hearts, and teenage dreams of all who knew and loved him.

Grab your softest flannel. Liberty High is up next.

My So-Called Life

(1994–1995)

Before there was Lindsay Weir, Rory Gilmore, Felicity Porter, or any other fictional young woman fighting her way through the trenches of growing up, there was Angela Chase.

The fifteen-year-old was introduced to audiences on August 25, 1994, in the quiet drama **My So-Called Life**, *which chronicled the pain, pleasure, and confusion of being a girl.*

"School is a battlefield for your heart," Angela's voiceover says in the first moments of the pilot as we watch her race up the steps of Liberty High.

Cut to the bathroom, where she's dyeing her light-blond locks a deep shade of red. Her new friend, Rayanne Graff, had told her that her hair was holding her back. "I had to listen, because she wasn't just talking about my hair," Angela explains. "She was talking about my life."

For the first time, a television show was about to go deep inside the psyche of a teen girl—in all its beautifully complex glory.

A television revolution was born one afternoon in a production office sandwiched between storefronts in bustling downtown Santa Monica. Writing and producing partners Ed Zwick and Marshall Herskovitz had just wrapped up their series *thirtysomething*, an ABC drama that followed the lives of a group of friends as they navigated their careers, marriages, and families.

Now Zwick and Herskovitz were ready for their next project and, this time, they had a third partner on board. Her name was Winnie Holzman. She had cut her teeth as a writer on *thirtysomething*, where she impressed the duo with how authentically she got inside the minds of the characters. Zwick and Herskovitz had an idea for a series they wanted to develop with her . . . or at least, an idea for an idea.

Zwick told Holzman that he had run into creative difficulties at the first show he wrote for, *Family*, when he tried to pitch certain story lines for the teen character Buddy Lawrence.

The conversation went something like this:

"Well, she gets in trouble for smoking."

"That's not our Buddy."

"She drinks too much and—"

"That's not our Buddy."

"She, you know, has sex and—"

"That's not our Buddy."

Herskovitz had hit a similarly frustrating roadblock. He developed a pilot for Showtime called *Secret/Seventeen*, which followed a seventeen-year-old boy trudging through the treacherous waters of adolescence. He wanted to tell a different kind of story about teenagers—not one that revolved around glamour and sexuality. His story would deal with the young man's internal struggles and all the specifically painful anxieties that come along with being young. Herskovitz was proud of his script. Then, there was a shakeup at Showtime. The old team was out, a new team came in, and the show was scrapped.

This would be Herskovitz's and Zwick's chance to finally capture adolescence on their own terms. "We're imagining you'll write about a teenage girl, and it's all the stuff we were told wasn't permissible," Holzman remembers them saying. "It's all the stuff—it's her real life."

It seems so crazy now, but a show centered entirely on a teen girl's life, told in frank, honest terms, was, indeed, a revolutionary idea. At the time, networks didn't think they could advertise to young girls, so what was the point of creating a show *about* one? Plus, *Beverly Hills, 90210*, packed with juicy drama and sun-kissed teens, had become a surprise hit, and executives thought they knew exactly what young viewers wanted: sex, explosive story lines, and beautiful people in wealthy enclaves. Not an unflashy drama about an ordinary girl in an ordinary suburb.

Before Holzman left Herskovitz and Zwick's office that day, Herskovitz had one last idea: "Why doesn't she keep a diary?" he asked. "We'll sometimes hear the diary entries and we'll see how the diary entries contrast with what is really happening."

The whole idea felt so daunting. Holzman didn't know any teen girls at the time. She had a seven-year-old daughter, and her friends either had kids her daughter's age or no children at all. Zwick offered some advice: "Don't think about the script right now," he told her. "Just write her diary."

So, that's how she started. Holzman sat down and tried to find her main character's voice, writing small moments and musings that would make their way into the pilot as a voiceover. "I'm in love," her protagonist says early on in the episode. "His name is Jordan Catalano. He was left back, twice. Once I almost touched his shoulder in the middle of a pop quiz. He's always closing his eyes, like it hurts to look at things."

(How painfully well does that bit of dialogue encapsulate high school crushes? The smallest interactions meant everything . . . I still remember the sharp *thrill* that came when my crush let his knee marginally brush mine during assemblies.)

Holzman decided to tap deep into the adolescent experience. She spent two days guest teaching at Fairfax High, a sprawling brick campus on Melrose Avenue in West Hollywood. In some ways, Holzman realized, school had changed a lot since she was a teen in the late '70s. But in other ways, it was exactly the same. Frighteningly so. That big clock on the classroom wall that always seemed like its hands barely moved. The dreamlike feeling of being propelled from one class to another. There was so much emotion going on in those hallways, and there was a sense of loneliness too.

For more research, Holzman got on the phone with the sixteen-year-old niece of *thirtysomething*'s script coordinator. The young woman's name was Angela, and the two had an honest, far-reaching conversation about life as a teen girl. "Boys have it so easy," Angela told Holzman at one point on the call.

"Well, I'm using that," Holzman thought, and mentally tucked the line away for the pilot.

As a nod to the teen, and because she found herself enamored by the name, Holzman decided to call the show's protagonist Angela.

My So-Called Life would tell the story of Angela Chase, a high schooler growing up in Three Rivers, Pennsylvania, a fictitious suburb outside Pittsburgh. Angela used to hang out with her best friend, Sharon, but lately she's been spending more time with Rayanne, a classmate with a wild streak and a substance-use problem, and Rickie, a closeted teen from an abusive household. Brian Krakow, her neighbor, has a secret crush on Angela, but she's infatuated with Jordan Catalano, a dreamy guy who has curtain bangs and wears a black choker necklace. And then there's Angela's parents, who are dealing with their own challenges as they struggle to navigate an increasingly bumpy relationship.

Selling the show to ABC was remarkably easy. Herskovitz and Zwick had a great relationship with the executives after working together on *thirtysomething* and the network was eager to snatch up another series from the duo. Still, director Scott Winant, who helmed the *My So-Called Life* pilot, wondered if the network knew what they were signing onto. "I think they were looking at it, and saying, 'Wow, that would be great, it's a show about a bad girl,'" he told me. "It's like, 'We'll make Shannen Doherty the lead, and it'll be controversial.'"

Fair enough, Winant thought at the time. On the surface, the pilot is about a girl who cuts ties with her straight-laced best friend, quits Yearbook Club, lies to her parents, and dyes her hair red. But that wasn't *My So Called-Life*. It was always going to be a coming-of-age tale that focused on its protagonist trying to find her way in the world, told through small, subtle story arcs.

Holzman didn't even want to think of her show as a teen show. She was too worried she'd channel the ways teenagers were normally depicted on television. The young characters of her world were going to talk the way kids talked, complete with plenty of "likes," "ums," and awkward pauses. They were going to be all the things that make teens such compelling characters: inarticulate, openhearted, inexperienced, insecure, and boldly overzealous.

In order to make any of this work, Holzman needed the perfect Angela. She was determined that whoever played Angela be her actual age, not an adult playing a teen as was (and still often is) the norm. The role, she knew, was a whole lot to ask of a fifteen-year-old actor.

"What if we can't find a person who's the right age who can do this?" Holzman asked Zwick.

"If we can't find the person, we just won't do the show," he told her, and Holzman breathed a sigh of relief.

Then he added: "But we're going to find her, and you're going to fall in love with her."

And indeed, when sixteen-year-old Alicia Silverstone walked into the audition room, Zwick thought they had found her.

"Oh my God. It's unbelievable, that's her. We're done," Zwick told Holzman and Herskovitz after listening to Silverstone read.

"No, it can't be her. She is brilliant, she's incredible. It can't be her," Herskovitz responded.

"Why?" Zwick asked.

"This girl is too beautiful to be Angela," Herskovitz replied. If Angela were that beautiful, he explained, she would have had a very different life.

The two went back and forth, arguing their sides fiercely. Finally—a stalemate. "OK, all right," Herskovitz recalls Zwick saying. "We'll just meet the other girl."

In walked Claire Danes. The thirteen-year-old read a scene from the pilot that takes place in the girls' bathroom, where Sharon confronts Angela about their unraveling friendship. At one point during the audition, Danes's whole face turned a deep shade of red. Herskovitz could feel all the pain and emotion in that moment. He wanted to reach out and hug her.

When she walked out, another fight ensued.

"That has to be her," Herskovitz said.

"I agree it has to be her, but it can't be her because she's thirteen years old. She can only work eight hours a day," Zwick replied.

A deal was struck and a template created. They'd expand the world of the show and focus more on Angela's parents and supporting characters, so that Danes wouldn't need to be available for every scene. There would be five or six scenes per act and four acts altogether. If they had two scenes in every act that Danes wasn't in, they could make the show.

On went the search for the rest of the cast.

Some entered the room, and Holzman just knew. Watching Wilson Cruz, a nineteen-year-old unknown actor, come in to read for the part of Rickie felt like a "fucking miracle." The character was born after Holzman watched *Paris Is Burning*, a documentary that chronicled the New York City drag scene in the '80s. The people in that community were all so beautiful, she remembers thinking, and they had created a family with one another. Rickie was a successor to those drag queens—sexually androgynous and Black and Puerto Rican. He'd wear eyeliner, hang out in the girls' bathroom, and wear beautiful, colorful, feminine outfits. This was a groundbreaking character description alone; there had never been a Rickie on television.

My So-Called Life was Cruz's first audition ever. "You should read this, there's a part in it that you might relate to," his agent told him when he handed off the audition scene. Cruz later told *Elle* he had a feeling that was code for: "Hey homosexual, you should play this!"

He read the script and saw his own high school experience right on the page, as if Holzman had trailed him with a pen and paper. Before the audition, Cruz donned red jeans, a rainbow shirt, and teased his hair up high. He was greeted by a roomful of guys in the waiting room, all wearing khakis and boat shoes. "You SO don't know who this person is," he thought.

Cruz made it to the next round. When Herskovitz met him, he was struck by this wonderful, sweet young person standing in front of him. He was *also* very aware of the fact that Cruz did not have any acting experience. "We knew that we were making a choice at that moment to go with the authenticity of this human being, and that we would somehow have to teach him the mechanics of acting," Herskovitz told me.

Then, there was Brian Krakow. When fourteen-year-old actor Devon Gummersall read the description for the character—"fifteen, nerdy, soulful, a diamond in the rough"—he immediately understood the part. That nerdiness was something he had tried to keep hidden for most of his life. Missing from the character description, and what would become an iconic part of Krakow, were those very big, very long blond curls. When I asked Gummersall the all-important journalistic question—his haircut's origin story—he laughed. "Yeah, this has to be discussed," he said. "The hair's important."

Gummersall had always hated his curly hair. He wanted that sleek look that Johnny Depp had. When he was twelve, he went to a School of Fish concert with his dad, who pointed to the lead singer and said, "Hey, you should grow your hair out like that guy. His hair is really cool and curly."

So, he did. Gummersall stopped cutting his hair in hopes that it would look just like that guy from School of Fish.

"Dad, this is crazy. It looks like a lion. It's huge," Gummersall complained, deep into the growing-out process.

"You've just got to stick with it, dude. Keep growing it out," his dad told him. "It's going to fall eventually."

And so it was in that painful transitional period that Gummersall came in to audition for Brian. He got the part and, of course, Holzman, Zwick, and Herskovitz didn't want him to change his look. It was perfect for the character.

When twenty-year-old Devon Odessa read the audition scene for the role of Sharon, she saw a slice of her own life. She and her best friend had gone through a big breakup and stopped speaking for a year. The confrontation between Sharon and Angela in the bathroom gave her chills; it all felt so eerily similar. Also, there was just something about the characters that spoke to her. She was so used to playing one-dimensional mean girls on television. The people who populated Holzman's world felt refreshingly complex.

Rounding out Angela's friendship world was Rayanne, played by A. J. Langer. The actor already had a number of television credits on her résumé, including *Blossom, Beverly Hills, 90210,* and *The Wonder Years*, when she stepped into the role of Angela's new pal. She'd inhabit a new kind of bad-girl character—one who was damaged and funny, kind and reckless.

There was one missing piece: Jordan, Angela's crush. He was originally written as a bit part who would only make an appearance in the pilot. Then, Jared Leto walked into the audition room. The twenty-three-year-old had a few Noxzema commercials and a handful of TV appearances under his belt when he came in to read for the role of one of Jordan's buddies.

Winant took one look at him and knew that he should be Jordan. The part had been written as a thuggish type, but Leto was something different—quiet and sensitive. Winant led the young actor into the hallway. There was a line in the pilot where Angela muses that she "loves the way that he leans" as the camera dreamily focuses on Jordan, his back pressed against his locker. Winant practiced that lean with Leto outside the audition room and then brought him back in.

Only, Leto didn't want to do the lean. "No, I'd rather not," Holzman recalls him saying. He also informed the room that he wasn't entirely sure he wanted to be an actor at all.

In the end, he begrudgingly did the lean. It made for a great audition, and the interaction, Holzman told me, felt "so Jared." Leto's performance would bump him up from a fleeting role in the pilot to a series regular.

It was a deceptively difficult role to play. "The show is subjective in the sense that it was through Angela's eyes. And so the Jordan we saw was Angela's Jordan," Herskovitz explained. "Not necessarily the real Jordan. He was playing the Jordan of Angela's imagination half the time. Which is a very hard thing for an actor to do."

There was one minor problem. The character was originally written as Jordan Veniziano, and Winant kept mispronouncing his last name. Holzman eventually grew tired of the confusion and decided to change it to something Winant could easily remember. His assistant at the time was Jennifer Catalano, so she renamed the character Jordan Catalano. A heartthrob was born.

Odessa still remembers the first time she saw Leto. The whole cast had gathered for their first table read. Holzman handed out character backstories she had typed out for each actor, and later that day they'd improvise scenes in character. Leto walked into the room wearing a beige sweater. "I can't even imagine if I went to high school with somebody who looked like that," she told me. "There's just no way anybody would be able to function."

When it came time to create the look of the pilot, cinematographer (and Winnie's brother) Ernest Holzman wanted it to appear cinematic, almost like a feature film. Most television shows set up lights in the set's ceilings, while more and more films were being shot on location, setting up lighting through windows or down below to give a more naturalistic look. The decision was made to shoot all scenes as if they were on location. A ceiling was designed on top of the sets so cameras could get more angles in.

The crew filmed the first episode at San Pedro High School, a campus of stucco buildings in the port neighborhood of San Pedro, Los Angeles. There's a misconception, perhaps, that teen shows need to look light and bright. But that's not what high school is. It's a hothouse bubbling over with intense emotions, deep insecurities, and bodies that are confusingly changing. Ernest captured that feeling by shooting on 16-millimeter film, which would give the show a grainy, textural look, a little like the viewer was watching a memory. Throw on an episode now, and you'll find yourself entering a surreal time capsule, a soft, dreamy moment frozen in time. There would be no sharp details on the screen, and Winant imagined it would look like a watercolor painting. Filters were taken off the camera while shooting at the high school so that it gave the fluorescent lights a sickly, institutional green glow.

Patrick Norris, who would go on to become a prolific director of teen television shows like *Dawson's Creek*, *The O.C.*, and *Gossip Girl*, signed on as costume designer and pulled inspiration from the grunge era. He had always been fascinated by album covers from the late '60s and early '70s, and he kept those images in the back of his mind as he shopped on Melrose Avenue, a mecca at the time for Doc Martens and up-and-coming designers. Along the way, he met a young fashion designer named Tommy Hilfiger, who had recently opened his first store on Rodeo Drive. Hilfiger was just starting to dress stars like Snoop Dogg and was making a name for himself with his rugby polo shirts.

"God, give me some of that stuff, man," Norris remembers saying to Hilfiger, loading up on the pieces and bringing them all back to his warehouse for Brian Krakow.

Norris decided he was going to dress both Jordan and Angela in soft, muted plaids and plenty of layers. One day, when he spotted Leto wearing a black ribbon-like necklace off-set, he exclaimed: "Dude, you've got to wear that!" The small, signature piece of jewelry would make it into every episode of the show.

When it came to Rickie, Norris took inspiration from Prince and Jimmy Hendrix. He dressed the young actor in bold colors that popped—a pink linen button-down shirt with a bright checkered vest, a maroon plaid button-down paired with a sunshine yellow tee. "I wanted you to look at him and go, 'Wow this kid is really cool.'"

The network's Office of Standards and Practices had a different take. They worried that Rickie was too "effeminate." He shouldn't be wearing eyeliner, someone told Holzman on the phone, and he definitely shouldn't be hanging out in the girls' bathroom.

Holzman was being backed into a tight corner, and she scrambled to get out. "Look, Michael Jackson was just on *Oprah*, it was probably her highest-rated show and he was wearing eyeliner, looking feminine, looking beautiful," she said.

Then, she referenced *The Crying Game*, a film that had recently nabbed a British Academy of Film and Television Arts Award and an Academy Award, in which a man falls in love with a trans woman. If there could be a trans character "starring in a movie [with] people falling at her feet," Holzman argued, "this is not going to shock anybody."

Standards and Practices backed off on that one. But there was another concern.

Each character got their own small closet, which meant that actors would re-wear articles of clothing from episode to episode. It was a purposeful decision to help make the world feel all the more authentic. That idea didn't sit well with some people at the network.

"Did you know she's wearing the same dress that she wore last week?" an executive asked Holzman.

"Yeah, I know," she replied.

"But . . . "

"Yeah, well, she has a closet, she hasn't got that many clothes, and you know, she's gonna be wearing stuff over and over," Holzman explained. She won that one too. Angela can be seen re-wearing the same long flannel shirts throughout the show, a small victory in a battle for television realism.

As shooting for the pilot began, Winant started to get to know the young actors. During Langer's first scene, he quickly realized that she had worked with an acting coach and had shown up overprepared. Langer was taking the network approach, that Rayanne was the very bad girl who was going to have a very bad influence on Angela. But that wasn't Rayanne, Winant thought. She wasn't one-dimensional. Winant was in a time crunch, but he put a pause on shooting. The two stood there, put their heads together, and created the character of Rayanne together in that dingy girls' bathroom.

Strangely, as a viewer, the best example of *My So-Called Life* skirting TV norms happens during a fleeting moment between Angela and her dad in their house's hallway. She's wearing a small towel when she runs into him and the whole thing is painfully awkward. They're immediately uncomfortable, skirting eye contact with each other and then parting ways. How often do shows—especially youth-oriented ones—tackle those really small but defining moments that so many teen girls experience but are just way too uncomfortable to talk about, even with friends? The emotionally jarring time when you no longer feel like a child around your dad? That one always stayed with me.

Winant was making decision after decision that wouldn't normally fly on television. When Danes stood on her mark during the pilot, Winant noticed she would cross her ankles and weave back and forth. That made life tricky for the camera operator to set up over-the-shoulder shots, because she kept leaning directly into the frame. He asked Winant to get her to stop but he refused. Winant liked how real and natural it felt, and he had boards laid down so that the dolly could adjust left and right as she swayed.

Then, Winant took the concept of realness one step further—all for the sake of good TV.

Toward the end of the pilot episode, Angela arrives at a party and almost immediately trips, falling into a pile of mud. She's drenched with muck and her dress is ripped as she rushes inside the house. There, Jordan sits in a darkened room. Winant decided to do something sneaky. He had a sense that Danes was nervous around Leto in real life, so before shooting the scene, he secretly locked the door that she had been instructed to exit out of. Winant knew her. He knew that if he didn't yell "cut," Danes was going to stay in character. And he was right. She didn't break. Instead, she continued to struggle with the doorknob until, realizing that she was stuck, she crumpled and slid down into a chair next to Leto.

Angela and Jordan have a short, unremarkable exchange ("This doesn't seem like a Friday," he says. "It's Thursday," she responds), and then some of his friends appear. They tell Jordan they're headed to Grungus, a real-life spot that Winant used to frequent when he was in high school, where teens would drink and smoke.

Jordan disappears with his friends and Angela is left alone in the room, equal parts mortified and pleased. She had just chatted with her crush, albeit for less than a minute, and it felt so, so big.

A normal shooting day goes for twelve hours. They only had Danes for five, which meant Winant needed to get creative. In one early scene Angela sits in a yearbook meeting, feeling lost. Brian moves his camera up to his eye to try to snap a picture of her, but she quickly pulls her loosely knit sweater over her head, where she continues to watch everyone from behind the material.

Danes had to be tutored that day, so they shot the scene quickly. Before she arrived, Winant got all the coverage he needed from the other characters in the scene. When Danes arrived, they only had a few minutes to shoot her dialogue. There wasn't enough time to film her from underneath her sweater. So later, Danes was called into a production office and Winant used a small hand-held camera called an Eyemo to shoot that point-of-view moment when she peers out at her classmates.

One of the last scenes of the episode finds Angela on her dark, empty suburban street, silhouetted against the warm glow of streetlamps. She's just been dropped off by the police after encountering a sexually aggressive man, and she spots her dad, laughing and talking outside with a woman who is not her mom. She stands there with Brian, who tells her that they've picked a theme for the yearbook. The song "Everybody Hurts" is playing in the background. It's a beautiful, now-iconic shot—all dreamy streams of light and powerful, unspoken emotion.

The crew filmed the exterior scenes of the Chase family's house in Pasadena, a quiet, residential area outside Los Angeles. There was a hard ten p.m. curfew, both from the neighborhood watch and because of Danes's restrictions as a minor. Winant and Holzman stationed themselves with a long lens two blocks away from Gummersall and Danes. They only had about eight minutes to shoot. Winant had designed the setup, knowing that Danes would do her signature ankle cross and back-and-forth weave.

Right before rolling, Danes suddenly had to go to the bathroom. It was always a production for her to use the bathroom, because her character wore hard-to-remove tights, adding extra minutes on the clock. There were no trailers around, and a production assistant ran to a house in the neighborhood to ask for toilet access. The two hurried in there together so Danes could get help with her wardrobe.

A police officer stood behind Winant, looking at his watch. "I can't give you any leeway here," he told Winant. Danes came running back, stood on her mark, the camera rolled, she weaved, and they got the scene in one take.

With the first episode in the can, Herskovitz, Zwick, and Holzman anxiously waited to see what ABC thought. At best, the reaction was ambivalent. Holzman got the sense that the executives were worried that it was just too dark. *My So-Called Life* didn't get picked up for the spring, and for a time, it looked like it was all but dead.

Then, a funny thing happened.

Creative Artists Agency, the talent firm that repped Winant and Holzman, started hosting screenings of the pilot. It got such good word of mouth that more and more industry people requested viewings. "By the middle of the year, everybody was talking about it, and I think that the network felt guilty that they hadn't put it on," Winant told me. "So, I think that campaign actually got us picked up."

One year after the pilot had been shot, ABC ordered six more episodes. Winant questioned how much faith they could possibly have in the show because they planned to throw it on Thursdays at eight p.m., putting it up against juggernauts *Friends* and *Mad About You*. "Why couldn't it have gotten a nine p.m. or ten p.m. slot?" he wondered. It seemed too simplistic to think that the show needed to be on earlier just because it starred a fifteen-year-old.

Still, with a late episode order, the clock was ticking fast and there was so much work to be done.

Herskovitz and Zwick weren't fans of the typical writers' room setup, where a group of people are crammed around a table, spit-balling ideas, dialogue, and jokes. You can't write by committee, Herskovitz explained. So instead, they'd send writers off to pen a draft in their own voices and then Herskovitz and Zwick would give them notes. Never rewrites, just note after note after note. Herskovitz and Zwick always preferred to give copious feedback rather than taking the script away from them.

They had writers—great writers—who struggled to grasp Holzman's style. Only one person so intrinsically got Holzman's world that she felt she could fully trust him with Angela's voice. His name was Jason Katims, and he'd go on to become the Emmy-winning writer and showrunner behind the much-beloved *Friday Night Lights*, *Parenthood*, and *Roswell*.

Katims had found his calling as a student at Queens College in New York City. He signed up for English 101, an introductory class, where the students were required to write in a journal a few times a week. Then, they'd sit in a circle and share. One day, Katims read out loud an excerpt from his diary. At the time, his girlfriend, Kathy, was working as a waitress and he would pick her up from work at the end of her late shifts. As he sat at a table waiting for her, he wrote observations about the people around him—waitresses bustling from table to table, the janitor sweeping. These were the small, no-frills slices of life that would populate *My So-Called Life* and later *Friday Night Lights*.

"Do you realize what that is?" Katims remembers his professor asking when he was done reading.

"What? What is it?" he asked.

"That's a short story," she said.

It was the first moment, he told me, that he'd ever thought: "Oh wow, I'm writing." When Katims graduated from college, he decided he would become a playwright. He took a graphic-design job in Manhattan to make ends meet and entered a ten-minute playwriting competition sponsored by the Actors Theatre of Louisville. Titled *The Man Who Couldn't Dance*, Katims's script was an intense, intimate one, featuring an ex-couple discussing the unresolved issues in their relationship. It was based on a real encounter he witnessed between his friend and his friend's old girlfriend during a weekend getaway in New Hampshire.

The Man Who Couldn't Dance got Katims published. It also caught the eye of Zwick, who read it in a copy of the Actors Theater collection and decided to track Katims down to offer him a job.

Katims and Kathy traded their Brooklyn digs for a charming, weathered walk-up apartment in Pacific Palisades, an oceanside neighborhood in Los Angeles. Most writers on *My So-Called Life* would attend story meetings and write their scripts from home. Katims ended up with an office across the hall from Holzman. "I kind of just invited myself in," he said.

Katims would watch in awe as Holzman, Herskovitz, and Zwick worked. The conversation always started philosophically. "What do we want to tell a story about?" Zwick would manage to find the heart of the episode so quickly after just a short back-and-forth. Then, he and Herskovitz would fight over who got to be the one to use the computer. Holzman, Katims remembers, was always able to access the emotion in every scene in a way he had never seen before or since.

One evening, Holzman had to hunker down late to rewrite a script. She asked Katims if he wanted to stay with her and help out with the edits. Secretly, he suspected that she just needed someone who would keep her awake during the wee hours. As the two sat side by side in Holzman's office, in front of the computer, the night turned into a writing master class.

Holzman pointed to moments that she'd call "seg alerts," which is when the subject in the scene changes. "When that happens, it should be imperceptible," she told Katims. Then, she'd say a line that Katims would end up using for years to come in his own writers' rooms. "What would *really* happen?" she asked. It was never: "This is what we *need* to happen in order to get to the next scene." Every moment had to feel true.

Katims watched Holzman think deeply, letting herself get emotionally entrenched in the scene. She really looked at the show as an art form, he realized. "I never thought of TV that way," Katims told me. "I mean, now we all do because TV has gotten its golden age. But at the time it really wasn't. There were features, there were novels, there were plays, and then there was TV."

Episodes would center on seemingly small stories and then expand into much deeper emotional territory. When Katims heard that they would be doing an episode about Angela waking up with a pimple on her face, he pretended to be enthused by the idea. Inside, he was thinking, *This ain't gonna work.* Then, to his amazement, he watched the story unfold.

The episode, titled simply "The Zit," opens with Angela peering at the blossoming pimple on her chin and expands into a larger examination of beauty. Angela's mom, Patty, is struggling with getting older. Angela is struggling with insecurity about her looks. Sharon feels self-conscious about her developing breasts, a story line pulled directly from Odessa's own life. She used to be so embarrassed about having big breasts that she would cut the control top off her pantyhose and wrap it around her chest to flatten it.

Holzman was quick to stitch real-life details into scripts. Jordan Catalano, for instance, was dyslexic because Winant had a reading disability in high school, which he hid from everybody. Holzman had a way about her that allowed people to open up. I discovered that myself during our phone interview when, as a result of her gentle line of questioning, I ended up telling her that I had just moved to Los Angeles and was feeling very weird about everything.

Delia, a transfer student played by Senta Moses, would end up having a crush on Rickie because Moses confided in Holzman that she had a crush on Cruz. "I know that he's gay, I don't even care," she told Holzman. Cruz was the first cast member she had met, and the two immediately clicked while rehearsing a dance sequence together. He was just so talented and sweet and smart. She was smitten.

Moses was twenty at the time, and not so far removed from experiencing the intense emotional feelings of being a teenager. She remembered how those really small moments meant everything at the time—a prolonged knee brush, passing someone a drink on the off chance that your fingers might touch. Her character would develop a crush on Brian, who—in one heartbreaking scene—rescinds his offer to take her to the school dance. Moses remembers standing opposite Gummersall and watching him in action. There was always so much going on in his head, and she found that she, too, was trying to figure out what he was thinking, hanging on each word.

Gummersall, meanwhile, was developing a budding friendship with Leto. He was shy around girls, and Leto would encourage him to get out of his shell. "Hey man, come out with me, come with me to this party," he'd say. They both loved to snowboard and Leto once helped Gummersall get a girl's phone number (he ended up being too nervous to call).

Gummersall loved to share those moments with Holzman. He'd visit her office and tell her funny stories from his life. "You won't believe what Jared did!" he'd say, or "This girl is so cool." She was a great audience. Plus, his story about Leto helping him get a phone number ended up making its way into an episode of *My So-Called Life*.

Gummersall was falling in love with writing. He penned a book of poems, which he photocopied, along with photographs he had taken, bound the collection, and presented it to Holzman. She loved it. "This is so cool," he thought. "Maybe I could actually be a real writer because she thinks I'm good."

He pored over the scripts, which were carefully sprinkled with "likes," "ums," and built-in hesitations. Gummersall memorized every single ellipsis in the script—he treated it like it was Shakespeare, he told me. Leto, however, would get impatient.

"There's too many 'likes'; I'm crossing some of these out," Gummersall remembers Leto saying.

"OK, bro, you do you." Gummersall shrugged.

Because he was a minor, Gummersall had to spend a chunk of his day alongside Danes doing schoolwork. That was not where he wanted to be. He wanted to spend time with the show's writers and watch them work. So he negotiated with his studio teacher. "Look, man, I love writing and you've got to let me go hang out and be a fly on the wall when Winnie and Jason are working and let me count it as school," he said.

"I don't know about that," the teacher responded. But they struck a deal. If Gummersall spent an hour with the writers, it would count as fifteen minutes of school.

One day, Winant showed Gummersall some ads he had cut for *My So-Called Life*. He wasn't happy with the way ABC was marketing the show and was hoping to course-correct. The trailers had rubbed Gummersall the wrong way too. The network was trying too hard to make the show look like *90210*, hyping up the story lines on dating drama and love triangles. "They were trying to cram it into this envelope of making it into a lighthearted little goofy teenage show that it was not," he said.

At the time, shows were promoted almost exclusively on their own networks. It would be a few years until Winant got his first glimpse of real-world television advertising. Suddenly, a young man standing in a rowboat was all over buses and billboards. The WB had created a massive, widespread campaign for its new teen show *Dawson's Creek* and young James Van Der Beek, with his sweeping, sandy-blond hair and white buttoned shirt, was everywhere. But ABC wasn't quite there yet. With trailers that weren't cutting it and a crummy time slot, *My So-Called Life* was getting most of its attention from favorable press reviews. Critics were impressed but cautious.

"The built-in obstacle for a dramatic series about teen-age life that aims to engage an adult audience has to do with its level of sophistication," Bruce Weber began his review for the *New York Times*. "It needs to be authentic enough that, on the one hand, it's persuasive and maybe even instructive about the angst and perplexity and exhilaration of the adolescent Zeitgeist. On the other hand, you don't want it to be too authentic. That would be stultifying (or terrifying), like living with your neighbors' kids."

My So-Called Life, he wrote, "bravely" took on that problem, creating a compelling world both inside and outside Angela's point of view while juggling story lines about her life with that of her family.

Variety's Jonathan Taylor dubbed the show a quality drama but expressed concern about its eight p.m. time slot. "ABC will need to exercise parental patience in letting this child grow and develop, but the show looks to be a critical hit and has the makings of a ratings contender," he wrote.

Taylor was right to be skeptical about the network. Holzman watched as ABC grew more and more antsy. She'd hear stories about the rough cuts being delivered to the studio office and young employees excitedly rushing to watch. But the people who were *actually* in charge of the show's fate didn't share their enthusiasm. They didn't seem to think it was financially viable. "How were we going to market products to teens during the ad breaks?" was the big question.

"There's no audience for teenagers on television," Zwick remembers them saying over and over again.

"Who is it for?" was another concern. Executives couldn't figure out if they were marketing the show to teens or adults. And then came the complaints about the content. It was too depressing. It was too dark.

"Have you ever watched the news? Like, ever?" Holzman responded. "Our show is not depressing compared to that."

My So-Called Life would get nominated for four Emmys—Outstanding Directing in a Drama Series for Winant, Outstanding Writing in a Drama Series, Outstanding Achievement in Main Title Theme Music, and Outstanding Lead Actress in a Drama Series for Claire Danes. Danes took home a Golden Globe for her performance and fielded questions after the ceremony on why the show wasn't getting more traction.

"I think it's on a weird kind of time slot and it's a really complicated show and it's very confusing to figure out how to market it. It's pretty fragile," she told reporters. "Hopefully maybe this will at least make more people aware that it's out there. Any recognition is wonderful."

Despite a mostly ambivalent network and unsatisfying ratings, the creative team pressed on. The show was filmed in a converted factory building, and Winant would often work late in his office, just above the stages. Every evening he would see Danes there, across the bullpen in a conference room, doing her homework. When Danes wasn't rehearsing or shooting, she was sleeping or studying between scenes. Holzman rarely spent any time alone with her. Once, when the two wound up in an elevator together, Holzman found herself suddenly shy. She was so in awe of Danes.

My So-Called Life had a small budget, but they would load their sets and locations with fake snow for Christmastime, despite the expense. The same went for night shoots on location. Equally expensive and difficult, but necessary. Patrick Norris suspected his job was constantly on the line because he was hitting the high-end stores of L.A.'s Rodeo Drive, spending money on pieces from Saks, Barneys, and Ralph Lauren. He'd blend those items in with vintage looks, like a rented kimono from a costume house. People from the network would call constantly, asking him to spend less. "OK, I'll watch it, I'll watch it," Norris replied. And then he'd head straight back to Saks.

Norris made his directing debut with the show's sixteenth episode, "Resolutions." He didn't get the impression that Danes was particularly impressed by his work. Norris thought if he didn't give the actors a note after each scene, they wouldn't think he was a proper director. So he overcorrected. And then there was the one note, he recalled, that didn't land at all.

As Norris was trying to get Danes into the mindset of a scene between Angela and Jared, he said: "This is that feeling, when you just made love to someone for the first time and you're really in the space of lust and you're really into the relationship."

"There's only one problem," Norris remembers Danes saying.

"What's that?"

"I've never made love to anybody," she said.

"Oh fuck," Norris thought. "Bad note." He learned in that moment to be sensitive to where the teen actors actually were in their lives.

The first time Angela and Jordan kiss is in his parked car. Finally, *finally* she's alone with him. She watches his profile with pure wonder. "What's amazing is when you can feel your life going somewhere, like your life just figured out how to get good," her voiceover muses.

Then, just as she starts to speak, he leans over and kisses her in a brisk, aggressive way. Absolutely zero romance. Angela had been waiting so long for Jordan to kiss her. And now that moment, which she had probably designed and played in her head on loop so many times, was happening—and it wasn't anything like she hoped it would be.

"I'm sorry—I was—I was talking," Angela said, pulling away from him.

She starts to try to continue her train of thought, and then he comes for her again. She pushes him off. "Quit it! I mean, you have to work up to that," Angela says. "I don't open that wide at the dentist."

For a long, long time, on-screen kisses were always magical. Lips would meet at a non-awkward moment, a great, romantic song would swell, and both parties seemed to know exactly what to do with their mouths. Here, it was the opposite. Not only did the kiss Jordan give Angela—for lack of a better term—suck, but the timing was all wrong. And yet we get to see the young female protagonist set clear, firm boundaries with her body. Not only that, she was *pissed* that he was ignoring her while she was trying to have an interesting conversation with him.

Then, the next moment makes it all the more real.

Jordan stops trying to kiss her. He moves away, leans back in his seat, eyes closed, looking sad and vulnerable. Part of his sleeve is touching her arm and they sit there quietly. He's evolved back into the Jordan Angela has fantasized about, the version of a person who doesn't really exist. And that makes him, suddenly, so appealing all over again.

"Everything started to feel perfect for some reason," Angela says in the voiceover. "The feel of his shirt against my elbow. The fact that I still had an elbow. It was the perfect moment for him to kiss me, for him to anything me."

And of course, it's then that Jordan opens the car door, firmly putting a close to their evening.

"Well, I gotta go," he says coldly. "So, later."

As the characters explored their coming-of-age journeys, the young actors were going through their own moments of growth. Herskovitz watched as Cruz had his first big acting breakthrough in the episode "Guns and Gossip." The pivotal scene happens when Angela finds Rickie alone in the backseat of a Cadillac. It's pouring outside and she runs over and hops in the car.

There's a rumor going around that Rickie brought a gun to school, but he admits to Angela that it was actually his cousin who did, and he was trying to stop him. He didn't mind that people thought it was him, though. Maybe that would make his classmates less inclined to pick on him. He then reveals some of his deeper insecurities to Angela.

"You know, it's weird, I always think of you as Rayanne's friend," he says. "I mean, you just think of me as someone who's just, you know, around."

Herskovitz directed that episode. The night before they shot the scene, his neck started itching. When he woke up, he looked disfigured. The whole left side of his face was swollen so badly that he couldn't see out of one eye. Turns out he had a very bad reaction to poison oak. The idea of going onto set looking like that was absolutely mortifying.

"What does the day of shooting cost? Seventy-five thousand dollars. Is it worth $75,000 to me for no one to see me?" he remembers thinking. "I don't care if I go into debt for ten years."

But Herskovitz decided against canceling the shoot. "I had to go in there and face everyone, literally looking like a monster," he said. "And it was so perfect for that show. I mean, we did a whole episode about a zit."

That day, he watched as Cruz struggled with his monologue inside the car. He just couldn't quite get it. Herskovitz called for a break and slid into the Cadillac beside the actor. They sat there for hours as the fake rain battered the windshield. He used his own vulnerability about the way he looked to nudge Cruz to open up about his pain.

"Most young people, when they act, it's about pretending, you know?" Herskovitz explained to me. "When the best acting is the opposite of pretending. It's being who you are."

They talked about who Cruz was. He was a young man who was going through a lot of pain. His father had kicked him out of the house after Cruz told him he was gay. For a time, he was crashing at Odessa's apartment in Studio City. Before that, he was sleeping in his car or on friends' couches.

"I feel dizzy," Cruz said.

"Yes, good," Herskovitz replied. Cruz looked at him like he was crazy.

"It *should* be that scary. That means you're going to the right place."

Later, Holzman and Katims would pen an episode where Rickie gets kicked out of his house at Christmas, the same time Cruz did. He wanders the street cold, hungry, and alone, eventually ending up in a dark, abandoned building where other teens without homes are living. The episode premiered a year after Cruz had been thrown out of his own house. About ten minutes after it finished airing, Cruz got a call from his dad. He had watched the episode and thought they should talk.

"It was through his watching of the series that he was able to understand what my life was really like," Cruz later told *People*. "And so you look at this man who was incredibly conservative. Growing up, I never thought he would ever accept my sexuality, but because of a TV show, he was able to change his mind."

Cruz's dad was far from alone in feeling the show's impact. Despite the show's sluggish ratings, there was a devoted fan base who were fiercely determined to keep it on the air. Steve Joyner, a twenty-seven-year-old writer based in San Francisco, fell in love after watching the pilot and logged onto message boards like AOL and CompuServe to swap notes with fellow fans. When the group found out that the season finale might be the end of the road, an uprising began to build.

Joyner penned a two-thousand-word email to all the fans on the forums with the subject line, "A *So-Called* Call to Arms." In it, he introduced the idea of Operation Life Support, which would involve raising $2,580 to place a full-page ad in *Variety*, written as a direct plea to ABC executive Ted Harbert. "[*My So-Called Life*] is well-observed, superbly written and brilliantly acted. The plots are intricate, the characters frighteningly real—in short, a breath of fresh air," Joyner wrote in his email. "I believe my love for this show to be a reflection of yours. And like you, I am shocked and dismayed that the end of the honeymoon is nigh—that, alas, the last episode of *My So-Called Life* MIGHT be less than two months away."

Joyner created Operation Life Support T-shirts and doled them out in exchange for donations. In the end, he raised a whopping $90,000. The ad would run the same day that *My So-Called Life* aired its final episode, "In Dreams Begin Responsibilities." It marked the first online campaign created to save a show, something that has become a recurring practice in the age of social media, from *Family Guy* to *Friday Night Lights*.

About a week before the finale, the *Washington Post* ran its own plea to keep the show on the air, with the headline, "A TV Show Worth Saving." Writer Judy Mann shared her love of the show, which she said offered just as much to her as to her teen daughter. "It's important that Angela make mistakes, that she's allowed not to be a nice person," Holzman, who spoke to Mann for the piece, said. "I believe in the kind of storytelling where people aren't always flawless, where people grow and stumble."

The network and, perhaps, viewers at-large weren't quite ready for Angela Chase. Only now are we in an era where strong, complicated women are—mostly—allowed to take center stage. Female characters don't have to be quite so likable anymore and, in fact, it feels reductive if they are. Angela's messiness and less-than-perfect edges would be a footnote now, but back then she felt too big and too bold. Sometimes, she was painful and frustrating to watch. She could be mean too.

But the fans who loved *My So-Called Life* really loved *My So-Called Life*. When Gummersall and Leto went to a Christmas concert at Universal Studios, they were spotted by a crowd of young people. Teens began climbing over sections just to get to the two of them. "Um, what the fuck? OK, I guess some people are watching the show," Gummersall thought at the time.

Before shooting the final episode, Holzman called *NYPD Blue* director and producer Elodie Keene in for a meeting. She wanted her to direct what could possibly be the last installment of *My So-Called Life*. At the time, Keene had grown used to being one of the few women on-set—in fact, she and the script coordinator were the only women working behind the scenes of *NYPD Blue*. She was so accustomed to taking on a masculine energy that when she sat down to meet with Holzman, she told me that she sprawled her legs wide out and leaned forward.

Keene quickly realized that this was not that kind of environment. She eased herself back on the couch and relaxed.

The script wasn't quite done yet, Holzman told her. She didn't know if this episode would be the last of the series or if they'd get picked up for another season, so the finale would need to feel like a satisfying-enough conclusion for fans while leaving a door open for future episodes just in case.

Keene had watched the show and marveled at its unique syntax. Was that in the writing, she wondered, or were the actors given leeway to speak how they wanted? Then the script arrived. Every punctuation, every hesitation was right there. The front page included a personalized inscription from Holzman:

This script is dedicated with love and gratitude to the brilliant, beautiful cast and crew of "My So-Called Life."

"How far that little candle throws his beams!"—Shakespeare

Love, Winnie

On-set, Keene remembers being in awe of Holzman. She had this very feminine, airy way about her, with big glasses and flowing hair. She always spoke with her hands. One day, she turned to Holzman.

"I get it. I get it now," Keene said.

"What are you talking about?" she remembers Holzman replying.

"You hide this prodigious intelligence behind all that so no one will feel threatened," Keene said.

In the film industry at the time, Keene told me, men were unnerved by women in charge. It wasn't a comfortable place to work. "All of us had to figure out a way to be OK, to be good in the company of all these guys and to have influence without making them feel like we were taking something from them."

The final episode would break television ground during a conversation between Rickie and Delia. Rickie knows Delia likes him and decides to bite the bullet and ask her out. Only, she's pretty certain that he's gay, which she gently asks him about. Moses sent me the script, with her carefully marked notes for each line in the scene, which you can see on the next page.

This was the first time a teen had ever come out on television. Holzman, Keene, Herskovitz, and Zwick were determined to get that moment right. Keene had directed the first network kiss between two women on *L.A. Law,* and she knew how significant something like this could be. After that *L.A. Law* episode aired, total strangers came up to Keene at parties and asked: "Do you have any idea what you've done for our community?"

Herskovitz and Zwick had already had their own share of battles with ABC over a same-sex scene they shot on *thirtysomething.* Executives were OK with two men being in bed together but definitely not OK with them kissing. Five years later, Herskovitz could feel the culture changing—at least a little bit. This time there was no pushback from ABC higher-ups.

RICKIE (cont'd)
Uh... Delia?
(beat, not looking at
her)
Maybe we should-- you know.

It's happening!

DELIA
What?

-heart is beating 1000 miles/minute

RICKIE
Go somewhere. Sometime.

DELIA
Oh, okay-- *(trying to be casual w/out screaming)*

RICKIE
To a movie or something. Okay?

DELIA
Okay! I'd like that!

RICKIE
(still can't look at her)
Cause I really like you. I really
think we'd be like-- good together.

DELIA
Okay. *Realization →* *I have to ask! Just in case he says NO.*
(just to clarify)
But umm. You're gay, right?

RICKIE
(in shock)
Well...

Did I offend him? Is gay the wrong word? Did I make it sound like being gay was bad?

DELIA
I'm sorry, I didn't--
...mean it like that.

RICKIE
No, that's okay--

DELIA
--that came out so <u>rude</u>.

RICKIE
See I try not to label myself as--
I mean, I don't like to limit
myself to any-- *He's babbling + won't answer the question. Still hope!*
(beat, Delia is just
staring up at him)
Yeah, I'm gay. I don't usually
just-- say it. Like that.

(CONTINUED)

They shot that coming-out scene fifteen or sixteen times. At one point, when Cruz said the line, "Yeah, I'm gay," he flicked the pencil he was holding out of his hand. The improvised moment would make it into the final cut.

"That was something he added," Moses told me. "The brilliance of Wilson Cruz."

The episode closes just where the first episode ended, on a darkened street between Angela and Brian's house. Angela is crushed to learn that a heartfelt letter Jordan gave her was in fact written by Brian. Her anger turns to softness when she realizes that Brian was just trying to express his own feelings for her. The two have a moment where maybe, possibly, they're going to kiss. And then Jordan pulls up in his car and Angela hops in, leaving Brian alone on the street.

It felt so real, Gummersall later told me. "I just remember it was easy to relate to that because, I think as any teenage boy can tell you, there's a lot of heartbreak and there's a lot of missed connection where you're like, 'If only this person knew this part of me, it would work out.'"

If the show was made now, Brian could have easily been the love interest. Funny, smart, and kind, he exists well within the realm of future television love interests like *The O.C.*'s Seth Cohen and *Never Have I Ever*'s Ben Gross. Jordan Catalano represents a dusty heartthrob of television's past—brooding, unpredictable, and largely unexpressive. Rewatching the show now, it's hard for me to imagine what was so appealing about Jordan. But maybe I've just grown too old for his curtain bangs and monosyllabicness. Later, I'd have the same revelation about Ryan Atwood when I went back to rewatch *The O.C.* (another classic bad-boy protagonist with a choker necklace).

Brian Krakow was just born a little before his time.

The last episode of *My So-Called Life* was scheduled to air on January 26, 1995, and Zwick fought one last battle to keep the show alive. He went to Bob Iger, then-CEO of Disney, the parent company of ABC, to make a final plea.

"You have daughters. This show is about teenage girls who are absolutely invisible in our culture. They have no voice whatsoever. Nobody speaks for them. No one listens to them," Herskovitz recalls Zwick telling the studio executive.

Renewing the show would simply be "corporate good work," Zwick explained. "You are giving a voice to a group of young people who go through a lot of pain, who no one sees or hears."

And the amazing thing was—Iger really listened. Herskovitz was sure that the network was prepared to pick up the show. But there was one problem.

"By then, poor Claire, she was ready to do movies. She wanted to move on. She had given three years of her life to do a season of a television show, and it was like, 'Enough already,'" Herskovitz said. "So it was really too late. That moment had passed."

ABC's decision to pick up the show in dribs and drabs had sealed its fate.

Then, something momentous happened. MTV began re-airing episodes of the show, in a move that the *Los Angeles Times* called "highly unusual" for its time. The network was a hub for young-adult content, and this go-round, upper-level management knew exactly who they were targeting.

"*My So-Called Life* speaks dramatically to our audience," Joe Davola, senior vice president of original programming and development for MTV, told the *L.A. Times*. "It's a true portrayal of teens today. We always bring to our audiences the coolest things—music, movies, personalities. We thought we should bring them the coolest show. Hopefully we can expose it."

Mission absolutely accomplished. Herskovitz told me that if it hadn't been for MTV re-airing *My So-Called Life* and introducing Angela to a wider audience, we would not be sitting there, having a conversation about the show today. And the impact marches on.

Years later, in 2019, Sam Levinson, the creator of the hit HBO teen drama series *Euphoria*, would pull from his love for *My-So Called Life* as he filmed night scenes with a whole new generation of teens.

"We drew on their style of photography, which captures how the world feels a little dangerous and unsettling and big and when you're young and sneaking out and wandering around," Levinson told *Vulture*. "The backlighting of the trees, the light streaming out. It's just beautiful."

But we're getting ahead of ourselves.

Way before Levinson, a writer named Kevin Williamson would settle down to watch the pilot of *My So-Called Life* as he tried to figure out how to write act breaks for his new show. He was going to tell his own version of the adolescent experience, this time set in the idyllic town of Capeside, Massachusetts, featuring four whip-smart, hyperverbal teens.

Another television revolution was about to be born.

Dawson's Creek

(1998–2003)

In January 1998, on the outskirts of a small town called Capeside, childhood best friends Joey Potter and Dawson Leery settled in for their usual movie night. Only this time, Joey tells Dawson, things are starting to feel different. They've both turned fifteen, freshman year is just around the corner, and she's worried that newly raging hormones will ruin their friendship.

The two argue their sides fiercely, with Dawson promising that nothing has to change between them.

"We're friends, OK?" he tells her. "No matter how much body hair we acquire. Deal?"

"Deal," Joey relents.

The camera zooms out on the two lying together, Joey curled to one side, Dawson on his back. The beginning notes of Paula Cole's "I Don't Want to Wait" start to play.

Dawson, it would turn out, could not have been more wrong.

Everything was about to change, and we, as the viewers, would be along for the whole tumultuous, aching, bighearted ride. In that sleepy creekside house, a new generation of television teens was about to emerge.

B efore there was *Dawson's Creek*, there was a television executive named Paul Stupin.

Every day after lunch, he would settle down at his desk and comb through *Variety* for news on up-and-coming writers. Stupin had landed a deal with Sony to develop TV projects and was on the hunt for fresh talent. One day, buried in the paper's back pages, he stumbled on a small blurb for an upcoming film titled *Scary Movie*. Something about the film's brief description spoke to Stupin, and he requested a copy of the script. Penned by a writer named Kevin Williamson, the story—later renamed *Scream*—followed a group of young people who were being tormented by a masked killer. The horror movie had a tongue-in-cheek edge to it, laced with pop culture references and high schoolers who were wiser, funnier, and more self-aware than their predecessors.

Stupin was impressed. He set up a meeting with Williamson in his office, and the two bounced around concepts for a possible television show. Stupin pitched the idea of a younger *X-Files* series, with action-packed sequences to play to Williamson's strengths in that genre. Williamson didn't particularly respond to that. *But* he did light up when Stupin began discussing a potential young ensemble show, featuring a group of teens who all lived on the same block. One week later, Williamson returned to Stupin's office with two characters and the beginnings of a story. He introduced Stupin to Dawson Leery, a Steven Spielberg–obsessed teen who loves movies and desperately wants to become a filmmaker. He lives across the creek from his best friend, Josephine (Joey) Potter, in a town called Capeside. The story was loosely based on Williamson's own adolescence in New Bern, North Carolina, where he would shoot movies in his backyard with his childhood pal. Stupin could relate. As a kid, he used to sneak onto studio lots just to get a peek at movie magic until an assistant director shooed him away.

Stupin suggested that Dawson have some sort of confidant, perhaps a Jim Belushi type, and Williamson came back with Pacey Witter, a wisecracking pal who had grown up with both Joey and Dawson. Filling out the group was Jen, a young woman with a mysterious past who moves to Capeside to live with her grandmother.

The teens of Capeside were going to speak differently from other teens on television. The young people who populated Williamson's world were deeply introspective, with dialogue that was dense, highly articulate, and capped with poetic flourish. Their hearts were big and their vocabularies even bigger. (I can credit *Dawson's Creek* for teaching me the word "proverbial" at the tender age of twelve.) Stupin thought of the show as a form of wish fulfillment. It was how teenagers *wanted* to express themselves.

The pilot script headed to Fox and, much to Stupin's disappointment, they passed. The voices felt dated, he was told, and the writing wasn't contemporary enough.

Next, he tried NBC.

"I really want to do *Dawson's Creek*," Stupin told a table of development executives. "It's one of these amazing scripts that I'm so proud of, and I don't think comes around all that often." Once again, the response was tepid. Executives told Stupin that they just weren't interested in a show about teenagers.

Williamson, meanwhile, had quietly given up. He decided to name his new dog Dawson as an homage to the show that he figured would never come to be.

Then Stupin got a call from the WB. The network was in its infancy and building up a stable of shows targeted at young adults. Though that's not what they called the demographic at the time, former head of the WB, Garth Ancier, told me. Rather, they said they were going after an "alternative audience," a group of viewers that no other network seemed to be single-mindedly pursuing. *Dawson's*, with its crew of teens exploring love, friendship, and growing pains, sounded like the perfect fit.

The WB didn't order a whole episode. Instead, they asked Stupin and Williamson to create a presentation, roughly twenty-six minutes long, which would be shot on ultra-low-budget 16-millimeter film.

Marcia Shulman, who had cast the WB's first big teen hit, *Buffy the Vampire Slayer*, was tapped to find the kids of Capeside. Shulman came from the indie film world, where she had spent her career casting small, low-budget films. She had no interest in working in TV.

But here she was, in Los Angeles, assembling a cast of young actors whom the network insisted fit the WB's definition of attractive. "It was just very cut and dry," she told me. "They had a very white-bread approach to what pretty is."

"Coming from my indie world, that drove me crazy. I was like, The weirder the better. I guess they felt, and it's true, that *Buffy* was a very attractive cast and since that was the show that launched the WB I think it kind of became a template for them."

Shulman took on the difficult if not impossible task of trying to hire actors of color for *Dawson's Creek*. She would try to have conversations with producers about casting non-white actors, and the coded response Shulman recalls receiving was "I don't see it." Or "They wouldn't be friends in real life." Those actors never made it to screen testing.

Beauty standards for young women cast on WB shows were exceedingly high. "Not pretty enough," Shulman was often told. Young men didn't face the same scrutiny, and there certainly wasn't as much judgment. If a male actor had charisma, that could make up for a lot.

It's hard to believe now, but when Michelle Williams, a sixteen-year-old from Kalispell, Montana, came in to read for the part of Jen, it wasn't an easy yes. Shulman had to fight for Williams after getting pushback that she wasn't really "WB pretty." There were also complaints that she looked older than the rest of the core cast.

"I'd be like, 'She's actually two years younger than everybody and she's beautiful. She has her own look,'" Shulman recalls pushing back. "She's like a young Simone Signoret. Like a young Ellen Barkin. It's interesting. It's not that Midwestern-pretty thing."

Katie Holmes would be a much easier sell.

A few years earlier, while casting for *Buffy*, Shulman had stumbled on a tape of the young, unknown actor and was immediately impressed.

"Oh, this is Buffy," Shulman thought. Then she found out that Holmes was sixteen. The show required actors to take part in extensive night shoots, which wouldn't be possible for anyone under the age of eighteen. Holmes was out of the running, but Shulman kept her in her back pocket. Maybe there would be another part better suited for her.

When the role of Joey Potter came along, Shulman reached out to Holmes's manager right away. "Put her on tape," she told him. Holmes's audition arrived in the mail, and Shulman flagged Stupin and Williamson down.

"I've got a good kid for you to see," Shulman told Stupin. Whenever she said something like that, he knew they were in for something interesting. Holmes had taped her reading for Joey in her basement in Toledo, Ohio, with her mom playing the part of Dawson.

"OK, there's Joey," Stupin thought immediately as he watched Holmes, all big, expressive brown eyes and charming tête-à-tête. He wanted to fly her out to Los Angeles for an in-person audition immediately.

There was one problem.

Holmes was the star of her high school musical *Damn Yankees*, and her manager explained that she didn't want to let down her cast members by missing a performance. If Stupin did indeed need her that week, she'd have to pass. That dedication won Williamson and Stupin over even more, and they booked an appointment around her musical's schedule. Holmes came in and won the role of scrappy Joey Potter.

There was *something* about Joshua Jackson, a young actor from Vancouver, Canada. Shulman had seen him in *The Mighty Ducks*, a '90s hockey movie, and thought he had a "charming pretension" to him. Jackson originally auditioned for the role of Dawson, but it didn't feel quite right. Then he read for Dawson's best friend. It was the perfect fit—Jackson, with his quick wit and confident ease, was a natural Pacey Witter.

The longest, biggest struggle was finding the show's lead. Dawson needed to be a delicate balance of so many things: wildly self-assured yet painfully vulnerable, incredibly self-aware but deeply misguided. As the pilot's shooting date inched closer, Stupin and Shulman frantically read actor after actor to no avail. Toward the end, Stupin stopped coming into his office because there were no more live casting sessions left. All that remained were the audition tapes from New York.

Shulman had her eye on James Van Der Beek, another unknown actor with only a few credits to his name. Van Der Beek, it turned out, wasn't interested. "These are the days when people didn't do television; they wanted a movie career," Shulman told me. "So he wanted to do starving, independent films in New York and not a TV series."

Still, a phone call was arranged with Van Der Beek and his agent. They tried to persuade him to simply shoot an audition tape and by the end of the call he relented. Van Der Beek felt like Dawson, Shulman sensed. He had an intelligence and eruditeness about him. And a pretentiousness, like Jackson—also in a good way.

Van Der Beek was flown out to Los Angeles to read for the network. But first, he needed a haircut. Van Der Beek, Williamson, and Stupin rushed around town trying to find a hairstylist who would create the signature Dawson Leery Season 1 look: long, wavy styled bangs. A stylist was tracked down, and Van Der Beek headed to the WB offices for his audition. It was an easy, quick sell. The next day, the three of them were on a plane to North Carolina to begin shooting.

Dawson's Creek was filmed in Wilmington, North Carolina, a small coastal city surrounded by dreamy creeks and with a charming downtown. Even now, if you head to the Wilmington Riverwalk, a quaint stretch dotted with restaurants and shops, you'll feel like you've been transported right back to the world of Capeside. The Leery's Fresh Fish building, those lamp-lined streets along the Cape Fear River, home to so many emotionally charged conversations—it's all still there, like a living, breathing set.

Alan Hook, the show's production designer, was given a small budget for the pilot, and that money needed to be stretched as far as possible. The first and second floor of Dawson's house were built on a soundstage, and only pieces of Jen's house—part of the kitchen, a slice of the living room and hallway—were constructed. They couldn't afford to build much scenery around those sets.

Hook found an old rowboat, turned it on its end, and created a bookshelf for Dawson's bedroom. Steven Spielberg gave permission for his movie posters to hang on the wall, and even autographed a picture of himself.

During the early days of filming, the show's director, Steve Miner, handed an old, clunky camera called a Bolex to Williamson and Stupin. "Why don't you guys shoot some footage for the main titles?" he asked.

The two of them didn't really know what the hell they were doing, Stupin later told me. They wandered around Wilmington, the four actors in tow, offering up directions, like: "Katie, do you mind climbing that tree?" In one shot, Jackson, Holmes, and Van Der Beek lay down on a creekside dock. In another, Williams snuggled close to Van Der Beek as Holmes looked on, arms crossed. The credits closed with the foursome walking along Wrightsville Beach together, arm in arm, all scored to Paula Cole's catchy, crooning tune "I Don't Want to Wait."

The presentation was finally ready to be turned over to the network.

WB executives watched the episode for the first time in a small screening space called the executive conference room. "There's a tradition at The WB where every year one pilot was just really special," Susanne Daniels, president of network, later wrote in her book *Season Finale: The Unexpected Rise and Fall of the WB and UPN*. "It was a great feeling of sitting in that little network conference room and putting up that standout pilot and you'd say, 'ah' because you just knew."

Dawson's Creek was that year's pilot. Those executives knew that they very likely had a hit on their hands. Now the challenge was getting eyeballs on it when it aired. The marketing, sales, and management departments gathered together to create the season's lineup. A scheduling board was set up in the front of the room, with magnetic cards for each of the shows, which they'd rearrange until they settled on the schedule. If the network really loved a show like *Dawson's Creek*, they'd figure out the best night for it to air, and then they *would not move that card*. "If you really believe in a show, you staple it to the board," Ancier told me.

The WB broke new ground with its *Dawson's Creek* marketing strategy, becoming the first network to advertise a television show in movie theater previews. Large posters for the show were installed in theaters as well, designed to look like a feature film. "It's the same font that's used in all kinds of motion picture posters," Lew Goldstein, the head of the network's marketing, later told *Entertainment Weekly*. "We used all of the tricks."

Films were king at the time, and the marketing team was huffing and puffing to catch up. Posters for *Dawson's Creek* were plastered on billboards, featuring a darkly evocative shot of Van Der Beek standing in a rowboat, gazing into the distance. "It's the end of something simple," the ad read. "And the beginning of everything else."

In another clever marketing move, the four actors were featured in a J.Crew catalog, modeling the latest clothing line while palling around Wilmington. You can still find those vintage pictures online, a glimpse of the young actors before their careers took off, hugging under a treehouse, lounging on a rowboat, and snuggling by a marsh.

Every shot of *Dawson's Creek* was going to feel storybook picturesque, down to the sunlit creeks and waterside homes. "Does this feel like the most idyllic, perfect sort of setting that it could be in?" Hook asked himself over and over. Sets were decorated with soft earth tones, and shooting was scheduled around mid-to-high tide. Both Joey's and Dawson's houses were on tidal creeks, and at low tide, the muddy banks and oyster beds were exposed. Not so idyllic.

During sit-downs with new directors, called "tone meetings," Stupin gave the same well-worn speech.

"I would always say, 'Capeside is the kind of town where sunlight shimmers off the water, where the colors are golden and beautiful.' I wanted every scene that showed Capeside to pull you in and make you wish that you lived there."

He added to me: "I still do when I watch it. I wish I lived there."

Wherever they filmed, Hook was instructed to wrap the location in twinkle lights—miles and miles and miles of twinkle lights. When the crew filmed the show's prom episode, Hook calculated that they used nine miles of twinkle lights on the riverboat alone. Sometimes, he grew tired of the lights and tried to quietly skip out on them. Then, Hook remembers, the phone call from Stupin would come: "Hey Alan, I noticed that in that scene, there were no twinkle lights. What happened?"

"OK, Paul, we'll make sure we get them in there," Hook relented.

Capeside was so beautiful, Hook sometimes found himself wondering: "What are these kids complaining about?"

One of the show's frequent directors, David Semel, still remembers an early nugget of wisdom he kept in his back pocket about Williamson's world. Semel had mentioned to the show's creator that the characters seemed very advanced for their age, but it worked. Kids are far brighter than we give them credit for, he said.

"I know when I was that age, we had all these feelings and emotions. We had difficulty articulating those feelings," Williamson responded. "I wanted to write a show where those characters could actually articulate what they were feeling in their heart."

"Wow, that's really beautiful," Semel thought. "That's a beautiful way to approach writing a show."

The marketing tricks for the pilot worked. The show premiered to 6.8 million viewers and would climb to become the network's highest-rated show within two months. *Dawson's Creek's* unique storytelling and syntax caught the eye of critics, as well, who struck an amusing balance between compliments and confusion. They couldn't quite wrap their minds around the way the teens of Capeside spoke, but they admitted there was definitely something intriguing there.

In *Variety's* first review, Ray Richmond wrote: "*Dawson's Creek* is *My So-Called Sex Life*, a hyperventilating soap that finds hit-making horror scribe Kevin Williamson pigeonholing the adolescent experience as a Freudian misadventure of boiling libidos and roaring psychobabble."

All that to say—Richmond dubbed *Dawson's* "an addictive drama with considerable heart."

Caryn James, a critic for the *New York Times*, decided that the show had officially "rejuvenated" the primetime soap opera. "Less earnest than the series it superficially resembles, like *Party of Five* and *My So-Called Life*, *Dawson's Creek* is also far more entertaining as it takes the characters' submerged fears and fantasies and turns them into action," she wrote.

And we hadn't even gotten to the love triangle.

Dawson's left one of its most memorable marks on pop culture history with a messy romantic battle for the ages: Pacey and Dawson duking it out for Joey's affections. We weren't quite there in Season 1—though in the tenth episode "Double Date," we got the first glimpses of a Joey/Pacey spark. The two are forced to paddle through a creek, searching for snails for an extra-credit science project. It was a long, muddy day and Semel, the episode's director, remembers throwing on waders and getting into the water alongside them. While Joey and Pacey were just friends at the time, with a side of heavy verbal jousting, Holmes and Jackson were embarking on a real-life romance.

Their chemistry was so clear and the attraction so obvious that Semel had to figure out ways to rein it in. "Katie, doesn't Josh just bug the shit out of you when he does this?" he'd say, throwing out examples of Jackson's shortcomings and trying to get her back into the combative dynamic.

That day, Joey and Pacey get soaked in water and muck. They head back to Pacey's car, where Joey changes her clothes just outside. Pacey gets a few quick glances of her bare back from the rearview mirror, and breaks into a warm, delighted grin. Semel wanted to strike the perfect balance of sexy but not sexual, while staying appropriate for broadcast television. After Pacey gets his glimpse of Joey in that mirror, she hops in the car and, with a smile, says, "Home, Jeeves."

In that moment of filming, everything felt right. Perfect, even. The sun set just when it needed to. Wilmington looked particularly beautiful that day.

On the van ride back with Jackson and Holmes, it was unusually quiet. Looking back, Semel wonders if the two actors were having the same thoughts he was. "Hey guys," he said. "You did something really special today."

Later, Semel told me: "I just knew. I just knew what we had captured. It was one of those moments where it was just like, 'Oh, that works. That's a moment. That's a memorable one.'"

We'd have to wait a few more seasons before anything romantic happened between Pacey and Joey, but for one brief scene, we felt the magic.

The show's Season 1 finale, directed by Semel, finds Dawson and Joey visiting Joey's father in prison. It was filmed one chilly, late night at a real Wilmington correctional facility. "Holy shit," Semel remembers thinking as he watched Holmes perform the emotionally charged dialogue behind the barbed wire.

There was this thing she did where she would hide behind another actor and the camera could only catch half her face. The camera operators approached Semel with complaints, but he'd always respond: "Don't you dare tell her anything. Don't change a thing." She did that hiding move again that night, during the shoot.

Semel wasn't entirely sure if Holmes knew how talented she was at the time. Often, he would avoid giving her direction because he wanted to capture whatever it was she was doing without making her self-conscious.

Dawson and Joey stay in a motel that night. Things are just beginning to change between them. Dawson is starting to realize his feelings for Joey are more than platonic, and Joey has grown tired of watching him pine after Jen. Semel re-created the exact shot from the pilot, when the camera moves slowly in a bird's eye view of the two, Dawson on his back, Joey curled up on her side. Semel had always revered the pilot, and he wanted to pay homage to it.

We end the episode with Joey and Dawson back in Dawson's bedroom. The big moment has finally arrived. The two kiss by the window as Beth Nielsen

Chapman sings "Say Goodnight Not Goodbye." Semel didn't talk through the kiss with Holmes and Van Der Beek before they shot it. He didn't even really want to rehearse the scene. The kiss needed to capture the pure, genuine mixture of nerves and newness that the two characters were experiencing.

"It's about making something that an audience is going to relate to," he explained. "Having had my own version of that experience, I would have to imagine one of the common universal truths is, you're scared to death."

As Joey and Dawson's chapter opened, Dawson and Jen's chapter closed. That left Michelle Williams wondering what role, if any, she'd continue to play on the creek. One hot, sticky summer night, before the filming of Season 2 began, Semel, Williams, Holmes, Jackson, and Van Der Beek gathered at the Rhino, a bar in downtown Wilmington. As the gang played pool, Williams pulled Semel aside and expressed her concerns about what direction her character would take.

"It wasn't coming from vanity. I didn't feel like it was coming from a place of insecurity," Semel told me. "I think she really understood the necessity of it."

The two continued to check in with each other about Jen as the second season went on. Semel would encourage her to find what was unique and relatable about Jen, a challenge he said she took on admirably.

Jen unravels in Season 2, pining after Dawson, feeling the awful sting of romantic rejection, drinking way too much, and hooking up with guys who were either unkind or far too old for her. It's painful to watch and exceptionally performed by Williams, who captures the heart-wrenching messiness, sadness, and loneliness of sixteen-year-old Jen Lindley.

Season 2 would introduce us to two new core characters, a brother-and-sister duo named Jack and Andie McPhee. Jack was played by Kerr Smith, who had recently driven from New York City to Los Angeles in a U-Haul to kick-start his acting career. There were two shows he was really hoping to land: *Party of Five* and *Dawson's Creek*. Smith had watched the pilot of *Dawson's* and remembers seeing Joey climbing up that now iconic ladder. "This show is going to be huge," he thought. But first, he auditioned for *Party of Five* and lost the role to Jeremy London. "I blew the audition," he told me. "I remember sitting in front of the casting director's desk and it just wasn't—I knew it wasn't that great."

Six weeks later, he was having a meeting with the head of the WB casting, Kathleen Letterie. By the end of their conversation, she said, "Kerr, I don't know what it's going to be yet. But I'm going to put you on one of our shows."

True to her word, Letterie called Smith in for the role of Jack McPhee, who's introduced as a new love interest for Joey and a foil for Dawson. Smith found himself packing up to move again, this time to Wilmington, where he crashed at the St. Thomas Inn, blocks from the Cape Fear River. It was the go-to spot for guest actors and writers to stay in Wilmington, each room furnished with a Hollywood theme, like Charlie Chaplin or Marilyn Monroe. Nobody seemed to have fond memories of staying in the kitschy hotel, and several were pretty certain it was haunted.

"Dude, get ready," Jackson told Smith. "Your life is about to change." Within a couple of months, Season 2 started airing and Smith couldn't walk down the street without being stopped, even when hidden under a hat and sunglasses.

At first, Jack's arc seemed to follow the same kind of love-triangle story line one might expect from a teen television show. A new kid in town, he develops a friendship with the show's protagonist, that friendship turns to a crush, and she kisses him one night while still in a relationship with her boyfriend.

But Williamson had other plans for Jack. A few months into shooting, he flew out to Wilmington and asked Smith if he wanted to get a cup of coffee. The two went to a local shop, and Williamson broached an idea. "I want to go down a different avenue with Jack," he told him. Smith understood, in that moment, exactly what he meant.

"I knew Kevin was gay," he explained to me. "At the time he was in the closet, and I think he wanted to come out to the world through Jack McPhee because on *Dawson's*, every character on that show is a little piece of his personality. Obviously he wanted Jack to represent his sexuality."

Back then, the decision to play a gay character felt risky, Smith said. They were few and far between, and *My So-Called Life*'s Rickie Vasquez was still the only openly gay character to appear on a teen show. It was 1999, and two men had never even kissed on network television.

"Look, give me a day," Smith told Williamson. "Let me call everybody whose opinion I respect." So he did. The overwhelming response was that he should do it.

We first get a glimpse of Jack's true identity during the episode "To Be or Not to Be . . . " when he's forced to read a poem he wrote about another man out loud. Some of his classmates torment him, writing a slur on his locker, and he insists that the poem wasn't a love poem. If he were to write a love poem, he reassures Joey, it would be about her. Then, his estranged father returns to Capeside. He's gotten a call about what's been happening at school and, steely-eyed, asks Jack if he's gay. Jack won't answer, and his father informs him that it *would* be a problem if he were.

Later, as Jack's father prepares to leave the house, Jack confronts him. He demands that he ask him the question again. "Ask me if I'm gay. Ask me."

"You are not gay," his dad responds resolutely.

"Yes. I am. You know it. I see how you look at me and I know you know . . . and as hard as you've tried to stamp it out and to ignore it, I've tried harder. I've tried harder to ignore it and to be quiet and to forget about it and to not bother my family with my problems," Jack says. He's crying now and slumps down onto the staircase. "But I can't try anymore because it hurts. I'm sorry."

It was a long, tough day on-set. They shot that scene over and over again, and by the end Smith felt completely drained. The response after it aired was immediate. Letters started arriving in the mail for him, stuffed with personal stories and asking for his advice. One note from a teenager read: "I watched that episode on the stairs and I immediately turned off the television set and walked into my parents' room and told them that I was gay."

That was the last of the mail Smith could bring himself to look at. It was really great that this kid was honest about who he was, he thought, but what if it changed his home life for the worse?

"Right there, that's when I really realized the responsibility that comes along with not only playing a character like this, but to the writers and everybody else who's involved in telling a story like this," he said. "You gotta be honest. You gotta be truthful. You gotta be responsible because that's the kind of impact you're gonna have on these kids."

Smith had expressed to Williamson early on that he wasn't going to play into stereotypes. "I'm going to play Jack McPhee straight, and I want the writing to make him gay. I want the situations and the story line to do that," he told Williamson.

And he reinforced that to the hair team as well when he arrived on-set one day and saw that they wanted to cut and style his hair in a new way.

"I'm like, 'Guys, no, no, no. We're not doing this.'"

Williamson left *Dawson's Creek* after the show's second season to work on the ABC drama *Wasteland*. The entire writers' room—with the exception of a young writer named Greg Berlanti—was gone as well. And so, as the show geared up for its third season, Stupin started from scratch, assembling a whole new team.

Tom Kapinos, who would go on to create hit series like *Californication* and *Lucifer*, discovered *Dawson's Creek* after listening to Howard Stern rave about it on his radio show. "I started watching and I was like, 'Oh, this is awesome,'" he told me. "It combined my love for John Hughes and Cameron Crowe. You forget, but it was about a guy who wanted to make movies. There was nothing else like that on TV, so I was like, 'I can relate to that.'"

Kapinos remembers walking into the office building on the corner of Olympic Boulevard and Bundy Avenue in Los Angeles for the first time. He got on the elevator next to a woman who was twisting a strand of her curly brown hair around her finger. "I wonder if she's a colleague," he thought as the two exited the elevator and headed in the same direction. Her name was Gina Fattore, and he was right—it was also her first day on the *Creek*.

Fattore had gotten her start as an assistant to Greg Daniels, creator of *King of the Hill* and future creator of *The Office*. There weren't that many women working in comedy in the late '90s, and she remembers being told by people in the industry: "You should write on a teen TV show." At the time, she interpreted that statement as: "Eh, women aren't funny."

So, when Fattore got the call to interview for *Dawson's Creek*, she wasn't particularly over the moon. She knew the show was a phenomenon, but she had only seen a handful of episodes. "I had given my heart to *My So-Called Life*," she explained to me. "I was thirty, and I was like, 'I'm done. I am done with teen shows.'"

"Just take the meeting. See what it is," Fattore's agent advised her. At the time, showrunners and producers asked for a "spec script," which involved picking a TV show already on air, and writing a hypothetical episode for it. Stupin loved Fattore's *Ally McBeal* spec. "If you can nail *Ally*, you can nail *Dawson's*," he told her.

A few weeks after a meeting in his office, she was offered a writing position on the upcoming season of *Dawson's Creek*.

Fattore called her friend who loved *Dawson's* and borrowed the VHS tapes he had recorded of all the episodes. She settled down with a spiral-bound notebook and created a "Beat Sheet," something Greg Daniels has taught her. After each scene, she'd hit Pause and ask herself: "What happened in that scene?" Then she'd sum it up in one sentence in her notebook, to get a sense of the structural rhythm of the show.

Fattore started to see cracks forming in Season 2. There were moments that really worked, like Jack's coming-out story, but by the time she got to the final episode, the Ice House was burning down and Joey was wearing a wire to implicate her father. "OK, is this the same show that it was when it first started out?" Fattore remembers thinking.

She was right to be concerned. *Dawson's* was starting to head in the wrong direction. On the first day in the writers' room, Kapinos recalls a *Risky Business*–like story line being kicked around where a mysterious woman comes to Capeside and seduces Dawson. Her name was Eve, and most of the *Dawson's Creek* people I spoke to remain baffled by that story line to this day. The first episode was broken out by the writers and the new showrunner, Tammy Ader. About a week later, the room was introduced to the show's co-showrunner Alex Gansa, who would go on to executive produce action-packed hits like *Homeland* and *24*. Running a teen television show, Kapinos remembers, was not what Gansa wanted to be doing. He kept joking that he had only taken the gig to buy a new house.

Ader would be gone after delivering her first script, Kapinos recalls, leaving Gansa in charge. Kapinos got a kick out of the showrunner, who kept a huge calendar in his office where he would mark an X next to each day that brought him closer to the *Dawson's Creek* finish line. At one point, Kapinos remembers Gansa telling him: "Tom, get out while you can. If they ask you to run [the show] don't do it. You're too much like me."

Kapinos didn't understand why they were doing the Eve story or this sudden film-noir twist. He was quiet in the writers' room, mostly because he was shy, and also because he didn't really know what to say. At one point, he remembers Gansa turning to him.

"Hey, Tom, do you have anything to contribute here?"

"I think it's a colossal mistake," Kapinos blurted out. A silence fell over the room.

Kapinos and Fattore were tasked with writing the episode "Indian Summer," which pushes forward Dawson's quest to unravel the Eve mystery. The script was divided up and Kapinos was assigned all the Eve scenes. Figuring out how to capture the unique denseness and lyricism of the show's dialogue proved challenging. Sometimes, Kapinos feared he was trying *too* hard to mimic that quintessential *Dawson's* voice. It just sounded a little over the top.

Fattore, meanwhile, decided to quietly forge another path—far away from Eve. She wanted to write a story between Jack and Jen and develop a friendship between the two, both radical outsiders in their own way. She approached Berlanti, the show's only veteran writer, with the idea. "Do you think that this is a story?" she asked. "That's a story," he replied. "You should totally pitch that."

Fattore, who had interviewed for a staff writer job on *Will & Grace*, always liked the relationship between Will, a gay man, and Grace, his straight best friend. She wanted to bring that same humor and intimacy to Jack and Jen. "True to my own life experience, my very best friend from college is gay," she told me. "So I enjoyed writing that dynamic."

It ended up becoming so much more than that.

Years later, in 2018, the *Dawson's Creek* cast reunited for the show's twentieth anniversary. As Smith sat down with an interviewer to discuss the impact of Jack's story line, Williams came over and put her arms around him.

"The thing that people always come up to me and say is: 'That changed my life,'" she told him. "The best story that I ever heard was somebody who came up to me and he [said], 'When I was growing up, I had this best friend and everyone said, 'Aww, you're like Dawson and Joey.' And the way that he came out, he [said], 'Actually guys, it's Jack and Jen.' And they were like, 'Oh, OK, we understand what that means!'"

The chaos of Season 3 would come to a head when Gansa approved a script that involved Pacey and Jen hooking up in the school bathroom. The network, Kapinos recalled, "threw a shit fit." The actors, Fattore added, were also unhappy with the story line. And when the actors were unhappy, they headed straight to the network, creating a double-whammy effect. Berlanti, Fattore, and Kapinos were forced to rewrite the whole script in one night, and it turned into the Thanksgiving episode, "Guess Who's Coming to Dinner." They wrote it so quickly that there really wasn't enough time to make it perfect.

"That episode contains my personal career low," Kapinos said. "I got made fun of it for years afterwards . . . I remember Pacey shows up at the Thanksgiving dinner and Andie is there and Pacey says to Andie, what'd you bring? And she goes, apple pie. It was an exchange completely devoid of any subtext, cleverness."

The season's turning point came when Berlanti was tapped to replace Gansa as showrunner. With Gansa out, Berlanti, who had a firm finger on the pulse of Williamson's original world, brought the show back to its roots. He also ushered in the story line that, in just one moment, would save *Dawson's Creek*. Pacey kisses Joey, Dawson finds out, and an iconic love triangle is born. To this day, the actors are hard-pressed to leave an interview without being asked: "Team Pacey or Team Dawson?"

The kiss happens in "A Cinderella Story," after several episodes of teasing viewers with some titillating will they/won't they material. Pacey picks Joey up following a disappointing experience with A. J., a college guy she's been dating. As Pacey drives her back to Capeside, she tells him, "I'm sixteen and there's been two people who actually know me, Pacey."

"This A. J. guy didn't know you," Pacey responds. "I don't care how you felt about him, Joe, he didn't know you, because if he did, he never would have walked away."

"I was going to say you, Pacey."

It's then that Pacey pulls the car to the side of the road.

"All right, what did you mean by that?" he asks.

"By what?"

"About me knowing you better than anybody else."

"Exactly what I said, Pacey. You know me, OK? In a way that nobody else besides Dawson ever had."

"I'm not talking about Dawson right now. We're talking about me. You can't keep on doing this to me, Potter."

"Doing what? So I count on you and I tell you secrets and . . . "

"And you call me in the middle of the night to pick you up. Why?"

"I'm sorry that I called. I thought that I . . . "

"I'm not mad that you called me, I just want to know why you called me."

"You were the first person that I thought of, Pacey."

"What does that mean, Joe?"

"It means that . . . I guess it . . . It means that I can talk to you, and that you're there for me."

"Don't you ever get tired of talking?"

"No. I don't."

"Well, I get tired of talking . . . I don't want to talk anymore," Pacey says, exasperated, and then pulls her toward him for a kiss. As the episode closes, she kisses him back. Of course, in classic Joey fashion, the beginning of the next episode opens with her freaking out, shoving Pacey, and fixing him with a glowering look on the car ride back.

As the writers began to navigate this new story line and a rejuvenated season, they delighted in finding new ways to play with the show's structure. *Dawson's* had started to feel a little bit too packed with exposition, Fattore noticed, along with a steady stream of conversations revolving around the recurring question "Can you explain to me how you're feeling?" The writing team began mixing and matching different pairings of characters. "What if Joey talks to Andie?" they'd ask. "What if Jen talks to Joey?" Some of the season's strongest moments happened that way, like a sleepover between the core group of female characters that was thoroughly fun and remarkably melodrama-free.

Then, they broke the structure altogether. Fattore was assigned the episode "The Longest Day," a pivotal turning point when Dawson discovers Joey and Pacey's secret kiss. The big reveal was originally written for the end of the episode.

Suddenly, Berlanti had an idea. He popped his head into the room.

"Make the third act break the first act break," he said.

"What do you mean?"

"That's when they tell Dawson."

The episode turned into one of *Dawson's Creek*'s most memorable. We, as the audience, are taken through a twisty story line, putting together the puzzle pieces of Dawson's discovery. Fattore still remembers the first time the cast came together for the table read. At that point, Kapinos recalled, those gatherings had become "hostile."

"They were so over it, and that year was so chaotic that we'd show up down there [in Wilmington] and they'd be making fun of the script right in front of you."

For the first time since working on *Dawson's*, Fattore watched as the core group of actors read the episode out loud, completely riveted.

"I could see it working on them, when the story rebooted at the top of the second act, I could see them sort of actually going like, 'Oh wait a minute, we need to pay attention to this,'" she told me. "'This one is going to be different.'"

At the end of the read, Fattore thought she overheard Jackson say, "Thank God for Gina Fattore."

"Oh my God, I just got a compliment," she thought, quietly delighted. In that moment, Fattore felt the writers had finally earned back some of the actors' trust.

The response to the show's love triangle was immediate. Fans were deeply invested, and they were taking sides.

Daisies began arriving at the *Dawson's Creek* writers' office, an homage to the flowers Dawson gave Joey on their first date. Team Pacey fans called themselves "Project Hellmates," alluding to the fact that Dawson and Joey were not soul mates, but rather the dysfunctional opposite. They sent their own memorabilia to the writers—including a mug Fattore kept on her desk.

The story line had a hidden bonus: Jackson and Van Der Beek were not getting along at the time. Their characters' tiff meant that the two actors wouldn't have to appear in as many scenes together. Whenever they did have to share the screen, Kapinos remembers, it was always a bit of a "pain in the ass." The only time Kapinos recalls things running smoothly between the two of them was when Dawson's dad dies in Season 5, and Pacey is there to comfort him.

A small but gratifying moment happened for members of Project Hellmates in the episode "The Anti-Prom," written by Maggie Friedman. Joey is still torn between her two friends, and she decides, in one spontaneous moment, to dance with Pacey at their prom. Everything slows down. Every touch is electric. Pacey runs his hand over the diamond earrings that Dawson had given Joey.

"Where did you get those?" he asks. "They're not you."

"Why, because I'm just a poor tomboy, or 'cause Dawson gave them to me?"

"Neither. You see this?" He touches the bracelet around her wrist. "This is you. It's not showy or gaudy. Just simple. Elegant. Beautiful."

"It's my mom's bracelet."

"I know."

"How do you know?"

"Well, because you told me. Six months ago. You were wearing that blue sweater with the snowflakes that you have. We were walking down the hallway at school. I was annoying you as per usual. You said, 'Look, Pacey. I just found my mother's bracelet this morning, so why don't you cut me some slack?'"

"You remember that?"

Pacey leans in close and whispers: "I remember everything."

How, I asked Friedman, did she write a line like that? One so deeply romantic that, when I first watched it as a teen, I *furiously* hit the Rewind button over and over again.

"I could still remember what it felt like to be in high school," she explained. "You're at the prom, and you're dancing with the boy you like, and it's been tumultuous, and what would you hope he would say? What would be the dream thing? What would make you swoon?"

After each episode aired, Friedman headed straight to Television Without Pity, a message board where viewers would congregate online to talk about shows. "They were often very snarky and mean, and somehow I just had to read it all, even when they were breaking my heart with stuff they were saying," she said.

Much to her delight, that scene with Pacey and Joey went over very well.

The "Anti-Prom" episode is just as much Jack's story as it is Joey's, if not more. In it, he tries to buy a ticket to the prom for himself and Ethan, a guy he likes. A student named Barbara John refuses to sell to him because he's going with a boy. In response, Dawson decides to throw an "anti-prom" at Leery's Fresh Fish, where everyone can come and be themselves.

The episode was inspired by the passage of California's Proposition 22 in 2000, which declared that marriage was between a man and a woman. Friedman watched commercials that would run in favor of the bill, and they made her blood boil. This would be *Dawson's Creek*'s chance to offer a searing rebuttal.

"We used the character of Barbara Johns selling the prom tickets as a voice of the people who wanted to discriminate against gay people," Friedman recalled. "I named her after one of my very best friends, who was the opposite of her, so progressive and amazing and cool."

Berlanti, who is gay, was on a fervent mission to see Jack's love story through to the end of the season. Jack was going to kiss Ethan, which would mark the first kiss between two men on network TV. Berlanti still remembered seeing the first *almost* kiss between two men on *Melrose Place*, when the camera moved away just before their lips met. He felt robbed of a pivotal moment. Here was his opportunity to right that wrong.

Fattore was on-set the day of the kiss, negotiating between a deeply determined Berlanti and a very nervous network.

"We want to have this from across the street. We want to do a really, really wide shot," she was told by an executive. Then, she got a call from Berlanti.

"Gina, I want to see tongue, I want to see a real kiss, I want it to be hot," he insisted.

She approached the episode's director, James Whitmore Jr. "I need this to be both incredibly wide and also incredibly close," Fattore explained. "We need to please all of these people."

To his credit, she remembers him saying: "No problem, I got this." The final scene would show a close-up of Jack putting his lips on Ethan's, for one quick meaningful moment, before Ethan pulls away.

That day, Smith was nervous, really nervous. "This is my first time kissing another dude. We made fun of it a lot back then. We wouldn't do that today. But we had to, at least I had to, to kill the fear, I guess."

Smith wasn't privy to any of the drama going on behind the scenes. He decided to kiss Ethan the way that he thought was right for Jack—gentle and sweet.

Jack's first kiss with a man starts with triumph and ends with crushing disappointment. It turns out that Ethan has gotten back together with his boyfriend Brad.

"It's so heartbreaking because of course it doesn't work out, which is maybe the essence of *Dawson's* in a way," Fattore said, looking back on that moment. "How great would that be if it had actually been euphoric and perfect? But how much more realistic is it that this is what happens to so many of us when we're teenagers?"

After the episode aired, Smith walked past the Screen Gems Studio gate for lunch and spotted a group of people protesting the show. "Holy shit," he thought. "This is suddenly real."

Dawson's Creek would garner two awards from GLAAD. The organization was particularly pleased with the next kiss Jack shared with his future boyfriend, Toby, in the show's fourth season. "I timed it," Scott Seomin, a spokesman for GLADD, told *USA Today* at the time. "A five-and-a-half second, mouth-to-mouth kiss. We haven't seen anything like this before on network TV."

In response, Heather Cirmo, who worked for Washington D.C.'s Family Research Council, an evangelical activist group, told the outlet, "The first kiss was disturbing enough," adding that the scene could have an impact on "impressionable teens who have questions about their sexuality by promoting a myth that homosexuality is something you're born with."

Berlanti rebutted by explaining that being born gay is *not*, in fact, a myth. Also, he had watched many teens kissing on television growing up, and those visuals didn't turn him straight.

By all accounts, Season 4 felt like smooth sailing after a tumultuous year. Berlanti was in charge, Joey and Pacey were dating, and the show was free to explore new story lines with Jack, Jen, and Dawson. To keep drama going, the writers decided to introduce a new character, pot-stirrer Drue Valentine, played by twenty-one-year-old Mark Matkevich, who would meddle in the lives of the core Capeside four.

Matkevich won the role of Drue over Zach Braff and Andrew Keegan. He was flown out to Los Angeles to read in front of network executives and, much to his delight, got to stay in a cool West Hollywood hotel, where they offered him turndown service and chocolate-chip cookies.

By the time Matkevich arrived in Wilmington, there was a feeling of senioritis in the air. He got the sense that Williams, Holmes, Jackson, and Van Der Beek were itching to move beyond Capeside and try their hand in films.

Matkevich was mostly concerned about holding his own against this group of actors who so innately understood the world and the verbiage of *Dawson's*. "Just don't screw up" was his mantra. Matkevich fell back on his theatre background to master the lyrical, dense dialogue, pulling from his experience with those strange, old plays he used to perform, which had a similar prose and poetry to them.

He studied Jackson and Williams, who took that language and made it feel believable. Matkevich remembers working with Williams fondly and flashed back to the scene where Drue presents Jen with ecstasy (one of *Dawson's* few "Very Special Episodes"). She opens the little box that contained two large cinnamon Altoids, the labels scratched off, which the props department hoped would pass as drugs. He broke down in laughter.

The fourth season is a light, enjoyable watch. By that point, the writers had discovered which characters came most naturally to them and comfortably settled in. Jeffrey Stepakoff, who had joined the show in Season 3, loved writing Jen's grandmother, and could craft her wise soliloquies like no other. Kapinos found his way in through Pacey and Dawson. "If you're a guy, you want to hope you're like Pacey, but on your bad days you feel like you're like Dawson," he told me.

Fattore put a lot of herself into Joey. "I look back and I realize that I wrote so much of my own anxiety into Joey," she said. "We went through this era where it was preferred to have a ballsy female heroine who was very confident. And I thought, 'Oh my God, thank God I got to work on *Dawson's.*' Because I'm not a ballsy person like that."

Rina Mimoun, who had been writing for the WB's teen show *Jack and Jill*, entered *Dawson's Creek* halfway through that season. It was nerve-wracking at first, she remembers, and felt a little bit like high school. All the writers already picked out their favorite chairs in the room and had worked together for so long, fighting through the television trenches as a team.

To prep for her first day, Mimoun gathered a stack of VHS tapes and watched every episode of *Dawson's*.

"I think the main thing I personally zeroed in on was 'OK, this is not funny,'" she told me. "This is a drama, and this is sort of veering towards melodrama in a lot of ways. Which isn't to say that it wasn't witty and smart. My instinct was to always find the humor in things, and this show was definitely not that. That was a little bit of a switch-up for me."

She found her match with Pacey, the show's wittiest, quickest-tongued character. He was so fun to write for, and Jackson always elevated the material he was given. She struggled with Jen, though. "I wasn't that girl; I didn't know that girl. Her voice was always the most difficult to capture."

It was so strange heading to Wilmington and meeting the cast for the first time. When she was in the writers' room, she thought of them as their characters. How jarring it was to talk to the actors in real life and think of them as separate people. Holmes surprised her the most. Joey was such a tomboy, Mimoun recalls, especially in the beginning when a lot of male writers were writing for her. Yet Holmes, she discovered, was so sophisticated and had a natural elegance. She kept a collection of European fashion magazines that she enthusiastically showed Mimoun, pointing out outfits she liked from Paris.

Dawson's Creek was never about the fancy clothing brands, so when Joey attended a cocktail party for Worthington, the fictional college she'd end up enrolling in, Mimoun nudged Holmes. "This is an opportunity," she told her. "Talk to wardrobe, get the dress you want." So she did. It was an elegant tan-and-brown striped number with cap sleeves.

The love triangle would continue into Season 4, though with far less urgency. For one brief moment, Dawson and Pacey reunite, alongside Jack, to pull off a senior prank in the episode "The Usual Suspects." A chunk of scenes were filmed with the school's principal, played by Harry Shearer, a comedy actor who voiced several characters on *The Simpsons*. Smith remembers shooting his scenes opposite Shearer and watching between takes as the actor closed his eyes and seemed to nod off. "This guy, we're kids to him," Smith remembers thinking. "Am I ever going to be at that point in my career?"

And then, one day, he was. In 2019, Smith headed to *Riverdale*, the hit CW teen show helmed by Berlanti, to play Principal Honey. It was all very surreal, being back on a high school set, with the same school colors as Capeside High. As he spoke to the group of young actors in character—"Boom, it hit me," Smith realized. "I'm Harry Shearer." Some of the cast members asked him about his experience back then on *Dawson's Creek*. Sometimes, Smith found himself closing his eyes between takes.

Riverdale handled the sticky situation of high school graduation by fast-forwarding several years and bringing the characters back home. Smith wondered if Berlanti made that decision after watching *Dawson's Creek* go through the murky challenges of the college years.

"It just doesn't work as well because people want you in Capeside," Smith said. "[Audiences] want that feeling, they want those relationships. Now all of a sudden we're in college and there's different stories and different sets."

The writers were grappling with those very same fears as they, too, started thinking beyond Capeside High. Berlanti was exiting *Dawson's* to start his new show, *Everwood*, and Kapinos was offered the showrunner reins for Season 5. He took them, albeit with apprehension.

Kapinos still remembers his first day in charge, standing absolutely terrified in front of a room full of new writers staring back at him. Newfound responsibility in hand, Kapinos was interested in starting to tell smaller stories and moments à la *My So-Called Life*. He would often sit with Stepakoff and Fattore and muse: "Why can't it be more like that kind of TV?"

But as Kapinos explained to me, the WB wasn't interested in small stories. The network didn't like the first script he turned in for that season. They were even more unhappy with the second script. There's not enough plot being set up for the year, they complained.

Then Berlanti, who had remained on as a consulting producer, offered Kapinos an idea. Why not kill off Dawson's dad? It could open up so many new stories, bring the cast of characters together, and add an emotional richness to the season. It sounded promising enough, so off they went.

Here's where Kapinos's biggest regret comes in.

Mitch Leery goes to the store to buy some milk. He picks up an ice cream cone on the way back and eats it as he's driving, singing along to the radio. When he spills some of the cone on the floor, he quickly tries to scoop it back up. Then, a car crashes into him, killing him.

An explanation, in Kapinos's own words, of that divisive scene:

"I remember writing that script. Yeah, what can I say about that? I think I liked the idea of being a mishmash of tones—something tragic happens but weirdly happens in a nice moment . . . can it even be funny? Again, what was I thinking?"

Mitch's death cast a pall over Season 5, and the writers struggled to dig their way out of the darkness. Then, real-life tragedy hit. One early morning in Wilmington, Mimoun got a call that she thought was from production.

"I'm sorry I'm late," she said, picking up the phone. "I don't think I'm going to be able to make it to the tech scout."

It was the show's director, Perry Lang. "Turn on your TV," he said.

She flipped on her television set. Two hijacked planes had flown into the World Trade Center, killing almost three thousand people. Terrorists hijacked a third and fourth plane, one of which crashed into the Pentagon and another in Shanksville, Pennsylvania, killing all passengers. Production was shut down for forty-eight hours. Everything felt like a sad, confusing, isolating daze. Holmes really wanted to go home, Mimoun remembers, but instead her boyfriend at the time, Chris Klein, took a train to be with her.

Production resumed faster than felt appropriate. While trying to shoot a scene during their first episode back, Williams burst into tears. "Everyone in the room was like, 'It's too soon,'" Mimoun said.

The rest of that season for the writers, as Kapinos remembers it, was a "white-knuckle ride to the finish line." Jen and Dawson get together for a bit and then break up. Dawson sees a therapist to deal with his anxiety following his dad's death. Jack struggles with his studies.

Kapinos, meanwhile, was still figuring out his duties as showrunner while navigating a newly intimate relationship with the whole cast, one that had previously been handled by Williamson, then Gansa, then Berlanti.

Going to Wilmington never felt like a pleasure trip for Kapinos, and he tried to limit the amount of time he was there. Upon arriving in the city and checking into The St. Thomas Inn, he'd have a message waiting at the front desk that Van Der Beek was waiting for his call back. The pair would have extensive conversations about the actor's issues with the scripts, Kapinos recalls. "Dawson wouldn't say that," Van Der Beek would often tell him.

"There were a lot of long-winded phone calls that, when you got to the end of the call, you realize could have been a five-minute call," Kapinos said. "It was really just about moving some words around or cutting a couplet. But we sort of chewed on it for a long time. So I'm remembering a lot of nights in a Wilmington hotel just talking to James."

Van Der Beek's phone calls and feedback began to wear on the showrunner. Kapinos stopped returning his messages and, by the middle of the sixth season, they were no longer speaking. When Kapinos returned to Wilmington for the show's finale, they didn't make eye contact.

Kapinos was well aware of the cast's discontent. While watching the dailies back in L.A., he could hear them making fun of the show.

"There was a Halloween episode that was legitimately bad. It was called 'Four Scary Stories,'" Kapinos recalls with a laugh. "I realized in the dailies they were referring to it as 'Four Shitty Stories.' So I was like, 'Well, I gotta hand it to them for that one. Because that's relatively entertaining.'"

Smith sometimes got the sense that, by the time the college years rolled around, Michelle Williams had grown bored with her role. "I'm trying to think if I should tell this or not," he mused before he launched into the tidbit. "What the hell, she's been nominated for an Oscar."

He remembers having to try to rev Williams up for one of their scenes when it was clear that she had no real interest in being there. "We shot this scene [and] I'm like, 'Michelle. Come on. You're so much better than this. I know you don't feel like being here right now, but will you please just bring it? Can we just make this fun? It's you and me and we're gonna have a good time.'"

The college years of TV shows are quick to be maligned. Here comes my defense of this one: those last two seasons of *Dawson's* were funny and sharp, with plenty of heart. And particularly in the sixth season, it feels like they're going back to the roots of *Dawson's Creek*. A scrappy Dawson is making movies again, and his Capeside friends rally around him, just like when they were sixteen, holding boom mics, organizing shoots, and acting as producers.

Plus, that last season would deliver us a surprisingly subversive finale. Joey doesn't end up with Dawson *or* Pacey. She goes to Paris for the first time, breaking away from her life in Capeside and her group of friends. It had been her plan for years, while in high school, but she didn't go because she wanted to spend the summer with Dawson.

For Fattore and Kapinos, the love triangle no longer mattered. They were more interested in Joey's own journey post-Capeside.

"As much as I like the Pacey/Joey of it all, I struggled with—is it really a huge victory to end up with your high school boyfriend?" Kapinos explained. "I always liked the idea that she had these experiences with these guys, then she goes off into the world. Maybe she's better because of the experiences but she doesn't necessarily have to end up with someone."

Fattore agreed. "I don't think that coming-of-age stories for women should be love stories," she said.

That's a significant point—especially for the time when *Dawson's* was filmed. Back then, movies and television shows always ended with the girl getting the guy or the guy getting the girl. That was the ultimate triumphant conclusion, and no other life event could stack up.

Later, while working on the final season of *Gilmore Girls*, Fattore would fight hard for Rory not to end up with her college boyfriend, Logan. Instead, she encouraged the idea of Rory, a fledgling journalist, following Barack Obama on the campaign trail. (She won.)

With Joey's story line figured out, there was one last *Dawson's* plot point to tie up: Pacey and Dawson. They were still on the outs, and the time had come to bring them back together . . . at least a little.

"In a funny way, because Josh and James actually did refuse to work with each other, essentially we did have this other story that needed to be resolved, which is these two people who you had met in the pilot as friends," Fattore recalled.

And so, as the end of Season 6 comes to a close, we see Pacey and Dawson reunited in Wilmington's Airlie Gardens. The two characters are embroiled in yet another fight, and Joey maneuvers the meeting with a tricky sleight of hand: she tells both of them to meet her there, though she's nowhere to be found.

It was drizzling that day, Michael Lange, the episode's director, remembers, drops of rain falling through the canopy of trees. He liked that the location felt like a tunnel, trapping the characters together and not allowing the two actors to move too far away from each other.

"You know, it makes sense," Dawson says, as they face each other.

"What does?" Pacey asks.

"Why it never worked out for either one of us. All we wanted was her. So much so that we destroyed our friendship . . . and in the end, all she ever wanted was for us to be friends again."

"OK, I'm gonna ask you this once, and then I promise you I'll never ask it again. Is it possible?"

"For us to be friends again?" Dawson thinks for a moment. Then, a small smile. "Anything's possible."

"Fair enough," Pacey says with a chuckle.

It's the perfect *Dawson's Creek* moment. Openhearted optimism and heartache rolled into one.

Then, we see Joey. She's in Paris, working at a pastry shop. She clocks out for the day and wanders outside. The crew filmed the scene in Montreal, and Lange played Joey's pre-recorded voiceover on speakers so that Holmes could hear the words as she walked down those cobblestone streets. That wasn't typical, he told me. Usually the actor doesn't hear the voiceover or, if they request it, a script supervisor will read the lines out loud. But it felt important that Holmes hear that final monologue in her own voice while wandering around this new city as Joey.

Joey's final words were deeply personal to Kapinos, who co-wrote the episode. It was his way of quietly saying goodbye to the show.

Here's what Joey says:

"I used to be afraid of so many things. That I'd be trapped in the same place for all eternity. That my dreams would forever be shy of my reach. It's true what they say. Time plays tricks on you. One day you're dreaming, the next your dream has become your reality.

"And now that this scared little girl no longer follows me wherever I go, I miss her. I do. 'Cause there are things I wanna tell her—to relax, to lighten up, that it is all going to be OK. I want her to know that meeting people who like you, who understand you, who actually accept you for who you are, will become an increasingly rare occurrence.

"Jen, Jack, Audrey, Andie, Pacey, and Dawson. These people who contributed to who I am, they are with me wherever I go, and as history gets rewritten in small ways with each passing day, my love for them only grows. Because the truth is . . . it was the best of times. Mistakes were made, hearts were broken, harsh lessons learned, but all of that has receded into fond memories now."

We then see Joey gazing at the Eiffel Tower in an almost dreamlike state. A cameraman in Paris had been hired to shoot that shot, which was superimposed around Holmes, who stood on a platform with a green screen.

"I can't swear this is exactly how it happened," Joey concludes as she looks around with such wonder. *"But this is how it felt."*

I've always felt like that could have been the perfect ending. It's sweet, moving, and unpredictable and I cry every single time I watch it. But there was one more chapter to come.

Kevin Williamson returned to write a second finale, alongside Berlanti and Friedman, and offered a very different ending. The two-part conclusion took place five years after the gang graduated from college. Joey is working as a book editor in New York. Jen is living in New York with her daughter. Jack is a teacher at Capeside High and dating Pacey's brother, Deputy Doug. Dawson is the successful showrunner of *The Creek*, a series based on his teenage years.

Two significant story lines are realized in the finale. First, in a shocking twist, Jen dies. "The thing about *Dawson's Creek* was that it was always supposed to be my version of a coming-of-age story . . . so I thought, it's coming-of-age—what was the one thing they haven't dealt with?" Williamson later told *Entertainment Weekly*. "They dealt with first love, first sex, first everything, but they hadn't dealt with the death of a core member of their group."

Williamson chose Jen because she always felt like the misfit of the group. And her death would serve as a breaking point for the love triangle, as her dying wish was for Joey to finally decide who she wants: Dawson or Pacey.

When Williamson started writing the finale, he was sure Joey would choose Dawson. Then, as Kapinos recalls, Holmes stepped in. "Katie freaked out. 'I don't want to end up with Dawson,'" he remembers her saying. "So it got replotted, or rewritten."

Stupin has a similar memory. "I think [Kevin] wrote the first half, if you kind of watch it, it leads you to think Dawson and then I think Katie kind of did weigh in and wanted it to be Pacey," he said.

The last time we see the Capeside kids, they're all grown up. Jack and Deputy Doug are raising Jen's daughter in Capeside, Joey and Pacey are together in New York, and Dawson just got some major news: he's landed a meeting with Steven Spielberg, the perfect end to a different love story.

Dawson's Creek, in all its wonderfully emotional glory, would make it OK for teens to feel everything. The absolute crushing devastation of rejection. The euphoria of a first kiss. The agony of yearning. All set against a beautiful riverside backdrop, dusted in heavy wish fulfillment.

Joey, Pacey, Jen, and Dawson were early iterations of teen characters who would populate our screens for years to come. The writers of *Dawson's Creek* had set a precedent—young people are whip-smart and not to be underestimated, they told us. Sure, no show would ever replicate the dense, poetic dialogue of *Dawson's*, but the savviness and self-awareness of the Capeside crew lives on in the DNA of teen shows.

For the first time, television was giving us a soapy show with substance. And it was just the beginning of teen TV slowly but surely subverting genre expectations. Or, in the case of our next show, ripping them up altogether.

Back in L.A., a struggling actor and filmmaker named Paul Feig was about to redefine what teen TV could be. Dubbed "the anti-*Dawson's Creek*" by one television critic, Feig's show, *Freaks and Geeks*, explored the pain and awkwardness of adolescence without the pretty backdrop and beautifully crafted dialogue.

Freaks and Geeks would be grounded deeply in reality, based on funny, traumatic, and mortifying moments that happened to the show's writers when they were teens. And it would change the world of television as we know it.

Freaks and Geeks

(1999–2000)

It's a gray, overcast day in small-town Michigan. A blond cheerleader and a handsome football player sit on the bleachers.

"You seem so distant these days, Brett. Is there something I did?" the cheerleader asks.

After some prodding, the jock responds, "Ashley, it's just, I love you so much. It scares me." The two embrace. Sweeping music plays.

The camera pans down, under the bleachers, where the school's burnouts, stoned out of their minds, discuss the godlike nature of Led Zeppelin drummer John Bonham. Around the corner, three freshmen swap Bill Murray impressions until they're picked on by a gang of bullies. A lone young woman wearing a green army jacket rescues them from the wrath of the boys, and then mutters to herself, "Man, I hate high school."

On a Saturday evening in 1999, the time had finally come for the freaks and geeks to step into the spotlight.

Paul Feig needed a break. He had just poured $40,000—all the money he made playing Mr. Pool, a science teacher on *Sabrina the Teenage Witch*—into his own film. Feig had written, directed, produced, and starred in a micro-budget movie, a dramedy called *Life Sold Separately*, which featured four strangers meeting in a field, trying to figure out how and why they had gotten there.

Then, in the middle of post-production, Feig got the call. Mr. Pool was being written out of *Sabrina*. He was jobless, spent all his savings, and *Life Sold Separately* hadn't made it into a single film festival.

Feig was becoming disillusioned by show business. After years of playing the sixth or seventh lead on television shows that swiftly got canceled, he thought he had finally landed a regular part with a steady paycheck. Now that cushy job had been snatched away.

Feig once fancied himself becoming an Albert Brooks type who wrote and starred in his own films. But on sets, he found himself hanging out with the writers, producers, and directors instead of the actors. Sometimes he'd pen spec scripts for shows he was on and share them with the writers. They always liked them.

Feig was wondering if he should quit the business altogether when his film was accepted by FlixTour, a traveling film festival that flew filmmakers to small colleges around the country for screenings.

He decided to go on the tour—and to keep writing. Otherwise, he figured he'd go crazy during the long days and nights on the road. Before leaving, Feig sat down to watch the pilot of *Felicity*, an hourlong drama about a young woman who had just graduated from high school and was navigating her first year of college. Feig was struck by how much this network television show felt like a movie. "That would be cool," he thought, to try something like that. And he already had an idea for a TV show. Or a seedling of an idea.

Feig had long felt that high school shows and movies didn't reflect his own adolescent experience. The core characters were too often a bunch of sexually active cool kids. The geeks—*his* peer group—were played supergeeky: tape on their glasses, suspenders, calculator in hand. But that's not what he and his friends were like. They loved comedy, discussed Monty Python over lunch, and were terrified of girls.

Then he thought about the burnouts in his high school: an ostracized group from the other side of the tracks. Feig had befriended some of them in drama club. Those types of kids never had their moment on television either.

"What would I call this show?" Feig wondered. "Well, I want it to be about the nerds—we were all nerds—and the burnouts, or the freaks. Maybe *Nerds and Freaks*. That sounds weird. *Freaks and Geeks*, that kind of rhymes."

The night before he left Los Angeles for FlixTour, Feig went out for a sushi dinner with his wife, Laurie. "While I'm out on this tour, I think I'm going to write the pilot for that high school show," he told her. "I'm gonna call it *Freaks and Geeks*."

She put her hand up for a high five. "That's it," she said. "You should write that. That sounds like a great idea."

Years before, Feig had written a book to immortalize his high school years on an IBM electric typewriter. Titled simply *School*, it relived the tortuous days of bullying, locker-room group showers, and humiliating dodgeball games—painful stories that were always crowd-pleasers when he recounted them to friends.

"Well, who cares?" his dad said when Feig told him about his manuscript. "Why would anyone want to read a book about when you were in school?"

"Oh God, you're right," Feig replied. He put the chapters in the bottom drawer of his desk and forgot about them.

Before leaving on the tour, Feig dug out the manuscript and threw it into his bag.

The booking manager for the tour collected $750 per college event. Feig wouldn't see any of that money, but the manager footed the bill for his lodging as they traveled from city to city, town to town. He stayed in no-frills hotel rooms—a bed, desk, and bathroom. It was a little depressing.

One night, Feig was wandering out to dinner in Wilkes-Barre, Pennsylvania, when he spotted a group of loud high school girls smoking and swearing. One girl in particular caught his eye. She was trying to smoke a cigarette, but it just didn't look quite right. She seemed desperate to fit in.

"I kind of love that girl," Feig thought. "I get what she's trying to do." He had always wanted an older sister, and he decided to fashion his show's main character—Lindsay Weir—around that childhood wish, and this out-of-place young woman. Her younger brother in the show would be Sam Weir, the fictionalized version of Feig, a wide-eyed kid with a tight-knit group of like-minded friends who had a big crush on the cheerleader.

The first words Feig wrote in his Wilkes-Barre hotel room were the show's opening scene, featuring the jock and the cheerleader. He wanted to acknowledge the high school shows that featured beautiful young people speaking in eloquent prose—and immediately let viewers know this was *not* going to be that type of show.

The rest of the script poured out of Feig. Whenever there was a free moment on the tour, outside the auditorium, inside someone's basement, Feig pulled out his laptop and wrote. He returned to Los Angeles with a completed pilot, which he handed off to Laurie.

"Send this to Judd," she told him after reading the script. "This is your guys' sense of humor." Judd was Judd Apatow, a producer whom Feig had met while they were both stand-up comedians. Apatow had produced and written for *The Larry Sanders Show*, a single-camera comedy starring Gary Shandling, which earned the creative team a multitude of Emmy nominations and awards and, later, a deal with DreamWorks for Apatow to develop more television shows.

Feig sent his pilot script to Apatow. Within twelve hours, he had gotten a call back. "I'm going to buy this, DreamWorks is going to buy this, we're going to do this," Apatow told him.

Freaks and Geeks' path was relatively charmed by television standards. NBC scooped it up and executives told Feig they loved it. "Don't change a word," they said. Apatow had other plans. He had learned from Shandling that he should be hard on his writing. Ruin it, and you can always go back to the original. Feig fought back at first. He didn't want to tear apart a script that NBC executives had already deemed perfect.

It took him a week to get on board and loosen his grip. "This can be better," Apatow would tell him. He pointed to the father character, Mr. Weir, whom Feig had originally written as an affable dad.

"This character could be funnier," Apatow said. "Was your dad like this?"

"Well, my dad was nice but he had all these crazy things he would tell you," Feig responded.

As a child, his father would often scare him, Feig told Apatow, by saying that someone had died. Once, when they were flipping through a *National Geographic* magazine together, they came across a picture of a man shooting up. "You don't see it, but this guy killed himself!" his dad informed him. The trick worked—Feig never tried drugs.

"I want you to bring that in," Apatow said.

Feig, along with Apatow and the show's supervising director Jake Kasdan, penned a visual manifesto, which they would hand out to directors before shooting an episode. "The kids of William McKinley High School, their parents and all the people of this small Midwestern town are real," it began. "We are simply documenting their lives."

It continues:

* The lighting is naturalistic. It is not lush, or edgy, or hip. It mimics the fluorescent lights in the school, the gray overcast filtering through Sam's bedroom window, or the warm reading light beside his dad's favorite chair.

* Longer lenses allow our cameras to film the action without feeling obtrusive. Except for the rare occasion, no filtration will be used. The truth is not diffused and fuzzy.

* Every episode of *Freaks and Geeks* will look and feel like an independent feature film. When asked about his acting philosophy, James Cagney said "stand up and tell the truth." That's all we need to do.

It was important to Feig that the show run an hour long. He wanted to linger on real moments with the characters, not merely ones that revolved around plot or exposition. He loved the idea of just watching people talking.

Casting director Allison Jones was tapped to put together an ensemble of misfits, and was given surprising instructions from Feig and Apatow. The main characters shouldn't be cool, and they definitely shouldn't be "WB Network kids who were 25 playing 16." All this invited a sigh of relief from Jones, who was fresh off casting the pilot of *Roswell*, which featured yet another group of beautiful teens. Jones wasn't particularly interested in beautiful people.

"In many, many cases, looks and humor don't go together," she would later say in an interview with the *Hollywood Reporter*. "It's always a compromise if you go with the beauty queen and she's just not very funny. It hurts your project."

Feig had a clear picture in his head of the characters, many of whom were drawn from his own adolescent experience. But he quickly had to learn to shake those images off. When nineteen-year-old Jason Segel walked in to read for the role of Nick Andopolis, Feig was struck by this tall, goofy, handsome young man, who wasn't anything like the person he had in mind.

"This guy is great," Apatow told Feig.

"But he's not like the guy," Feig replied.

"Well, rewrite him to make him like Jason."

John Francis Daley was another surprise. The thirteen-year-old came in to read for Sam, the character Feig based on himself in high school. Feig had been a goliath of a kid, and all his bullies were small—they ganged up on him knowing he wouldn't fight back. Daley was such a tiny kid, but he was *so* good. You could read everything going on in his head, Feig thought, his eyes were that expressive.

Then it hit him. "What I love about high school and I'm trying to get across with this show is, everybody goes in there at completely different maturity levels," he realized. "Some of the kids look like they were in grade school. Other kids looked like they were in college or in their thirties." Daley landed the role of Sam.

Some actors walked into the audition room and they were exactly what he'd pictured all along. Martin Starr was a doppelgänger for the kid from Feig's high school whom he based Bill, Sam's best friend, on. James Franco looked just like a real-life version of the sly, charming Daniel Desario.

And then there were the unexpected actors who arrived along the way. Busy Philipps, clad in a black leather jacket, auditioned for the role of Kim Kelly, a tough-talking member of the freaks group. The character was supposed to show up in the second episode, but Philipps felt so special that Feig decided to write her into the pilot. Seth Rogen, an unknown actor from Canada, deadpanned his way through Ken Miller's lines and left the whole room in hysterics. And Samm Levine landed the role of Sam's other best friend, Neal, largely because of his William Shatner impression. Apatow watched the tape later and the moment made him laugh. He brought Levine in to meet with him and Feig and requested the Shatner impression again. This time, Levine threw in Beetlejuice, too, for good measure.

"None of them were good! That's the thing. In my mind, I was like, 'Oh, they're loving it!' I was a sixteen-year-old idiot, making an absolute fool out of myself. Which, of course I've come to realize now, is exactly what they were looking for," Levine told me.

The biggest aha moment for Feig came when Linda Cardellini walked in for her audition. He had conjured an image of Lindsay in his head, the way she would look and sound, and there, standing in front of him, was that exact young woman.

"That's her. We have to hire this woman right now," Feig told the room after Cardellini finished her audition.

"We have to see other people," Apatow responded.

Later, Feig was in the bathtub unwinding after a long audition session when he got a call on his cell from Jones. Cardellini was being offered a role on another show and they were about to miss out on her. Feig panicked and called Apatow.

"We're gonna lose Linda Cardellini if we don't hire her now. I'm telling you now, I'm quitting my own show. We have to get her," he told him.

They made the call and got their Lindsay.

Rounding out the cast were seasoned stage performer Becky Ann Baker as Mrs. Weir and *SCTV* comedy veteran Joe Flaherty as Mr. Weir. Flaherty read the pilot script and was impressed. It wasn't the typical sitcom show. It was actually offbeat and intelligent.

Everyone gathered for the first table read at Raleigh Studios in Los Angeles. Natasha Melnick, who was cast as Cindy, Sam's crush, hadn't slept in days, reading her script over and over because she was so excited. Watching everyone in action proved even better than she'd expected. She was particularly impressed by Rogen. He didn't have many lines, but he was so funny that he'd run away with whatever scene he was in.

Flaherty was taken with Starr and his thick glasses. "That's perfect casting," he thought, and decided that Starr would be the show's breakout hit.

One of the young actors arrived late that day, and Apatow used the opportunity to make a statement to the whole cast.

"I'm telling you now that's the last time anyone comes late to a table read or a rehearsal or a shoot without getting fired," Baker remembers him saying. "I hate to make you the butt of this but that's it. This will be the last time we tolerate any of that."

Apatow would become known as the disciplinarian on the set. He was quick to make sure the young actors knew their lines and took the work seriously. During the filming of the episode "Noshing and Moshing," Levine showed up to the set for a lengthy monologue with his ventriloquist dummy, Morty. He remembered his lines just fine but stumbled over Morty's. After calling cut and sending Levine off to run the scene with a production assistant, Apatow pulled him aside.

"You get one warning. That's it. One. Don't ever do that again," he said. Not only was Levine never unprepared for a day on *Freaks and Geeks* after that, but he'd never show up unprepared to any set ever again.

Toward the end of the pilot's production, an opening sequence still hadn't been shot. One afternoon, on a lunch break, the cast filed into the gymnasium of Grant High School in Van Nuys, California. They were short on time that day, and Apatow had each actor cycle through, posing in front of a camera.

"Smile! Goofy smile! Serious face. Try to look cool. But you're not cool," Apatow called from off-camera. They needed someone to play a photographer, who would be seen briefly between shots, so Daley's father slapped on a fake mustache and took on the role. The now iconic opening sequence, scored by Joan Jett's "Bad Reputation," was shot in about fifteen minutes.

One of the most memorable moments comes at the very end of the pilot. Sam finally screwed up the courage to ask Cindy out to the school dance, only to find out that she already had a date. She'd promised him a dance though, and in that last scene, Sam shows up to the school gym in a suit and tie and makes his way straight to Cindy.

"Hi, Cindy," he says.

"Hi, Sam."

"I was wondering, um, you said you'd save a dance for me. So, can I have it now?"

She agrees, and he nervously leads her across the dance floor. Melnick, in her long blue silk dress, still remembers walking hand-in-hand with Daley, butterflies in her stomach. The gym had been decked out for the occasion and there was this feeling of everything being so much bigger than she ever imagined it could be. Looking back, it was such a sweet moment, she thought. Melnick had tried out for other cheerleader roles, and they were all stereotypical mean girls. In any other teen show, this girl would have laughed and made fun of Sam with her friends. Here, she was kind.

Of course, in true *Freaks and Geeks* fashion, we get only a few moments of that triumphant feeling. Life ebbs and flows, and Apatow and Feig were going to lean into every wave. The slow song transitions into a fast beat, and Sam looks absolutely horrified. He had *not* signed up for a fast dance. Then, he's forced to adapt. He ends up letting go and dancing, nervously at first and then joyfully. A small high school victory, ripped, in part, from Apatow's own experience at his junior-year dance. Elsewhere, Lindsay dances with Eli, the disabled kid who has gotten picked on throughout the episode.

Apatow sat in the editing bay, watching that scene, and cried. "This completely works, this is beautiful," he thought. "It's kids reaching out to each other and it's so hard to do that as a kid. It's so hard to offer your heart, it's so hard to try to connect."

Scott Sassa, an NBC executive at the time, felt very differently. He watched the pilot and wasn't particularly blown away. Still, he decided to pick the series up for thirteen episodes. Crunch time had officially begun. The show was filmed on location at a high school in Los Angeles for the pilot, and Apatow tapped production designer Jefferson Sage to build a look-alike set at Raleigh Studios for future episodes.

Sage decided to design a high school that appeared to be packed with a labyrinth of hallways as if it were swallowing the kids up in its vastness. He painted a swatch of pink on the walls as a potential color scheme and invited Apatow and Feig to come look at the set. They had one reservation.

"Maybe it could be scuzzier-looking," he was told. "It's not necessarily a happy place. It's not a chipper, 'Oh we go to school and life is great.' School is this necessary thing they have to do, they're finding their way with one another."

Sage swapped the pink for dingy greens and browns.

That palette crept its way throughout the entire design of the show. Debra McGuire was entering her sixth season as a costume designer on *Friends* when she came on board to create the *Freaks and Geeks* wardrobe. She pulled clothing from costume houses and vintage stores and overdyed each article of clothing with grays and browns. The wardrobe, she thought, was ugly. No way around it. "It was like the Midwest threw up," she'd later say.

When it came time to assemble a writers' room, Apatow and Feig populated the group with people like Bob Nickman, a former *Roseanne* writer; Jeff Judah and Gabe Sachs, a writing team who worked on Apatow's Fox show *Sick in the Head*; and Patty Lin, who had come off working on *Martial Law* (it was a show about martial arts—she was embarrassed by it, but Feig got a laugh out of it).

When Lin met Feig, she was disarmed by his friendliness. The two swapped stories about growing up in the Midwest and their mutual love of the band Styx.

Lin saw herself in Lindsay—she had also been a straight-A student who straddled two worlds in high school, taking honors classes while dating a pothead drummer.

A week before the writers' first day of work, a questionnaire arrived in the mail from Feig and Apatow. In it was a list of twenty questions about their high school experience. *What's the worst thing that ever happened to you? Who did you fall in love with? What was your best drug experience? Your worst drug experience?* They also received a copy of Feig's show bible, a binder packed with each character's life story. Notes lined the pages with beginnings of story ideas and thoughts on the themes and tone of the show.

The day started at 9:30 sharp at Raleigh Studios, in a conference room with black-and-white headshots of the cast tacked to the walls. The newly assembled team of writers gathered around a long table and took turns sharing their most humiliating high school experiences with a group of strangers. They munched on food from Astro Burger, a joint down the street on Melrose Ave., and listened as common threads emerged—rejections by crushes, embarrassing first brushes with sexuality, and gym class. Oh, how they hated gym class. No other show in memory quite nails the true horror that comes from standing in a line, praying someone will usher you onto their team.

The writers still loathe gym, to this very day. "I didn't like changing in the locker rooms. I didn't like jocks. I hated track," Nickman told me. "The gym teachers were some of the dumbest men I've ever met in my life."

"That's where a lot of my scars came from," writer J. Elvis Weinstein added. "I just remember shower horror. I was younger and skipped a grade, so I was less pubescent. It was a dark cloud every day on the horizon."

Sometimes Apatow would instruct each writer to take out a piece of paper and set a timer for five or ten minutes. "Write down every idea you have in your head," he said. "It doesn't have to be good; it doesn't have to be relevant." Afterward those papers were photocopied and passed around the room. It was a brilliant exercise, Lin remembers thinking. As a writer in the room, you're constantly self-editing before pitching so you don't risk getting rejected. Apatow was giving everyone permission to be as free as they wanted to be.

Seeds of real moments grew into story ideas. Nickman's tale about getting freaked out watching a Super-8 porn flick that belonged to his friend's dad was turned into an episode for Sam, Bill, and Neal. Maudlin poetry that Lin used to write as a teen helped shape the poem that Cindy would read in the episode "Girlfriends and Boyfriends." Writer Steve Bannos based his own character on the show, Mr. Kowchevski, on a miserable teacher he had in high school who hit kids.

An entire episode was built around a fashion snafu Feig experienced when he was sixteen. He was browsing in Silverman's, a clothing store at the mall, when a salesman pulled him aside to show him a new line of jumpsuits.

"This is the hottest thing going, man," he told Feig. "Everybody's wearing these."

Feig tried one on and agreed that he did, indeed, look pretty cool. He put on that jumpsuit and walked into school the next day, only to realize, with horror, that he had made a very bad decision. His outfit was *not* a hit with his classmates. Laughter and stares ensued, and he was forced to ride out the rest of the day in his disco ensemble. Feig sketched out the jumpsuit he wore for McGuire, down to the cut and powder-blue color, and she tracked down a re-creation for Daley, who wore the outfit—to similar mockery—in the episode "Looks and Books."

Feig was confident that these mortifying moments would resonate with an audience. "Who wouldn't want to relive the worst moments of their life from a safe distance, like a horror movie?" he thought.

NBC scheduled *Freaks and Geeks* for eight p.m. on Saturday night, which sent Feig into a panic. Anybody who might want to watch the show would be out on a Saturday night. But the pilot actually did pretty well. That is, until about half-way through the episode when there was a sharp ratings drop-off. Feig pinpointed that moment to one emotionally brutal scene when Eli, a disabled student, is called "retarded" and then sprints down the bleachers in anger, falling and breaking his arm. "You just heard America go, like, 'Nope,' and turn the channel."

Still, they nabbed a rating that was good enough to celebrate. Feig stood on a table in the cafeteria set and read the numbers out loud to the cast and crew. "It looks like we have a hit on our hands," Feig said.

Critics were complimentary but cautious. "In many ways, *Freaks and Geeks* is an original, as brazenly smart as *Dawson's Creek* is broadly idealistic," *Variety*'s Ray Richmond wrote. "But that's hardly a guarantee of a long and prosperous primetime life. There remains, after all, little evidence beyond *The Wonder Years* that viewers carry an overwhelming desire to revisit high school through their television set."

Entertainment Weekly's A. J. Jacobs dubbed the show "far from a hormone-soaked fantasy," and called it "funny but not zany, poignant but not melodramatic." He added: "Sad to say, but smart, frank writing about teen angst doesn't necessarily translate into huge ratings (R.I.P. the admittedly more earnest 1994–95 critical darling *My So-Called Life*)."

The critics were, once again, right. The show's numbers tumbled after the pilot. In fact, it was the lowest-rated show on NBC for multiple weeks in a row. Feig never announced the numbers again.

Flaherty, who had dealt with his own ratings struggles on *SCTV*, understood what was going on. "You can't be too complex on network television with each episode," he told me. "Each episode can't be a little masterpiece, with seriousness and comedic stuff. If they're not saying funny lines every third or fourth line, it doesn't work for the audience."

One miserably cold, icy day, Baker, Levine, Cardellini, and Daley headed to New York City to promote the show at the Macy's Thanksgiving Day Parade. Baker was thrilled—she had watched the parade for years and now she was actually going to be *in* it. The four of them got on the Mother Goose float, slipping back and forth, gripping the rails as sleet and freezing rain drenched them.

"Who are you?" someone called from a street corner.

"We're *Freaks and Geeks!*" she yelled back.

Then, more trouble on the horizon. NBC got a new network president. Garth Ancier had moved over from the WB after helping make *Dawson's Creek* a hit and was handed a stack of pilots to review on his arrival. He watched the first episode of *Freaks and Geeks* and thought it was "adorable," but he found the storytelling unconventional. It didn't quite fit in with NBC's comedies like *Cheers*, and it also wasn't a natural fit in the drama category alongside shows like *Law & Order*.

"Who's the lead?" he wondered. On *Dawson's Creek*, the show followed a tight-knit group of teenagers whose stories interconnected. But *Freaks and Geeks* felt like it revolved around two separate groups and two different sets of stories.

Ancier and Apatow would talk on the phone. A lot. Sometimes Ancier took him to lunch at a restaurant across the street from CBS Studios and spit-balled ideas.

"Maybe let's make James Franco a more central character," Ancier suggested to Apatow.

"Oh no, but he's not the lead."

"OK, so help me here. Who are we focusing on?"

The conversations were tense. Ancier couldn't understand why Apatow wouldn't throw some of these characters a victory—whether it be on the athletic field or with their school crushes. It drove him nuts that Cindy and Sam weren't getting together. "He's finally out with this girl and she says he's like her sister?" Ancier asked after finding out that Sam was going to be friend-zoned in an upcoming episode.

Sometimes costume designer McGuire would put a beanie on Franco for a scene and get irritated notes from the network. "No, you can't put a hat on James Franco. He's too good-looking. Why would you put a hat on him?" they would ask.

"Because we're not doing *Dawson's Creek*, OK?" she remembers thinking. "We're doing *Freaks and Geeks*."

When staff writer Mike White penned the episode "Kim Kelly Is My Friend," a painful glimpse at Kim's bleak home life, the network was so nervous that they decided to air it later in the season. Before designing the set, Sage remembers Apatow giving him a note: "They don't have a whole lot of money. It's a broken marriage. The boyfriend is kind of a construction dude. It's the kind of thing where the wife tries to get him to fix up the house and he never finishes anything."

Sage ran with that, creating a space filled with open stud walls and dangling wires. The bathroom has no door, just an old curtain. We see that Kim has no privacy in her home and nowhere she can feel safe.

The episode didn't sit well with Garth Ancier. "These kids have terrible lives and now they're going home to dysfunctional parents," he thought. "That's really—that's sad."

The show might not have been making waves with Ancier, but something special was happening at William McKinley High. Feig and Apatow were going to do things their way, creating a new kind of format for a teen show, where improvisation was celebrated and each episode was populated with unguarded moments ripped from reality. If an actor accidentally flubbed a line, that was gold. During the episode "Smooching and Mooching," Levine shot a scene where he explained to Starr and Daley the mechanics of Spin the Bottle. Halfway through answering the question "Do people French kiss?" Levine realized he had completely forgotten his line as he fumbled out, "Some people don't. I do," half laughing as he went. That was the take that made it in the final cut.

When Ken Kwapis, a frequent director of *The Larry Sanders Show*, came on board to direct, he was instructed not to be too precious with composition. In fact, Jake Kasdan told him that the shots should be framed like a family photo album, with way too much headroom above. Nothing slick, and a little bit unruly. Kwapis was struck by how different the show was from everything else on network television. He remembers Daniel making a wisecrack about Kim's period and thinking, "This isn't something you would expect to see on a teen show."

If Kwapis needed further proof of *Freaks and Geeks*'s commitment to realism, he saw it during the filming of "Tests and Breasts." In the episode's final scene, Lindsay sits with Daniel as he tries to prove that he didn't cheat on his math test. He starts to tell a sob story about his academic failings, and Cardellini lets out a laugh so spontaneous and unrehearsed-sounding that Kwapis, who was standing behind the monitor, was taken aback. In the same moment of marveling at Cardellini, he thought: "Oh God, she blew a lot of snot out of her nose." It was the cherry on top of that scene and, of course, the take that made it into the show.

Often, scripts would be used merely as jumping-off points. J. Elvis Weinstein was so excited that Feig and Apatow loved the school assembly scene he wrote for the beginning of the episode "Beers and Weirs." Then came shooting time. He watched as it was shaped into something completely different.

"Hey, say this!" Apatow would call from behind the camera, throwing out lines for the actors to use. There was enough of Weinstein's original material that stayed in, so he wasn't totally mortified, but he said, "I learned very quickly that nothing is sacred on the page."

The show's young actors took this unusual freedom and ran with it. While filming the pilot, Levine thought there could be more to the scripted line: "The dance is tomorrow, she's a cheerleader. What's wrong with you?" He approached Apatow with a pitch. "How 'bout I say, 'The dance is tomorrow. She's a cheerleader, you've seen *Star Wars* twenty-seven times. Do the math!'" He got the green light and, much to his delight, that ad-lib made its way into multiple *Freaks and Geeks* trailers.

Segel, Rogen, and Franco would take the new scripts that they were handed on Friday and meet at Segel's house on Sundays, poring over the pages, rehearsing, and looking for moments to punch up or add jokes. When Franco expressed to Apatow and Feig that he was interested in writing, the two took him into an office and wrote a scene in front of him, each improvising the different characters as they went. In between takes, Rogen would work on an early draft of the future comedy hit *Superbad* when he was supposed to be doing his schoolwork.

Sachs and Judah watched the young actors from behind the monitor and were impressed. Segel and Rogen were talented improvisers, and Rogen would usually come up with a line that was funnier than what was scripted. Philipps was funny, too, Judah recalled, and she could also break your heart. She'd tap into the emotions of a scene with just one look. Franco's improvisations, though, often missed the mark. They just didn't fit his character.

And then there was the time he took it way, way too far. During a scene in "We've Got Spirit," Philipps was instructed by the director to give Franco a light slap on the arm as she said the line, "Dammit, Daniel, do something!"

"He grabbed both my arms and screamed in my face, 'DON'T EVER TOUCH ME AGAIN!'" Philipps later wrote in her book *This Will Only Hurt a Little*. "And he threw me to the ground. Flat on my back. Wind knocked out of me."

There were other incidents of this erratic behavior on set. During one of the rare scenes that the trio of geeks shared with him, Franco got upset with the way the other actors were saying their lines. They were filming on the AV Room set, and the character of Daniel Desario was supposed to leave in a huff, declaring, "I'm not hanging out with these losers."

Instead, Levine remembers, Franco said: "I'm not going to stay here and hang out with this bunch of bad actors." Then, he slammed the door so hard behind him that the frame broke.

Starr, Levine, and Daley exchanged looks and let out uncomfortable giggles.

Decades later, more would come out about Franco's behavior over the years, including a 2018 lawsuit that saw five women accusing the actor of sexually inappropriate behavior, four of whom were students at his now-shuttered acting school.

But outside of the uncomfortable tension with Franco behind-the-scenes of *Freaks and Geeks*, the young cast developed bonds off and on set.

It was important to Apatow and Feig that Starr, Daley, and Levine feel like real-life pals, so the trio would hang out and run lines together in a workroom.

Starr and Levine had their driver's licenses (a fact that Daley, at thirteen, envied) and the two would hang out after hours, eating at Baskin-Robbins, going bowling, or catching a movie. In a way, it all felt a lot like high school. Starr and Levine developed crushes on their teenage co-stars, and Levine would make a few innocent overtures, like suggesting a chat over lunch in the cafeteria.

And then there was the kissing. Melnick and Daley shared their first on-screen kiss (and Melnick's first kiss ever) on *Freaks and Geeks*. She was buzzing with nerves before shooting the scene, building the moment up in her head. When it finally came, she realized that it really was just two pairs of lips touching. "Well, that's done," she thought, mentally checking the big moment off in her head.

In another scene, Stephen Lea Sheppard, who played Harris, one of the school's resident geeks, shared a kiss with his on-screen girlfriend Judith. Nickman watched from behind the camera as the two young actors nervously pecked. They were both so scared that the kiss lasted for just a quarter of a second. To elongate the moment, the camera cut to Sam, Neal, and Bill, who watched wide-eyed.

Those anxieties were exactly what Feig wanted to capture. He was tired of the teen shows that made young people look so cool with sex. "Who the fuck was that comfortable in high school to be sleeping with people?" he thought. Feig knew *some* people did it, because there were pregnant girls at his school— but certainly not him and his friends. They barely dated. They were terrified of talking to girls.

They wanted to shoot the small, real moments. Forget sex. Back then, for writers like Sachs, if a girl accidentally had her hand near his knee that was huge, and would prompt a larger, deeper discussion of what it could mean.

The young actors were coming of age alongside their characters. When Millie briefly joins the freaks group in the episode "Dead Dogs and Gym Teachers," she's handed a beer bottle and an opener. Sarah Hagan, who had never opened a bottle of beer before, struggled with the cap, and then handed it to Franco. "Can you open this for me?" she asked.

That day, Hagan watched Philipps, Franco, Segel, and Rogen in action. They were so confident and comfortable with one another, and ad-libbed so freely.

Sometimes she had a hard time keeping a straight face around Franco, who always had this sly smile, like he knew something she didn't.

Hagan was in an unusual situation. She wasn't a regular cast member, so she split her time between set and real-life high school. She was new to Los Angeles and hadn't made any friends at her new school, which wasn't helped by the fact that she was gone for chunks of time during the week. At the same time, it was hard to forge strong relationships on-set with the actors who were there all the time. Cardellini turned into a sort of big sister for Hagan. She would go to Cardellini's trailer between scenes and they'd talk through Hagan's troubles.

One day, Hagan came to work exhausted from juggling those two worlds, and completely forgot her lines. She was humiliated. Between takes, she broke down. Cardellini came and sat with her. "It's OK, it happens all the time to people," Cardellini reassured her. Hagan was so grateful for her friend at that moment.

The show was shot on 35mm film, one of the biggest costs of production. But Apatow hated to yell cut because he worried that it would take the air out of filming. Instead, he'd let the camera continue to roll between takes. Members of the hair and makeup team would scurry in, wardrobe would be adjusted, the lighting technicians would make tweaks to equipment, and still the camera rolled. *Freaks and Geeks* shot so much footage that, by episode twelve, Kodak sent them a case of Champagne because the production had used 1 million feet of film.

For his part, Bannos wondered if that was also Apatow's way of saying eff you to the network, by forcing them to foot the bill.

As the show reached the end of the twelve episodes that NBC had ordered, a big question loomed: Would they get an order for the back nine to finish out the season?

The ratings weren't talked about much on-set. But Baker recalls Apatow's frustration with the show's constantly shifting time slot. The show was on for two weeks, off for four weeks because of the World Series, on for another six weeks, and then off for two months. Baker's friends from back in New York would call her, confused. "I thought you were on tonight," they'd say.

One afternoon, some of the cast and crew headed to a baseball field to shoot a scene from the episode entitled "The Diary." Apatow and Feig had decided to throw Ancier a bone and give the kids a victory—sort of. Tired of being picked last in gym class, Bill maneuvers his way into becoming a team captain. After a frustrating start to the game, Bill finally, finally catches the ball. His two best friends come running over to him, jumping and whooping, as *Rocky* music swells. The trio are so busy celebrating, they don't notice that the opposing team's runners had tagged up and scored. It's a classic *Freaks and Geeks* moment of triumph—a small victory tempered by a real-life twist.

While filming that day, Levine noticed Apatow on the phone, pacing up and down alone on a nearby tennis court. He returned to the field and didn't want to talk about what had just happened. Only later did Levine realize that Apatow was begging the network not to cancel the show.

Kwapis was already beginning to think about the characters' lives post *Freaks and Geeks*. At the end of the episode "Looks and Books," Lindsay goes to find Daniel, Kim, Ken, and Nick. She spots them at their regular hangout, sitting on the hood of the car outside a local diner. She pauses for a moment and looks at them from afar.

Kwapis knew that Lindsay wasn't long for this small town. She had other things—big things—she was going to do with her life. Her four friends, though, would stay behind.

Before filming that day, Kwapis walked Cardellini through what was going on in Lindsay's head. "You think ahead about your future and it's almost like you're looking back on this moment, a precious moment that you're not going to have again," Kwapis said. "You want to put this moment into amber and hold on to it." You'll watch that scene a little differently thinking of Kwapis's note. There's Lindsay, who's coming into her own thanks to this scrappy, tight-knit group of teens. They won't always be in her life, but for that night, and for many nights after that, she was going to get into that beat-up car and catch a movie.

As uncertainty continued to loom, the writers stayed laser focused. Sachs and Judah holed up in their office and pretty much never left. The two put on the songs they listened to in high school—"Vienna" by Billy Joel, "Free Bird" by Lynyrd Skynyrd—and transported themselves back to adolescence. They kept toy blocks in the office so that Maude, Apatow's two-year-old daughter, could play while her dad had meetings.

Apatow would push Sachs and Judah with their writing. There had to be a reason that each scene was in the show, and it couldn't just be because it was relaying plot information. "OK, what's the real version of the story?" Apatow would ask. Both he and Feig wanted brutal honesty in every episode.

Closest to home for Judah was "The Garage Door," an episode that revolves around Neal finding out that his dad is cheating on his mom. He roams the neighborhood at night, trying to track down his dad's car with a garage clicker. The scenario was pulled directly from Judah's own life when he was fifteen. He had been home sick from school, watching an old Phil Donahue episode about the signs that a husband is cheating, when he realized that his dad fit the bill. "There were five signs," Judah recalled. "Worried about his teeth being yellow, losing weight, I was like, 'Oh my God. Oh my God.'" After he made that discovery, he set out to find his dad's car. Finally, after some searching, there it was, in another woman's garage.

They shot that scene right before Christmas. It was a cold night by California standards, and Judah bundled up in a big black coat and bright yellow cap. He watched as this painful real-life moment unfolded in front of the camera, Levine wandering the neighborhood on a bike, garage clicker in hand. It was tougher to watch than he imagined. Yet so satisfying. Satisfying that something significant that happened in his life could be shaped into a strong episode, and that it was being done really well.

He wasn't the only one on-set experiencing catharsis.

One afternoon, Feig watched from behind the monitor as Lindsay and her friends got into a car crash. The scene was based on a moment that happened to him when he was sixteen and had his drivers' license for only a week. His friend was in the passenger seat and the two were laughing, distracted, when the friend yelled, "Turn here!" Feig turned right into another car filled with a family of kids. It was the worst thing that ever happened to him.

During that day of shooting, he was downright giddy. When the car smashed into the other car, he felt a release. He started laughing. "Why are you laughing?" someone asked him. "We just did a car stunt."

"I can't help it," he replied. "I feel so good right now. I just made poor Lindsay go through the most traumatic experience of my life."

As shooting progressed, tensions mounted between Apatow and Ancier. Apatow loved the show just as it was; he didn't want to change a thing. Ancier continued to pitch him ideas that made his eyes roll. They were at a standstill.

"You should write the final episode," Apatow told Feig. "We should shoot it now in case we do get the plug pulled; at least we'll have the final episode."

So, Feig set out to tell one final chapter of his beloved show. As he mapped out where to leave each of the characters, a question stuck out. What should happen to Lindsay? He needed to close the book on the girl who started this whole journey, way back in Wilkes-Barre, Pennsylvania.

"Maybe she becomes a Deadhead," Apatow suggested.

"Oh my God, that's awesome," Feig thought. He didn't know the Grateful Dead's music well—just the hits like "Sugar Magnolia," which used to play on Detroit radio. So, he went out and bought their album *American Beauty* and immediately fell in love. He listened to "Box of Rain" over and over as he wrote the scene of Lindsay, alone in her room, twirling and grooving to the same song. He was going to have her lie to her parents, say that she was heading to a summer math program at the University of Michigan, and instead join Kim to follow the Dead. In the last act of the story, he wanted her to disappoint her parents.

Titled "Discos and Dragons," the episode opens with Nick entering a disco-dancing competition with his new girlfriend (played by a then unknown Lizzy Caplan, who would go on to play the iconic Janis Ian in *Mean Girls*). Lindsay watches Nick, who seems to have actually gotten his act together. The two sit down to *really* talk for the first time post breakup, as both pretend to be completely, totally fine. They're not, and as they walk away, the camera shows Nick in slow motion, heading back to the dance floor with all the soul-crushing heaviness that comes after having that kind of talk. Feig's one regret, he told me, was not shooting Lindsay in slow motion. Later, they'd have to optically slow her down in post-production.

Apatow had given Feig the green light to direct the episode. Throughout shooting Feig was desperate to take the helm but was told that he was needed on the writing side. Finally, he was being given the chance to get behind the monitor as a kind of consolation prize.

Feig was thrilled but nervous—his only other experience directing was his small feature film. Still, he had such a clear vision of the episode. He diligently did prep work ahead of time, deciding how he wanted to shoot each scene. Then, teaming up with Sage, he re-created the bowling-alley disco club from his childhood and picked out "The Groove Line" for the scene's soundtrack. He'd always thought that that was the world's greatest disco song.

"Ripple" by the Grateful Dead underscored the final moments of *Freaks and Geeks*. Lindsay said goodbye to her parents, her brother, Bill, and Neal at the bus station. Baker ad-libbed the line "I miss you already" as her daughter boarded the bus. Then, once safely out of view, Lindsay hops off, dons her green army jacket, and joins Kim in front of an old hippie van. They used a crane to shoot that day as the van drove around the corner and disappeared.

"We didn't often get a crane," Sage recalled. "I thought, Wow, we're going all out on this. Now I think, OK they knew. They were trying to make it something special."

At least, when the time came, Apatow and Feig would get to end this thing on their own terms.

They didn't get that order of nine episodes. Instead, NBC asked them to shoot one additional episode, with the option for more. Still, there was a bright side. That episode would be scheduled for Monday night, when there would be a lot more eyeballs—and a lot more competition. Ahead of the show's new time slot, the *New York Times* penned a piece about *Freaks and Geeks*, titled "Low Times at McKinley High," calling it one of those "rare birds": "a dramedy that manages to be brutally honest, unexpectedly hilarious and often touching all at once."

Within the article, the friction between Ancier and Apatow's opposing creative views hung heavy.

"I love the characters," Ancier told the *Times*. "I just want them to have less depressing lives. We felt they needed one decent sized victory per episode."

Apatow's take: "TV wants to show kids making it. But sometimes the victory is just that you survived something with your sense of humor intact."

Referred to as Pilot B, "Carded and Discarded," written by Feig and Apatow, would serve as an introduction to the world of *Freaks and Geeks* for new viewers just discovering it on Monday nights. In it, the freaks try to buy fake IDs to get into a concert. The geeks befriend a transfer student named Maureen.

The episode aired on January 8, 2000, and Scott Sassa told Apatow if it got an 8 share—that is, if 4.4 percent of households with television sets watched the episode, and 8 being the same size as Sassa's shoe—he wouldn't cancel the show.

For the first time, Levine remembers seeing a handful of ads promoting the show. The cast and crew waited anxiously for the results of the ratings. Then it came: they had gotten an 8 share. Exactly. The show hadn't been canceled, but it had been picked up for only four additional episodes, bringing the series to a total of eighteen, with the possibility of a second season.

There were still some loose ends to tie up. Throughout the course of the series, Ancier had pitched the idea of Sam finally landing a date with Cindy. Feig had no interest in the typical boy-girl relationship arc that played out on television. He decided to take an entirely different route.

Early on, in the writers' room, Lin had pitched the idea that Sam realizes Cindy isn't the girl he'd put on a pedestal. He should discover she has human flaws, like a really loud burp or a bit of a mustache. Apatow liked that idea.

"What about if she farts?" he asked.

Lin thought he was joking. What network would allow something like that on television? She brushed the comment off and changed the subject. But Apatow was adamant.

"No, no. What about the fart?" he said, circling back.

"Are you serious?" Lin asked. "Can we really do that?"

"Yeah, why not?" he replied.

And so, in one small yet revolutionary moment, a character's love interest farted on television. They largely got away with it, except Standards and Practices insisted that the word "fart" be changed to "cut the cheese." That was OK with Lin because, actually, she thought that was even funnier.

Apatow and Feig continued to dismantle the classic crush story line. Sam finally gets to date her, only to realize he doesn't like her at all. She wants to do stuff with the football players and really hates the necklace he gifts her. Plus—the ultimate faux pas—she's unamused by *The Jerk*, the classic comedy film starring Steve Martin, which Sam adores.

"She's kind of boring. It's weird hanging out with her friends. And, I mean, all she wants to do is make out and stuff," Sam tells Neal and Bill as he's becoming disillusioned by his crush. The fall of Cindy from Sam's pedestal is one of the show's strongest story arcs. You delight in watching the interesting, honest tumble, as—much like happens in real life—the pair slowly realize they're just not a match. Still, there's a sadness there when they break up, which makes it all the more real. The writers captured the pain of a relationship ending, even when both parties knew it wasn't the right fit.

Apatow had one more unconventional twist up his sleeve. He was listening to an episode of Howard Stern when a doctor came on to discuss intersex people. It sparked an idea for *Freaks and Geeks*. "There's a way to do that that's real and sweet and compassionate," he remembers thinking.

The concept was that Ken's new girlfriend, Amy, played by Jessica Campbell, would confide in him that she was born with both male and female genitalia. That would cause Ken to spin out about his relationship, his own sexuality, and his feelings for Amy.

When Apatow presented the idea to the room full of writers, he was met with raised eyebrows. Bob Nickman thought the idea felt a little too outside the box for a show set in the 1980s. Still, when Apatow looked over at him, he remembers saying: "If you wanna do it, I'm wrong all the time, so if you like it you should fucking do it."

The result was "The Little Things," the very last episode of *Freaks and Geeks* ever shot. Apatow brought Campbell and Rogen into his office to improvise the scene where Amy reveals that she is intersex.

"How would this go down if she was telling you this information?" Apatow asked Rogen. He shaped the dialogue around their improv, intent to make the moment as thoughtful and real as possible. Rogen was impressed. "That was the first time I saw you can make weird moments work if you treat them totally honestly," he later told *Vanity Fair*.

At the very end of the episode, Ken realizes that his feelings for Amy are stronger and more important than anything else. He chases her down right before she's about to give a tuba performance in the school cafeteria.

"I'm sorry and I—I don't care and I'm, I'm so sorry," he says. The two kiss—but not before Ken accidentally knocks his head on Amy's tuba. Another perfect *Freaks and Geeks*-style victory.

On their last day of shooting, Levine and Starr got up on their chairs in the middle of the cafeteria set and thanked everyone. Levine knew that he hadn't just filmed his final scene of Season 1, but likely of the entire show. There wasn't much hope that *Freaks and Geeks* would get picked up. All that was left was one last lunch and a wrap party.

Everybody gathered later, and Feig stood on a folding chair to give one final speech.

"I'm kind of flustered right now because I didn't think the last day would hit me this hard," he said. "That's going to be the hardest part—not getting to see everybody every day." The room broke into applause when Feig finished speaking. Cardellini, still in her green army jacket, had tears in her eyes.

Later, the cast and crew headed to their wrap party, a 1980s-themed prom. A paper banner hung above the stage that read: CONGRATULATIONS FREAKS & GEEKS 2000. The group gathered in rented formalwear, Feig in a ruffled orange number, Apatow in powder blue. Phillips put on her junior prom dress and a bright-pink wig. Daley donned the infamous blue jumpsuit.

Apatow awarded high school diplomas to the cast's "graduating class": Rogen, Levine, and Starr, all wearing their requisite caps and gowns.

"As it may be, this is the only graduation I'll ever have, so I'd like to thank y'all for coming down," Rogen said when he got up to the microphone. "And I don't know—every rose has its thorn and all that junk."

A paperback McKinley High School yearbook was printed and handed out, featuring snapshots Sachs had taken on-set. Stories and blurbs lined the pages from the cast and crew, and people passed around their yearbooks to sign. It really was like the end of high school.

Over at NBC, Sassa popped out the tape of the show's last episode. He had just watched Lindsay hop on the bus to follow the Grateful Dead on tour. "That's not how this thing should end," he remembers thinking. In that moment, Sassa knew once and for all that *Freaks and Geeks* would never be the show they needed it to be.

Apatow got a message from Ancier's office. "Garth is going to call you in a little bit," he was told. Apatow knew what that meant. The show was canceled, and he was being given an hour to collect himself so that he wouldn't argue.

Later, Ancier would say that he was having his own reservations.

"It's easy to cancel a show when the show is just god-awful. Then you're basically saying to someone without saying it, 'Your show is god-awful. I'm irritated that we gave you all this time and all this money to make it work and it didn't work,'" he told me. "The hard cancellation is when everyone thinks the show is very special but no one is watching it. Then you sort of get into this position of, Well, now I feel like I'm clubbing a baby seal."

It was around that time that Feig's mom died suddenly. Elaine Feig was Mrs. Weir: she was so positive, always upbeat, and tried to see the best in things. Feig was at his father's lawyer's office when Apatow delivered the news that *Freaks and Geeks* was being canceled. He was so devastated about losing his mom that he felt he couldn't deal with the double tragedy of the moment.

"That was crazy, because the show getting canceled felt like the death of all these characters that I loved and knew and wanted to keep writing for and then on top of losing my real mom," Feig said.

Apatow was angry. He was also determined. He wasn't going to let these young actors disappear. He was going to get them work and he was going to make them successful. As Segel would put it: "[It was] a *Count of Monte Cristo*–style revenge mission on Judd's part that he will systematically make every one of these people a star." And—from Seth Rogen to Segel—he did.

Feig, meanwhile, would go on to become a wildly successful, respected director with hits like *Bridesmaids*, *The Heat*, and *A Simple Favor*. Both he and Kwapis were frequent directors on *The Office*, a television show—much like *Freaks and Geeks*—that was based firmly in reality, with the ability to make you laugh and break your heart.

What was so revolutionary about *Freaks and Geeks* is mainstream now. Shows don't have to exist in the world of comedy or drama, they can find their place somewhere in between. Characters don't need big victories—in fact, it's far more interesting when they don't get them. Small, real moments are paramount. But for one season on NBC, *Freaks and Geeks* completely redefined what TV could be.

A few years later, Josh Schwartz, a young screenwriter and admirer of *Freaks and Geeks*, took his own stab at teen television. His series would have all the ingredients of the hit *90210*—a group of wealthy, beautiful teens living and loving in Southern California—but dig deeper and you'd find offbeat humor, quirky story lines, and a whole new kind of heartthrob.

As a young man in a seashell necklace once said: Welcome to *The O.C.*, bitch.

The O.C.

(2003-2007)

A sandy-haired teen steps onto a dark street just outside a tony mansion. He's wearing a gray hoodie, black leather jacket, and matching black choker. Just as he starts to put a cigarette in his mouth, he spots a young woman standing a few feet from him.

"Who are you?" she asks, intrigued.

Cigarette in mouth, he gives her a sideways glance. "Whoever you want me to be."

A gentle breeze ruffles the young woman's hair. She smiles. The teen approaches her and offers her a cigarette, which she lights with the end of his. The two slowly eye each other, sweetly and curiously. In that moment, on a quiet street in California's Orange County, a tortured, iconic teen television romance was born.

We've found our way to Newport Beach, a hamlet packed with juicy drama, misbehaving teens, and misbehaving adults, all set against an idyllic backdrop of piers, surf, and sand. On the outside, **The O.C.** *was neatly packaged as a drama-filled show about beautiful high schoolers. But scratch even a tiny bit below the surface, and you'll discover a series with the wit of* **Freaks and Geeks***, the intrinsic beauty and sadness of* **My So-Called Life***, and a fresh, new take on the way teen shows could be.*

If Josh Schwartz, the creator of *The O.C.*, were a superhero—and when it comes to creating teen television hits, he's certainly earned his cape—this is how his origin story would unfold.

When Schwartz was seven years old, his parents, toy inventors from Providence, Rhode Island, sent him off to sleepaway camp. There, the kids took part in an essay-writing contest, where his peers penned homages to horses and soccer. Schwartz wrote a review of *Gremlins*, a 1984 horror movie that had recently rocked his world.

"Spielberg has done it again," his opening line read. (He won the contest.)

As a child, Schwartz had all the ingredients of a future screenwriter: precocious, introverted, and a lover of pop culture. Back home in Providence, he liked to hang out in his room, read comic books, and write short stories in the garden. Some of his favorite memories were of going to the movies with his dad.

Schwartz's dreams of becoming a writer brought him to the University of Southern California, where he quickly made his mark by winning the school's prestigious Jack Nicholson Award for his screenplay *Providence*, based on his senior year of high school. The award was revoked the next day—it was discovered that he was too young to be eligible—though he did sell the script to Sony, who purchased the feature film for an impressive first-time deal of more than $500,000.

The studio didn't end up producing *Providence* but buzz around the script got Schwartz industry attention, landing him a meeting with McG, the director behind the tour-de-force hit *Charlie's Angels*, and his producing partner Stephanie Savage. Schwarz met them in a grand office at Fox Studios. It was all very intimidating.

McG and Savage told Schwartz that they had a seed of a show idea that would revolve around McG's hometown of Orange County. The producer explained that he never quite fit into that world—his friends were water polo players who spent their summers as lifeguards and surfers, and looked like chiseled Adonises. McG was very slight as a teen. He had a mess of curly orange hair and braces and wore an unfortunate neck brace.

That struck an immediate chord in Schwartz.

While in college, he had encountered the strange, unsettling world of water polo players, many of whom hailed from Orange County. These tall bros looked like they were straight out of an Abercrombie & Fitch catalog, with sandy blond hair, crisp polos, and flip-flops. Their new show wouldn't be about those guys. In fact, in this fictional world, jocks would be mostly peripheral characters who bullied the real protagonists and were slyly mocked by far wittier protagonists.

Savage, Schwartz, and McG began discussing who the show would *really* be about, riffing on the idea of a lost girl and a boy from the wrong side of the tracks. Then, Schwartz pitched the idea of a different kind of outsider—not of the leather-jacket, car-stealing variety. This would be a teen who grew up in a city filled with Juicy Couture sweatsuits and expensive cars but, much like McG and Schwartz, never fit in. He lived in his own bubble, where he got by with a sharply tuned sense of humor and a deep love of comic books and video games.

Savage slapped the arms of her chair. "It's like the fucking *Breakfast Club*," she declared.

The idea of a lovably gawky character being given top billing in this glossy world intrigued Savage. The more they discussed the show's possibilities, the more excited she became. The trio put their heads together and began to flesh out the group dynamics. Savage loved the idea of a close connection springing up between the show's two male leads. She had never seen a soap that was rooted in male friendship. This was their chance to do something really original. The final pitch came together like this: Ryan Atwood, a troubled teen from Chino, moves in with public defender Sandy Cohen, who lives in a glitzy mansion with his wife, Kirsten, and son, Seth. Down the street is Marissa Cooper, a popular high schooler who immediately catches Ryan's eye. From there, lots of romance and drama would unravel.

Savage knew teen TV. She had devoured *Beverly Hills, 90210* and loved *My So-Called Life*, which moved her with its emotional storytelling and ability to elevate the smallest of moments, like Jordan holding Angela's hand in the boiler room. The parents on the show also stood out to her. They were deep, fleshed-out characters who had their own insecurities and desires and made messy mistakes. Schwartz, meanwhile, had always been a fan of *Freaks and Geeks*. He liked the offbeat casting, the music, and the fact that it was populated with underdog characters.

Both knew they had no chance of selling something like *Freaks and Geeks* or *My So-Called Life* to a network. Teen shows with small, emotional stories and a confluence of genres were being canceled on a dime.

So, the duo did something sneaky. They developed what Schwartz would later call their "Trojan horse." A show that—on the surface—had all the trappings of a sexy romp: beaches, hotties in bathing suits, bonfires, and all the delicious drama you'd expect from teen TV. But dig a little deeper, and you'd find quirky humor, indie music, comic books, and an underdog named Seth Cohen as the star. The secret plan was to combine the ingredients of shows like *Beverly Hills, 90210* with *Freaks and Geeks* and create something completely new.

The two presented a collage featuring ripped magazine cutouts to Fox Studios. On one side, there were film posters for *St. Elmo's Fire*, *Diner*, and *Election*. On the other side, photos of California at its sandiest, surfiest, and most glorious. Executives were instantly tantalized by the prospect of another runaway teen hit like *90210*. Sure, they had their concerns. Seth's last name, which was originally Needleman, felt too Jewish. Schwartz changed it to Cohen.

With careful strategy and a winning pitch, *The O.C.* was sold. Schwartz, just shy of twenty-seven, was officially the youngest showrunner on network television. The hunt for Newport's finest could begin.

When it came to Sandy Cohen, Seth's father, the network wanted a big name. Sandy needed to be the lovable backbone of the show, a public defender from the Bronx who fell in love with his future wife, Kirsten (played by Kelly Rowan), back at UC Berkeley. Kirsten came from a powerful family with roots in real-estate development, and Sandy was an outsider in Newport Beach. He would be a warm, funny haven for viewers, keeping us safe in a complicated world of romance gone wrong, sketchy financial dealings, and outsiders arriving in rotation to stir up trouble. For every scene where future menace Oliver maniacally scared the crap out of us, there was Sandy in the kitchen of the Cohen house, fresh from surfing, making bagels with schmear.

Schwartz's initial casting suggestion was Jeff Goldblum, a veteran actor with a whimsical, eccentric charm who starred in hits like *Jurassic Park* and *Independence Day*. No dice there. "Too Jewish," Schwartz recalled being told.

The network was excited about Peter Gallagher, though. The actor's formative years were spent taking voice lessons at the New England Conservatory and performing with the musical theatre group Torn Ticket II. After graduating college, Gallagher made his stage debut in the 1977 revival of *Hair*, went on to perform in *Guys and Dolls*, and landed roles in big name films like Sandra Bullock's romcom *While You Were Sleeping*.

Gallagher was marquee enough that he didn't have to audition for Sandy, but he did need to go through a network test, where he appeared in front of Fox executives, casting director Patrick Rush, Schwartz, and Savage. Gallagher walked in and instantly charmed them. Gail Berman, the head of Fox at the time, jokingly suggested that he perform a number from *Guys and Dolls*, and Gallagher gamely broke into song. When he read lines of dialogue from the pilot, Schwartz turned to Rush with a note of disbelief. "I've never heard somebody that famous say my words," he said.

When it came time to find Sandy's son, Seth, the network had a pretty good idea of who he would be. "If Ryan is our Luke Perry, then Seth is our Jason Priestley," an executive declared.

No, Savage countered. "That's not the paradigm we're doing. We're trying to do something unique and different." They wanted Seth to be nerdy, something that definitely wasn't on Fox's heartthrob wish list. The creative partners would meet the studio executives halfway, keeping the soul of Seth alive but, as Schwartz later told me, moving him to a place that was more palatable for the tone of the show.

It could have been a tricky character road map to navigate. And then Adam Brody walked in. The twenty-eight-year-old had just come off a season arc on *Gilmore Girls* as Dave Rogowski, Lane's guitar-playing boyfriend. He was supposed to read for the role of Seth, but Brody told Rush that he'd prefer to audition for Ryan. "I think he probably wanted to be the leading man," Rush speculated. "Someone he characterized as our heartthrob leading-man guy."

Rush felt like it would be too rude to shoo him away. So, he let Brody do his reading of Ryan (if only we had footage of that . . .) and then politely asked him to read Seth's audition scene. As Rush suspected, that role clicked so much better.

Rush brought Brody in to read for Schwartz. The young actor decided to go off script then, ad-libbing his way through the scene.

Schwartz was not charmed. "What scene is he doing? Is this from our show? What is he doing?" he recalls thinking. "I hate this kid. Get him out of here."

After Brody left the room, Rush pleaded with Schwartz. "What if we brought him back again and made him stay on the page?" he asked. "I guess," Schwartz replied begrudgingly. Looking back, Rush suspects that Schwartz just gave him the green light to stop his badgering. He reached out to Brody's representatives to offer one final shot.

"You guys, he really kind of blew it. We'd like him to come back and stick to the material as written," Rush told them.

Brody returned, read directly from the script, and changed Schwartz's mind. Maybe he *could* be Seth. Brody landed the part, but Fox continued to have reservations about the character as a whole. They even attempted to leave him off the first poster for the show until Schwartz stepped in ("You gotta put him on the poster!").

When it came to the all-important role of Marissa Cooper, the show's very beautiful, very troubled protagonist, Schwartz and Savage were all-in on a young actor named Mischa Barton, whom Rush remembers as an "It girl." She had made her mark as a child in the horror film *The Sixth Sense*, appeared in ads for Neutrogena, and starred in the Marshall Herskovitz and Edward Zwick–created show, *Once and Again*.

The role of Marissa would come down to a choice between Barton and a young, unknown actor named Olivia Wilde. Wilde was clearly talented but, as Schwartz later put it, "Olivia Wilde needs no saving. She was pretty tough." There was more of a vulnerability and fragility to Barton, so essential to the core of Marissa.

Marissa's best friend and Seth's future girlfriend was Summer Roberts, who, when we first meet her, is a by-the-book superficial teen. She had only a few lines in the pilot, two of which were: "*Ew*, Chino," and "I have to pee, do you have to pee?" Twenty-two-year-old Rachel Bilson, a Los Angeles native, walked in and managed to sell that pee line.

Summer wasn't supposed to be a series regular, but Bilson immediately won over Savage and Schwartz, turning a potentially one-dimensional character into a funny, fierce young woman with a tendency for rage blackouts and a soft spot for her plastic unicorn, Princess Sparkles. It's a good reminder for struggling actors everywhere, Rush said. "Show up for an audition even if it's one line. Look what happened."

Finding Ryan, the outsider from Chino, would be the hardest battle. Then-unknown actor Garrett Hedlund impressed everybody with his effortless cool-guy persona. He made it to testing for the network before he suddenly had to pull out. He had just landed a role in the star-packed epic *Troy*, alongside Brad Pitt and Diane Kruger. Then it happened again. Chad Michael Murray, who also read for Ryan, bowed out after getting the lead role of Lucas on the WB's *One Tree Hill*.

After multiple false starts, there was a possible light at the end of the Ryan Atwood tunnel. A theater actor named Benjamin McKenzie had just unsuccessfully tested for a smaller role on a UPN comedy. An executive from Warner Bros. was in the room for his audition and reached out to Schwartz: "We just saw this kid. He's really good, you should see him."

From the moment McKenzie stepped into the audition room, Rush could tell that he was serious about his work. Sometimes actors would chitchat before the audition. McKenzie was not one of those people.

The young actor read the scene where Ryan meets Marissa for the first time in the driveway, with Rush filling in as Marissa. The producers were sitting behind Rush as McKenzie did his thing, and the casting director quietly prayed, "*Please* let them love him as much as I do." Thankfully, they did.

There was just one step left. The actor would need to read with Barton to make sure the chemistry was there. The duo arrived in a warehouse in Burbank for their first meeting and McKenzie had his game face on. From the moment he walked into the room, he refused to break character, remaining firmly ensconced in Ryan's simmering moodiness. The two performed the driveway scene, running through the memorable "Whoever you want me to be" dialogue.

As the audition came to an end, they were asked to face the camera. McKenzie was shorter than Barton, and she leaned over, gently resting her head on his shoulder. He looked taller than her in that final shot and Rush thought: "That was really sweet of her." He knew that she knew executives would be watching the footage and raise an alarm if Marissa were taller than Ryan. She was looking out for him.

"I remember when she did that, I thought, 'They both have the job,'" Rush said.

Tate Donovan, known at the time for *Hercules*, *Love Potion #9*, and a memorable story line as Joshua, Rachel's boyfriend, on *Friends*, signed on as Jimmy Cooper, Marissa's dad, who we quickly discover is embroiled in some pretty sketchy financial dealings. Marissa's mom, Julie Cooper, introduced as a steely-eyed social climber, would be played by Melinda Clarke, a regular on *Days of Our Lives*. Kirsten would be played by Kelly Rowan, with credits to her name like *The Outer Limits* and *Hook*.

Before shooting began, Schwartz, Savage, McG, and Loucas George, the show's producer, headed to Orange County to get a feel for the area. They hopped on little pontoon boats and explored the surrounding islands, noting the locals surfing and the kinds of cars people drove. It felt like an education, George told me. The city's officials had already decided that they wanted nothing to do with Schwartz. "Don't come down and shoot [here]," George was told by the powers that be. They thought that the show was out to trash their reputation.

McG wanted the pilot to be filmed at a series of sound stages all the way out at Manhattan Beach Studios, a schlep of over an hour, depending on where you lived in L.A. It was a pain to get to, but the location had a hidden bonus: no one from the studio would come down and bug them.

Doug Liman, who directed the 1996 comedy hit *Swingers* and the 2002 action flick *The Bourne Identity*, signed on to helm the first episode. Go back and rewatch the pilot, and you'll notice a different feel from the series as a whole. It's grittier and rougher, with sharper cuts and jerkier, handheld camerawork. Liman, Donovan remembers, was not the charismatic leader one might expect from a director. Sometimes he'd offer the direction: "Can you be better? Can you act better?"

The first scene that the show's editor, Norman Buckley, cut was the opening sequence. Ryan and his brother Trey try to break into a car and get caught by the police. "It's terrible," Liman told him after watching the cut. "It's the worst thing I've ever seen." The next scene Buckley showed him was Ryan and Seth attending a beach party. "It's perfect," Liman said. "Don't change a frame."

A lot of time was spent shooting those beach-party scenes. At night, Schwartz and Savage would hang out behind the camera in Malibu and listen to the same Missy Elliott song for what felt like the millionth time. Unbeknownst to them, one of the most memorable moments of the episode—and the series—would come out of their endless night shoots. Luke, Marissa's boyfriend, gets into a fight with Ryan, knocking him onto the sand at a beach party. He stands over Ryan defiantly, with his perfectly manicured bangs and half button-down J.Crew–esque shirt. "Welcome to the O.C., bitch," he declares, arms spread menacingly.

Schwartz came up with that line. He remembered how kids who went to USC would say, with a note of swagger, that they were from the O.C.—as if they were saying they were from Long Beach, a rougher area in California that was frequently referenced in rap songs.

Another *O.C.* Hall of Fame moment happened during those long night shoots. Ryan and Marissa meet for the first time on the characters' shared street, two houses nestled in the Malibu hills on Ocean Breeze Drive. The camera was shooting coverage of Barton that evening when a small breeze picked up, ruffling her hair in the most cinematic of ways. There was this feeling that the young actor could command the wind on her close-up. "It was magical," Schwartz told me.

That scene would mark the first and last time that we'd ever see a teen smoking a cigarette on *The O.C.* "The deal with the network was: it's a moment of Marissa showing a little bit of rebellion and, after this, Ryan will never smoke again," Schwartz said. "We were able to get it through that way." Fox had them reshoot the scene without the cigarette so they could show snippets of it for commercials. It didn't feel quite the same to Schwartz.

In the middle of filming the pilot, George got wind that McKenzie was asking production for a car. The producer was incredulous. "Why would I give him a car?" he thought. "If I give a car to one actor, then all of sudden all the other actors will be asking for it."

He approached McKenzie. "Ben? What's this, you want a car?"

McKenzie explained that he was out of money and his car kept breaking down on the way to set. In that moment, Loucas realized this wasn't a diva move; McKenzie was literally struggling to get to work. "I'm gonna give you a car, but don't tell anybody, because I don't want to be dealing with this with everybody else," he told the actor.

Later, when the show got picked up and the buzz around it was getting hotter and hotter, McKenzie appeared in George's office. "I just bought a car!" he told him.

"That's fantastic," George responded. "But don't let this go to your head. These shows, you're a hero today and you're a bum tomorrow."

He wasn't the only one trying to drill that message into the heads of the young cast. It was something Gallagher would continue to reinforce, too, as the show quickly transformed into a massive hit. "Peter was new to television. But he knew enough to know to enjoy it while we got it because nothing lasts forever," George said.

Something special was happening on-set, Schwartz was beginning to believe— at least with trepidation. He felt it most while sitting behind the monitor as a teen fashion show unfolded, where all Newport Beach's A-listers gathered to see and be seen. Girls are strutting down the runway in peak 2000s ensembles. Luke and his water polo buddies sit at one table. Seth, who is friends with none of these people, escorts his cool new pal Ryan over to the children's table, where a young boy refuses to make small talk with him.

It's a small but mighty example of what made *The O.C.* special. The glossy teen fundamentals mixed in with awkward humor. As Schwartz watched Seth try to chat up this unwilling child, a confluence of different worlds and genres melding together in one room, he remembers thinking: "This feels exciting and fun."

The series would work to elegantly find a balance between drama and comedy. Seth held the comedy torch in the beginning, his quick wit and observational humor balancing out dark scenes with ease. Later, Ryan got to be funny, too, a rare character move in itself. It's not often that the brooding bad boy is given witty one-liners and self-aware quips. "I think Ryan Atwood would be thrilled to know that you thought of him as witty," Schwartz said when I asked him about that development.

Early in the show's run, critics noticed that Schwartz and Savage were forging a different path. While Alessandra Stanley of the *New York Times* commented that *The O.C.* "owes a vast debt" to *Beverly Hills, 90210*, she was pleased to note that it *also* seemed to be paying homage to *My Man Godfrey*, the 1936 screwball comedy about an heiress who takes a homeless man under her wing as a butler, inviting him into the world of society and privilege.

"Like *My Man Godfrey*, Our Boy Ryan is not changed by his new environment. Instead he seems to quietly and with considerable savoir-faire alter the teenagers and adults around him," Stanley wrote. "Even Luke (Chris Carmack), Marissa's hulky, blond and brutal boyfriend, proves a little less viciously shallow than he seems in the pilot episode, and that tiny shift is, by television-drama standards, quite an avalanche of complexity."

The *Washington Post*'s review was oddly vicious. Writer Tom Shales heavily criticized Ryan, who "wanders, roams, stumbles, mumbles and stares"; called Sandy "a boobishly emasculated twit" (because his wife makes more money?); and deemed Seth "mealy-headed." It's head-scratchingly harsh and shows little interest in what teens—the people who would actually be tuning in every week—might be drawn to.

In one paragraph, Shales declared that the "drop-dead-stupidest dialogue" comes when Luke scoffs, "Welcome to the O.C., bitch." It's amusing to read now. There aren't a lot of television lines that outlast their shows. Luke's bit of dialogue did.

Every behind-the-scenes feature article written about *The O.C.* pointed out just how young Josh Schwartz was. In a *New York Times* article titled "No Experience Required," journalist Ari Posner began by writing: "When you see Josh Schwartz on the set of *The O.C.*, Fox's hit teen drama, it's easy to mistake him for one of the casually hip actors who pretend to be high school students on the show."

"I have never seen anyone take to this medium as quickly as he has," Marcy Ross, Fox's senior vice president of current programming, told Posner at the time. "I mean, sure, he's lost a lot of weight, he's falling apart, he does nothing but work. But he was born to do this."

The young actors were finding their way alongside Schwartz, navigating uncharted television waters. Sanford Bookstaver, who would go on to direct multiple episodes of the show, remembers watching Brody coming into his own as an actor and relishing the opportunity for improv. Bilson loved ad-libbing, too, and the duo's chemistry quickly clicked as they traded zippy barbs. Barton preferred to stay on-script, as did McKenzie, who was an intense actor. He did his homework, was calculated in his decisions, and knew what he wanted his performance to be. It helped bolster the show's delicate balance between light and dark. Seth and Summer's relationship lent itself to the spontaneous and lively. Marissa and Ryan's was entrenched firmly in the world of teen drama, where carefully crafted, beautifully written monologues and meaningful looks make up the DNA of the characters.

Barton did have one requirement when it came to being directed by Bookstaver. The two loved the animated show *South Park*, and she would only listen to him if he gave her feedback in Eric Cartman's voice. "The crew thought we were out of our fucking minds," he told me. But that silly little ritual helped Barton open up. "What I like about working on a teen show is that you have to figure out how to break through to younger actors, who don't have as much experience, and make them comfortable," Bookstaver said. "[The Cartman bit] allowed her to feel safe and comfortable and have some fun and try stuff."

From the outset, Schwartz and Savage had a clear idea of the first seven episodes of the show. They mapped out the stories and wrote them in a vacuum, without the noisy feedback of online message boards and with the benefit of a minimally involved studio. The show hadn't aired yet and, as Savage put it, the duo were writing from a very pure place, putting their heart and souls into the scripts.

They walked their characters carefully to the edge of an emotional cliff as they approached the seventh episode, "The Escape." Seth, Summer, Ryan, and Marissa would head to Tijuana, a trip that begins light and fun, with Seth and Summer at peak bickering/flirting levels (they share newspapers over breakfast like a long-time married couple) and Marissa and Ryan embroiled in full romantic tension (they wake up at a dingy motel spooning).

Later, Marissa discovers that her boyfriend, Luke, has been cheating on her. Bookstaver directed the episode and—in a career that's since spanned more than twenty years—it remains one of his all-time favorite nights of filming. They shot at Universal Studios, on a set designed to look like a Mexican village and was once used as a backdrop for *Butch Cassidy and the Sundance Kid.*

When Bookstaver first toured the space, he was dubious. It looked way too much like a backlot. "This is going to be great," the show's production designer Thomas Fichter said. "We're going to make it look like Tijuana."

"It kind of looks like *Three Amigos,*" Bookstaver replied. "It looks like a bad movie."

"No, just trust me."

Bookstaver returned for shooting and was floored by what Fichter had done. He had transformed this bare, stripped-down set into a living, breathing city, packed with outdoor bars, tables for vendors, and a two-story nightclub called Boom Boom. A "Welcome to Tijuana" sign hung at the entrance. They brought in three hundred extras and set the stage for the core four's misadventures.

When Marissa, in a fit of rage and sadness, splits from the group, she ends up getting drunk, taking pills, and stumbling around the city's darkened streets. To amp up the tension, camera operator Billy Nielsen crafted a 360-degree panorama, putting one camera on each shoulder and following her around in a circle to create a disorienting feeling.

The episode ends in an alleyway, where Ryan, Seth, and Summer discover Marissa alone, curled up on the ground and unresponsive. There wasn't really a budget for crane shots, but Bookstaver was adamant about using one for the moment that Ryan picks Marissa up, camera floating above him as he carries her limp body through the street.

"I just wanted it to feel incredibly powerful and emotional and you're kind of on the seat from God's point of view," he explained. "I wanted this swelling, emotional, beautiful music that shows he was in love with her and caring for her. The way he's holding her in his arms—and I'm not a religious person or trying to make this religious—had that kind of religious feel to it. He was the savior."

That episode would be the turning point for Schwartz and Savage. The show, which they had gotten to quietly write while holed up in Manhattan Beach Studios, was proving to be an early juggernaut of a success. The pilot was the night's highest-rated program among the twelve-to-seventeen-year-old demographic.

It was something to celebrate, but it was also terrifying. They received a super-sized order of twenty-seven episodes for the season—an unprecedented number, both then and now—and weren't quite sure what to do next. How, they wondered, could they possibly generate twenty more episodes' worth of story?

Schwartz and Savage assembled a writing staff, a slew of creatives who fit the mishmash of tone and genre *The O.C.* was shaping up to be. It was an Avengers team of sorts, each bringing their own strengths to the new series.

There was Allan Heinberg, a *Sex and the City* alum, who arrived equipped with a talent for crafting character-driven scenes and comedy. He also knew a lot about comic books, which lent itself swimmingly to Seth Cohen. John Stephens was a *Gilmore Girls* writer, with a sharp focus on characters and an ability to create stories that pleased both the network and fans. J. J. Philbin had a comedy background, with years on *MADtv* and *Saturday Night Live*. She loved writing the mother-daughter story lines and knew how to infuse the world of Newport Beach with humor. She could also, Schwartz and Savage told me, write an emotional Julie Cooper scene like no other.

Savage loved writing a good Marissa scene, particularly a dark, gritty fight with Ryan. She also reveled in developing Summer, fleshing her out into a three-dimensional character with an unexpected intelligence. When Savage felt like one of the characters was growing, she'd cry happy tears in the writers' room.

Schwartz felt most at home writing Sandy. There was just something so fun about interjecting the voice of this Jewish guy from the Bronx into a thoroughly

WASPy world. And it was particularly enjoyable juxtaposing him against someone like Kirsten's cold tycoon of a father, Caleb.

With the Tijuana overdose in their rearview mirror, the writers decided to introduce a character named Oliver Trask. The young man would enter Marissa's life after a chance meeting in a therapist's waiting room and end up becoming obsessed with her, strategically pulling her apart from Ryan. Fans hated Oliver. They really, really hated him. And, yes, Schwartz heard every complaint.

When Schwartz first started checking the message boards to see what was buzzing, it felt thrilling. "Look at all these people who like what we're doing!" he remembers thinking. Then, he started reading the negative comments. It was hard not to take them personally. He tried to reason with himself that the fierce backlash against Oliver meant fans were watching, and they were watching closely. They genuinely cared about what happened to these characters and the direction that the show was going. Plus, say what you will about Oliver, but that story arc was the highest ratings win *The O.C.* ever had.

Philbin joined the writing team just as Schwartz and Savage were dealing with the Oliver problem. She had gotten a taste of TV drama writing while working on the short-lived show *Dead Like Me*, and was also a teen television connoisseur in her own right, having devoured *Beverly Hills, 90210* while it was on-air. Philbin became thoroughly invested in the romantic story lines of Brandon, Brenda, and the whole Beverly High gang, so she fully understood the audience's fierce commitment to the Ryan/Marissa/Seth/Summer of it all.

Still, she was nervous for that first day of work. *The O.C.* was becoming a full-fledged phenomenon and she felt like a baby in the industry. To prepare, Philbin binged all the episodes that had aired. Then, she played each episode again with her eyes closed. This was a helpful trick she had learned long before; it helped her focus on the specific rhythm of the dialogue.

The writers' room was in Manhattan Beach, a surfside community in Los Angeles lined with picturesque piers. Most rooms that Philbin had worked in were miserable, windowless conference spaces. This one had a nautical, beachy vibe. There were seashells on the end tables and wicker furniture scattered about. It was still a conference space with the controlled chaos of a writers' room, scripts strewn about and whiteboards covered in marker scribbles . . . but way less depressing.

Schwartz and Savage were running as fast as they could to break stories and stay on track with the intense output of the first season. "How can we keep this up?" was always the central question. "How can we tell stories at this pace and not run out?" Philbin sat at the table and tried frantically to stay on track. The writers were talking about episodes five or six away from the last one she had seen on-air. It felt like showing up in the middle of a conversation. She didn't want to slow anybody down or ask too many questions, so she carefully pieced everything together as she went, making mental notes of which characters were hooking up and who was fighting.

"The Shower" was the first episode Philbin was tasked with writing. In it, Seth has a disastrous meeting with Summer's dad. Kirsten is named maid of honor to Julie (who is marrying her father, Caleb). Ryan's ex-girlfriend Theresa is seeking a restraining order against Eddie, her ex-boyfriend.

Philbin was intimidated when it came to writing anything to do with Caleb and his real estate company ("I remember being like, 'I don't know what I'm doing . . .'"). But she relished the Seth scenes, particularly when they involved Summer. It was especially fun getting to spend time in the Cohen house, where life was fun and cozy. "I felt the things that everyone else felt," she told me. "Which was like, it's nice to be in their home. It's nice to . . . live in a world where this is your family."

Yes, there were gritty things happening, but there were always moments of levity to be found. Like, in Philbin's first episode, when Seth pulls a disinterested Ryan into his bedroom for a frantic fashion feedback session.

"What about this one . . . too edgy?" he asks earnestly, holding up one possibility. "Too fashion-forward?"

"It's a white collared shirt," Ryan responds.

"That's a good point," Seth says, knowingly. "White shirts make my teeth look yellow."

The O.C., particularly in that first season, was all about yearnings and almosts. Seth pining for Summer and then Summer pining for Seth. Ryan and Marissa being perpetual star-crossed lovers, never quite getting their timing or communication right. Little moments would feel so big, ripping through the screen with all the throbbing of young lust and love. While the writers were well past their own high school heartbreaks, many were navigating the equally rocky and angst-filled relationships of their early to mid-twenties. "We were sort of on the brink of growing up," Philbin remembers. They were all dating people at the time, some of whom they'd end up marrying, and the writers' room would become a microcosm of the high school hallways, with the group analyzing one another's relationships, delving into the nuances of their problems, and diagnosing one another's neuroses.

When it came to crafting the show's all-important romances, the will they/ won't they dynamic of the core four became a challenge. "Can you make them yearn for this?" Schwartz would ask himself. "Or give the audience enough without necessarily getting them together?"

It was an education for Philbin, who learned the delicate art of bringing TV couples together and pulling them apart, determining where the characters align and the blind spots that keep tripping them up. Later, when Philbin joined the writing staff of *New Girl*, she would keep Ryan, Marissa, Seth, and Summer in her head as the group of writers meticulously mapped out the course of the show's central relationship, Nick and Jess. There, too, they had to determine how much the audience could take before the duo got together. "Once we do, what's the most interesting version of that?" the writers would ask themselves. "What's the most honest version of a breakup?"

"Even though *New Girl* wasn't a teen drama, I think when you're falling in love with your best friend it's very teenager-like," Philbin explained. "You don't know where the line is between your friendship and something more. It didn't feel that different honestly."

Ryan and Marissa finally kiss atop a Ferris wheel in the ninth episode of the first season. Helming that episode was Patrick Norris, who got his start on *My So-Called Life* as a costume designer and director. Norris had learned from directing Claire Danes and Jared Leto that it was important to keep those kisses spontaneous and organic. He didn't have McKenzie and Barton practice their Ferris wheel kiss ahead of time, nor did he give them instructions, like which way to turn their heads. It was always a surprise to see how long that first on-screen kiss would last and how they would approach each other in the last inch or two of meeting lips. The moment was awkward but in a wonderful way.

Norris let them sit for a moment after the kiss. "You got to see them go, 'That was kinda cool,'" he remembers. "If we rehearsed it, I don't think we would have had the same reaction."

Director Lev L. Spiro was tapped to lead the charge of another landmark moment of romance that season. He came aboard to direct the disastrously awkward first sex scene between Seth and Summer, which results in an even more cringey birds-and-bees chat with Sandy. Spiro watched as sparks flew between Brody and Bilson on-set. "Maybe they like each other, maybe they're just great actors," he thought at the time. "There was definitely chemistry. They played really well off each other . . . the fun that they had with each other was palpable."

Spiro could access, with great clarity, what it felt like to be a teenager, taking a big, scary dive into the unknown. He still remembers shooting the final scene of that episode, when Seth and Summer decide that they're going to slow down the physical stuff. They go back to the basics, with Seth playing "Wonderwall" on a vinyl and reaching his hand out to her.

"You are so cheesy, Cohen." Summer laughs.

"C'mon," he says, smiling back at her, "I'm sweeping you off your feet."

The two slow dance in Seth's room, camera lingering on them as they hold each other tight. Spiro hasn't seen the episode since 2005, but that moment still stays with him. He got exactly what he wanted, the perfect combination of sweetness and awkwardness.

Seth and Summer's first public kiss happens in the Harbor School's lounge. The two have begun to secretly date, but Summer, being the cool one of the pair, refuses to acknowledge Seth in the hallways. She agrees to take part in a kissing booth, which proves to be the last straw for Seth. He arrives on the scene and makes one final grand gesture, hopping ungracefully on top of the coffee cart and offering Summer the opportunity to stand beside him, so the whole school can see them together.

"You kiss all these other guys, but you won't kiss me?" Seth says. "Acknowledge me now or lose me forever."

Bookstaver directed that episode. The speech, he remembers, was a lot of Brody. The actor improvised that day, really going for it as he stood in front of a set crammed with extras. As Bookstaver looked around the room, he could feel an excitement that he hadn't experienced while shooting previous episodes. "The extras were looking at him like, 'Oh my God, this is *Seth Cohen* giving a speech.'"

The fandom had arrived.

McKenzie, Brody, Barton, and Bilson were splashed across magazine covers. The foursome, looking dewy and beautiful, appeared on the front of *Teen People*, Bilson placing bunny fingers behind McKenzie's head, and a headline reading: "Wild parties! Dating drama! Nasty rumors! The *O.C.* cast tells all!" Then there was the *YM* cover (remember *YM?*), featuring McKenzie, Brody, and Barton snuggled together, beaming at the camera, with the words "The O.C." printed in big red block letters and the subhead: "Behind-the-scenes shockers: 1. The ocean's not real! 2. Ben's arm muscles are!"

Go back in the archives of the Internet around when *The O.C.* was huge and you'll be transported to the early aughts. It's nostalgic and also a little depressing, a neatly printed reminder of the intense pressure and scrutiny famous young women were dealing with. It was a time when nip-slip shots reigned supreme and Perez Hilton, a popular celebrity blogger, drew ejaculating penises on actors' faces and called Barton "Mushy Fartone."

Years later, Barton would open up about the full extent of her experience with fame during *The O.C.* In an op-ed penned for *Harper's Bazaar*, she talked about the lengths paparazzi would go to get a photo of her.

"They tried to climb over the walls to my house. They'd track my phone and my car. They'd make deals with restaurants so that when I went to one, someone would notify them," she wrote. "They'd buy cell phones for the homeless, instructing them to call as soon as they saw me walking down the street. I was stalked. They'd shoot directly into my home to the extent where I couldn't even open my blinds. It was lockdown before there was a name for it."

Season 1 came to a close with a cast of unknown actors turned to stars, a first-time showrunner at the height of his game, and a whole lot of weighty expectations for another breakout season. The finale finds Ryan returning to Chino after discovering that Theresa is pregnant. Seth, meanwhile, goes on a solo sailing trip, leaving Summer behind. The episode culminates at Caleb and Julie's wedding, atop a mountain, with glorious views of the Pacific Ocean. The singer

Jem is performing "Maybe I'm Amazed" as Ryan asks Marissa to dance. It's the last time they'll be with each other before he leaves. "I just want you to know," Marissa says, her voice breaking, leaning close to him. "I understand why you have to do this."

"Thanks," Ryan whispers.

She's fully crying now. "But I wish you didn't have to."

"Me too," he says. Marissa almost kisses him but stops herself, moving her face toward his neck instead and softly says: "I love you."

Savage did a lot of the wedding planning for that episode, picking out the bridesmaids' dresses and flowers, and making sure that, despite the heaviness of all the heartbreaks, it felt like a celebration of sorts. "Even in the saddest scenes where people are breaking up and saying goodbye, it's going to be in a house on a cliff, and everyone looks gorgeous," she said. "We wanted that counterbalance to be something that was so visually beautiful. I think a lot of the actors had never looked better than they did in that episode."

Savage still remembers how emotional she got, watching Kirsten go into the pool house in the episode's final montage. Ryan has moved out, and his room is empty once more. As Kirsten begins to remove the sheets, she crumples, crying as she holds the material close to her. Savage bawled in the editing room when she watched that scene. The feeling, she later quipped, was like wanting someone to come over and hold her like a weighted blanket.

It all felt bittersweet in a way, the ending of that first season. "There was a real sense that whatever came after this, nothing would be the same," Schwartz remembered. "Everybody was about to go off and have their summer hiatus and do other projects and we would be returning with that first year behind us."

Schwartz still has some regrets about Season 1. If he could go back, he would have kept Anna around, Seth's friend/onetime romantic partner, and Luke too. There were still more stories to tell about them and maybe even some unexpected romantic pairings (wildly enough, there had been talk of a coupling between Anna/Ryan and Luke/Summer). Maybe the problem, he mused during an interview with journalist Alan Sepinwall, was that he never watched those hit teen television shows like *Dawson's Creek* for instruction. The shows he did watch didn't make it past the first season.

The writers had burned through so much story. As they mapped out a plan for Season 2, they discussed the idea of crafting smaller stories, à la *My So-Called Life*, where episodes would revolve around simpler concepts, all while keeping up the delicious drama that *The O.C.* had made its name on.

The writers tortured themselves by logging onto the popular message board "Television Without Pity" and reading fans' reactions. It was particularly brutal during the second season, as the room worked to find their footing. People would get so upset, Philbin remembers, particularly when Seth and Summer broke up, not realizing that the writers were setting a larger story in motion. Those message boards fed into a roller coaster of emotions—Philbin would read one comment and feel overjoyed, but then the next person would be furious about something she did.

"I think you get to a tough spot where you start writing for those four people on the message boards," she said with a laugh. "You're like, 'I really want them to be happy so I'm gonna add this scene in.' And that's never a good idea."

Season 2 would find Seth and Summer broken up and a new guy entering the fray, a water polo player named Zach, played by Michael Cassidy.

Cassidy was twenty-one, fresh out of college, and had worked a day or two on tiny independent films when he got the call to read for *The O.C.* Summer would date Zach after Seth leaves her behind for his sailing trip, and the new character becomes both a friend and foe to Seth, as Zach, too, is a comic-book lover but one who's dating his ex-girlfriend. Cassidy was booked for three episodes, with the possibility of three more, and he shacked up in a hotel close to the Manhattan Beach Studios. He hadn't seen the show, and a messenger arrived with DVDs of the first season so he could catch up. Cassidy popped a disc into the player and settled down with his friend, him on the floor, her sprawled on the bed. After the first episode, he turned around and looked at her. "This is a real TV show," he said with a note of disbelief. "Yeah," his friend replied with matching awe. "You're on a real TV show."

Cassidy wasn't sure he had done himself a favor by watching *The O.C.* By the time he was done with Season 1, *he* didn't want Seth and Summer to break up. "Even though I knew she was going to be dating me at the beginning of Season 2, as I watched it I was still like, 'God, they're just such a great couple,'" he told me.

On his first day of filming, Cassidy was instructed to kiss Bilson in front of Brody, who was dating the actor at the time. The added pressure of kissing her while standing right near her real-life boyfriend proved to be too much. During the first take, Cassidy got three inches from Bilson's face, turned, and promptly walked away, hoping that nobody noticed. The director asked him to give it another try.

It was so surreal to be inside the world of *The O.C.* "Holy shit!" Cassidy remembers thinking when he walked into Seth's bedroom for the first time. Then, he glanced over, spotting Captain Oats, Seth's plastic horse. "That's the horse he talks to!"

One day, the whole cast was summoned to Newport Beach, where Schwartz was handed a key to the city. There were roughly two hundred fans there, all screaming as they took to the stage. "I was so dumb that I actually thought it was staged," Cassidy told me. "It seemed fake that there would be a bunch of people that were excited to see Ben. Like, this guy that I just knew from work."

Cassidy wasn't a tabloid reader and didn't quite grasp how much the stars were being photographed and followed. During downtime on-set, Brody used to like to go to the movies at a theater near the studio. Often, he'd slip in after showtime. "The movie started ten minutes ago," Cassidy would remind him.

"I just go in late," Brody responded.

Cassidy thought Brody wanted to skip the trailers. Later, he realized it was because the actor liked the feeling of walking into a dark room alone and having an hour and a half of anonymity.

As the years went on, Cassidy found himself trying to copy Brody's seemingly effortless on-screen techniques. Brody would say his lines and then, if no one yelled cut, he just started ad-libbing. That wasn't how Cassidy was trained. He had learned to stop talking as soon as his lines were done. Cassidy was so in awe of how Brody could turn the smallest moments into comedy, and grateful whenever the actor would offer him ad libs about superheroes to incorporate into his own dialogue.

In the episode "The O.Sea," Zach and Seth reach a standstill when they have the opportunity to take Summer to the prom *or* meet legendary Star Wars creator George Lucas to discuss a comic book they created together—on the very same night. They flip a coin to see who goes to which event and, after the toss, Brody improvised putting the quarter in Cassidy's breast pocket, squeezing his shoulder like he was his uncle, and sending him out of the room. Cassidy immediately started cracking up. Look closely and you'll catch another moment of Cassidy subtly breaking character a few scenes prior, when he sits in the pier diner with Brody and Reed Carlson, the vice president of a graphic novel company played by Marguerite Moreau.

"Me and Adam are sitting on one side, Marguerite's on the other side. She's so mad at us and she can't speak for something we did in the prior episode. Adam's contrition is so funny, if you watch the scene, my giant triple-sweatered arms are up on the table and I'm squeezing one hand with the other hand because I'm trying not to laugh."

Michael Lange directed that episode and was thrilled to get to work with George Lucas, who was making a cameo. He expected that Lucas—the great George Lucas—would say something mind-blowing when they first met.

Instead, as he remembers, the conversation went something like this:

"You guys are shooting this on film?" Lucas asked.

"Yeah, it's film," Lange responded.

"Why are you shooting it on film? Don't you think you should be shooting it on digital?"

"Well, maybe, but we are shooting it on film," Lange said, and then tried to pivot. "So here we go, here's the scene . . . "

Then, Lucas began "mansplaining" the concept of film to Lange. Later, while shooting the scene, Lange paused so that they could reload the camera.

"You know, you wouldn't have to do that if it wasn't on film," Lucas reminded him.

"Yep," Lange said. "I do know that." He decided that he was beginning to dislike George Lucas.

By Season 2, Tate Donovan found himself getting restless. He got the sense that his character, Jimmy Cooper, wasn't long for *The O.C.* The writers seemed to have churned through all the stories they could with him, reaching an end point with all his financial misdoings. Donovan was bored in L.A. and kept busy by participating in triathlons. Acting just wasn't really inspiring him the way that it used to. Sometimes, he even wondered if he was any good.

Donovan also had some serious questions about his character. Week after week, his sister would call to tell him just how much she hated Jimmy.

"Tate," she'd say after finishing the most recent episode. "Jimmy Cooper is the worst goddamn father. Why are you such a horrible dad?"

Donovan approached Schwartz and Savage. "Hey," he told them. "My sister says Jimmy Cooper is the worst dad on television."

"Nah," they'd respond. "Jimmy's great! He's an awesome dude, don't be ridiculous." Donovan continued to feel suspicious of his character, all the way up to his very last episode, when Jimmy leaves Marissa behind to move to Hawaii, in what was supposed to be a way of helping their fraught relationship.

"At the end of that episode I was like, 'Oh my God. Poor Marissa. She has nobody. Nobody in her life.' I remember going to the director and saying, 'How would I become a better father by leaving?' He's like, 'I don't know. Just say the lines.'"

Then, finally, a victory. A few years ago, a magazine came out with a list of the five worst TV dads. Jimmy was one of them. "I was so vindicated," Donovan told me. He reached out to Schwartz and Savage immediately. "See?" he declared. "I was a terrible dad!"

All that to say, Donovan didn't mind bidding adieu to Jimmy. Now he could turn his attention to more important matters. Donovan had aspirations to work behind the camera. He began to shadow directors on the set of *The O.C.*, sitting in on every casting session, pre-production meeting, and location scout. He was there, alongside the director, as the first one on-set during rehearsals and the last one to leave every night. Then he headed to the editing room to watch how the episode was pieced together.

Donovan got to be in the room during tone meetings, which he remembers being "the greatest things on the planet." He equated them with getting to hear what your parents say behind your back. "The producer sits down with the director and says, 'Look, this is what we need from this scene. This actor has this problem. This actor is really good at this. Don't let this actor do that because he always does it.' It is so much fucking fun. My jaw dropped when I heard what the producers and directors really say about us."

He mentally filed away every lesson he learned from his shadowing days and, in Season 3, returned to helm the episode "The Game Plan." By then, the teens were well into their senior year of high school, trying to figure out the next stage of their lives as deadlines for college applications crept closer.

Behind the scenes, the attitude on-set had taken a turn. The four principal actors, Donovan noticed, seemed to have lost interest in the show. While the older cast members showed up on time, knew their lines, had ideas, and were open to suggestions, Donovan wasn't getting the same results from Barton, McKenzie, Bilson, and Brody. Getting them on-set, he said, was like "herding cats." They weren't reading the scripts ahead of time, he remembers, and it became a matter of just getting them to say their lines correctly.

"We didn't have much time because they often showed up late, so you're trying to beat the clock. The producer's going, 'Hey, we have to get out of here by five,' You're like, 'Shit. I've gotta get this scene.'"

Donovan looks back good-naturedly on the whole thing. He had his own experience with being a young actor and landing the big-budget movie *SpaceCamp* right out of college. While it would turn out to be a flop because of timing—a space shuttle blew up roughly three months before the film was released—Donovan remembers his ego ballooning while on-set.

"If you spoke to me when I was making *SpaceCamp*, I was the biggest, most pompous son of a bitch you'd ever met in your life," he said. "I thought I was gonna be a huge star. I remember telling myself that if I didn't win an Academy Award by the time I was thirty, I was going to get out of show business."

Donovan knew McKenzie a bit at the time; they had both performed at the Williamstown Theatre Festival. "Ben is such a bright, smart, talented dude. I think he struggled with playing this bad boy from the bad side of town," Donovan said. "I could relate to thinking, I'm better than the television show that I'm on . . . because that was a time when television was a separate class from film. Now it's totally changed. Back then doing a teen drama was not everybody's ideal."

Donovan just wished that he could tell McKenzie, "Hey, dude, this is a really rare, amazing experience. Enjoy it while it lasts."

When Lange came on-set to direct in Season 3, he tried to tell McKenzie just that. "Let me ask you a question," Lange said, pulling the actor aside. "I'm going to mention a name to you and you're going to tell me if you know who it is."

"OK," McKenzie replied.

"Ian Ziering."

McKenzie had no idea who he was talking about. "This is good," Lange responded. "Ian Ziering was one of the main characters on *Beverly Hills, 90210*, which was the biggest show ever. It had 30 million weekly viewers. It makes this show look like it isn't even on the air. None of those actors ever had this attitude that you have. So, if I were you, I would just take a deep breath and think about how lucky you are to be on this show doing the job that you're doing and getting to come to work every day and pretend to be someone you're not."

McKenzie actually took that pretty well, Lange remembers.

We've arrived at Season 3, which means we've reached the part of the story where I have to ask Schwartz and Savage about killing off Marissa Cooper, the heavily debated creative decision that rocked *O.C.* fans to their deepest core.

Some context: by the time Season 3 rolled around, Fox's head of network, Gail Berman, left and new management came in. Suddenly, Schwartz and Savage were being directed to take the show in a soapier direction. *Desperate Housewives*, an ABC series packed with sex, murder, and dark mysteries, was a runaway hit and Fox wanted *The O.C.* to use that formula as a blueprint. They were also pushed to write a big story line at the end of the season, which the network could heavily promote.

So, Schwartz and Savage tried to do just that. "What can happen that would really make anyone who had ever watched the show tune in?" Schwartz and Savage asked themselves. The idea of killing off one of the show's foundational characters began to crystallize. Marissa had always been such a tragic character. Maybe it should be her? Like this was her fate all along?

The last time we see Marissa she's in a car, driving with Ryan. Her ex-boyfriend Kevin Volchok chases after them and crashes into their car, causing it to flip over. Ryan saves Marissa from the fiery wreckage. He carries her limp body, much like he did in Tijuana, and sets her down, telling her he's going to go get help. She asks him to stay, head bloodied, and looks up at him, lovingly but barely conscious. That day, Barton encouraged the makeup artist to really go all in with the fake blood. "Squeeze it all over me!" she said. She didn't want the accident to feel glorified. A haunting rendition of Leonard Cohen's "Hallelujah" plays as Marissa dies in Ryan's arms.

Bloggers, message boards, and TV critics had always seemed so lukewarm about Marissa. So, Schwartz really wasn't prepared for all the sadness and fury that followed. Many fans took to Tumblr to express their grief. Angry fan art was drawn. Even Schwartz's and Savage's mothers were upset. Savage's mom brings it up to this day.

"All of a sudden it became clear that a lot of the audience watched the show for Marissa," Schwartz said. "It was clear that there was a whole big section of the show's viewers who really identified [with] and rooted for that character. I am someone who is naturally very conflict-averse. I'm a people-pleaser. So this was just not great for me."

While I was in the middle of writing this chapter, I met up with my friend Alex for dinner and told her I had gotten to the part where Marissa dies. "Oh," she said. There was a weight to her words. She had her *own* story about that infamous episode—complete with all the specific twists, turns, and heartache that comes from loving a TV show so much.

In her own words:

> There had been rumors leading up to the Season 3 finale that something big was coming, but no one was sure what that might be. I had dance rehearsal the night the episode aired, so I asked my mom to tape it. I got home from rehearsal and sprinted to the family room. Much to my dismay, I was met not by a wisecrack from Sandy Cohen but rather by an infomercial for a blender. Maybe I just need to fast-forward, I thought. But no dice. My mom had taped over an hour of QVC programming. Fuming, I stormed into her room. "MOM, YOU DIDN'T GET *THE O.C.*!" I screamed through tears. "Honey, I'm sorry. I must have taped the wrong channel."
>
> The next day I told all my friends what had happened, begging them not to spoil the episode for me. But inevitably, I learned of Marissa's tragic end in Mrs. Gonalez's second-period science class. I have since forgiven my mom for her indiscretion but to this day I mourn the fact that I didn't get to experience that moment live, and regret that, like everyone in her life, I completely let Marissa down.

The ramifications of losing Marissa were hitting Schwartz and Savage fast and hard. As they grappled with the backlash, there was a whole other mountain to climb. The group was making the oh-so-nerve-wracking transition from high school to college.

There was also the issue of the ratings. Each season, the show had slipped further from the top of the television heap. *The O.C.* averaged 9.4 million viewers in its first year. Those numbers dropped to 7.3 million the second year and 5.8 million the following year. The series had been moved from Tuesday nights to Wednesdays to Thursdays, facing off against juggernauts like *Survivor* and *The Office*. Now in their fourth season, they'd be up against two other television heavy hitters: *Grey's Anatomy* and *CSI: Crime Scene Investigation*. Fox tried to get creative, premiering episodes of the show on MySpace ahead of their TV airing dates, but Schwartz was getting the sense that the fourth season was going to be their last.

While the beginning few episodes of Season 4 lean into the melodrama (Ryan becomes a cage fighter so he can fight Volchok and avenge Marissa's death), it settles into something refreshingly different, shedding its teen drama trappings for a season that's—actually—quite fun. For reference: at one point, Che, played by Chris Pratt, serenades Seth in the nude with a song about polar bears. Ryan's new love interest, the neurotic, bubbly Taylor Townsend, brings a delightful concoction of kookiness and humor to his chronic brooding.

In a way, the fourth season felt like a welcome relief. Schwartz decided he was no longer going to care about ratings. All he wanted to do was make the best show possible, Trojan Horse be damned. They had tried so hard to juggle a mix of darkness, romance, and comedy over the past three seasons. It felt like walking a tightrope. Finally, out of the darkness of Marissa's death came light.

In one of the season's most memorable episodes, "The Chrismukk-huh?," Ryan and Taylor fall off a ladder, hitting their heads and entering into a strange, alternate universe of *The O.C.* There, we see what life would have been if Ryan had never moved to Newport Beach. It turns out that the boy from Chino had been the glue that had held a fracturing world together. Without him, Sandy marries Julie Cooper and becomes mayor of Newport Beach. Kirsten, cold and removed, ends up with Jimmy. Seth is still the same bullied, uncomfortable-in-his-skin guy we met in the show's pilot. Summer has turned vapid once more and is married to Che, *who*, incidentally, is having an affair with Julie.

A big question looms: Is Marissa alive and well in this alternate universe? Ryan thinks she might be. A maid at the Coopers' household tells him that Julie's daughter is arriving at the airport from college and he dashes over there, hoping that he'll get to see Marissa one last time.

It's not her.

It's her sister, Kaitlin, who just got back from UC Berkeley. She tells Ryan that Marissa died three years ago. She overdosed in an alleyway in Tijuana.

When they come to, Taylor tries to comfort Ryan.

"Ryan," she says. "You gave her three more years. She got to fall in love. She got to graduate."

"And then she still died."

"Which just means that you weren't meant to save her!" Taylor insists. "So if there's any part of you that's still blaming yourself for what happened, you have to let it go. You've done so much for everybody."

Was that a coded message to the fans from Schwartz and Savage? That Marissa was meant to have a tragic ending? It felt like this episode was them extending a hand to viewers who were still grieving Marissa's death and explaining that, sad as it was, it was always her destiny. Taylor knew it. Perhaps Ryan did too.

The fourth season drew in 4 million viewers, the lowest yet, and in January 2007, news dropped that the season's last episode would be the finale of the series.

As the show inched to a close, Philbin didn't feel like she was ready to wrap up Ryan's, Summer's, and Seth's stories just yet. She shoved her sadness down by leaning into the comedy and pitched an entire story line that involved Seth and Summer getting really into the fictional show *Briefcase or No Briefcase*, a take-off on *Deal or No Deal*. At first, Schwartz acquiesced. Eventually, he put the kibosh on it.

"Wait a minute, wait a minute. Seriously, we can't do this," he said. Philbin forced herself to switch gears then, leaning into the more emotionally substantial story lines.

Summer lands a job with GEORGE (Global Environmental Organization Regarding Greenhouse Emissions)—and, fun side note, the character who offers her the position is played by none other than Mike Schur, Philbin's husband, writer on *The Office*, future co-creator of *Parks and Recreation* and, of course, Moses, Dwight's cousin on *The Office*. At the very end of the *O.C.* finale, we see that Summer has married Seth, the ultimate happy ending to many years of tumultuous love.

When it came time to figure out where to leave Ryan, Savage and Schwartz asked themselves a few central questions: What do we want from him? What is Ryan's ultimate goal? "Obviously we wanted him to be a successful person but—this is making me tear up a little bit—did Ryan grow up to be a good person who would do for someone else what was done for him?" Savage asked.

The answer, of course, was yes. The last time we see Ryan, he's dressed in a button-down shirt and crisp pants, briefcase in hand, talking on his cell phone. He's a successful architect, miles from the scared, defiant teen we met in the pilot. Just as he's about to get into his car, he spots a boy in a gray hoodie straddling a wall. Ryan flashes back to his young self, kicked out of his house, desperate and alone.

"Hey kid," he calls out. "You need any help?"

Schwartz and Savage wrapped up *The O.C.* just as they started shooting their new show *Gossip Girl*, a series about wealthy teenagers living scandalous, glamorous lives on Manhattan's Upper East Side. As they said a final goodbye to this chapter of their lives, Schwartz looked back on everything the whole team had done over the course of four long, strange, joyful years.

"Well," he thought. "That almost worked."

It wasn't until *The O.C.*'s ten-year anniversary in 2013 that Schwartz and Savage began to fully understand the impact that their show had on a generation of fans. Suddenly, people wanted to talk about *The O.C.* Maybe, Schwartz thought, it was because it reminded them of a special time in their lives when they first watched it—whether in a college dorm room or at someone's parents' house after school, or (in my case) under blankets, late at night, clutching my dad's laptop when I was supposed to be asleep.

"I can't tell you how many people have told me they moved to California because they watched the show or they had just moved to California and they watched the show and then they stayed in California," Savage said. "People who went to college to meet their Seth Cohen. People had a really deeply personal connection to it and still want to talk about it, and that's the most gratifying part of all." Her voice starts to crack on the phone.

"There's those Stephanie happy tears coming," Schwartz said.

The O.C. dared to go where no teen show had gone before. It allowed an off-center cast of characters and quirky plot lines (*ahem* *Je Pense* . . .) to live comfortably on network TV, cleverly packaged in dreamy wrapping. It elegantly mixed genres in a way that felt effortless and cohesive. And it opened the door for the teen phenomenon *Gossip Girl*, which would fully embrace the finely crafted melodrama that Schwartz and Savage had so adroitly learned to cook up.

Were audiences and networks ready to accept teen shows for all that they could be—boundary pushing, grounded in realism, funny, dramatic, and maybe a little silly? We hadn't gotten there *quite* yet. But writers, directors, cinematographers, and actors were trying. Next up, a small Texas town called Dillon was about to become the new stomping ground for teen TV that dared to be different.

The cast and crew of NBC's *Friday Night Lights* would push the boundaries of network television with guerilla-like cinematography, a fierce appreciation for improvisation, and a gritty commitment to realness. And they were going to have to fight like hell to get the recognition they deserved.

Because after all, clear eyes, full hearts, can't lose.

Friday Night Lights

(2006-2011)

A car crawls slowly through the small town of Dillon, Texas, as a camera pans out to capture a pink sunset on the horizon and modest ranch homes below. In an empty football field nearby, Coach Taylor walks onto the turf with a look of gritty determination. The big game is coming up on Friday, and lots of folks are skeptical that this new guy has what it takes to lead their beloved high school team to victory.

We're shown snippets of his players, then. Tim Riggins, fullback, is passed out on his couch, shirtless and surrounded by beer bottles. Matt Saracen, backup quarterback, takes care of his grandmother's breakfast before he hurries off to school. His friend Landry gives him a ride and asks if he thinks he's going to get to play at all this season.

"Nope," Saracen says firmly.

"I can't keep driving you to this practice in humiliation," Landry tells him. "It's not good for either one of us."

Welcome to Dillon, a town that lives and breathes high school football. And welcome to **Friday Night Lights,** *a character study, a drama, a sprinkling of hilarious comedy—and a show that, secretly, wasn't really about football at all.*

In 1988, a writer named H. G. Bissinger implanted himself in the town of Odessa, Texas. He had decided to chronicle the story of a high school football team called the Permian Panthers and offer an intimate portrait of a community built around a fierce love of the sport. Characters included Coach Gaines, the school's devoted football coach leading the young men to the Texas state championship; "Boobie" Miles, a fullback who suffers a knee injury; and Don Billingsley, a halfback who has a rocky relationship with his former-football-star father.

Actor Peter Berg had only a few directing credits under his belt when he took helm of the film adaptation of Bissinger's book. It starred Billy Bob Thornton as Gaines, Connie Britton as his wife, Sharon, and a roster of young talent including Derek Luke and Garrett Hedlund. The film had a raw, documentary quality to it and an inherent underpinning of sadness, with strands of abuse, crushing pressure, and dreams unfulfilled—both for the players and the parents. It was an early aughts teen movie, certainly, particularly when it came to one-dimensional female characters. But something about it felt different from the breezy, fun romps being released around that time like *She's the Man, Napoleon Dynamite*, and *Freaky Friday*. It felt real.

When Berg finished shooting the film, he realized he wasn't quite ready to say goodbye to the world of West Texas football. He met with Kevin Reilly, then the president of NBC, and detailed an unconventional idea for a TV series about young football players. There were about ten NBC executives in the room that day as Berg made his pitch: this wasn't going to be a typical sports show, and it certainly wasn't going to be a typical teen show.

"I want to build up this all-American quarterback, this hero," he told them. "This wonderful, beautiful kid with his entire future ahead of him . . . He's got the hot girlfriend. He's got loving parents. And he's going to break his neck in the first game. We're going to create this iconic American hero, and we're going to demolish him."

That sounded good to Reilly. NBC didn't have any teen television shows on its roster at the time. Its headliners included dramas like *ER* and comedies like *The Office. Friday Night Lights* would add some demographic diversity to the lineup. Maybe it could do what the WB did and pull in droves of teen viewership.

Some changes would be made from the original film. Coach Gaines was renamed Coach Taylor. The town of Odessa was changed to the fictional hamlet of Dillon and the cast of characters were given new names and new backstories. With the show green-lit, Berg went on the hunt for a crop of high school students to populate this Texas community—and he knew just who to call.

"Get me the *Grey's Anatomy* casting director," he told the show's producers. Berg was connected with Linda Lowy, who had assembled the cast of the hottest series on television, a medical drama created by entertainment powerhouse Shonda Rhimes.

Berg told Lowy that the actors they cast should be relatively unknown, with few to no credits, and a raw, natural quality about them. That's exactly what he got.

Minka Kelly was working as a scrub nurse when she landed the role of Lyla Garrity, a devoutly religious cheerleader. Scott Porter, soon to be star quarterback Jason Street, was beatboxing in an off-Broadway show and crashing on a friend's couch. Zach Gilford had been folding clothes at a sporting-goods store before he got the part of Matt Saracen, our underdog and second-string quarterback. Just six months after graduating from Carnegie Mellon, Gaius Charles put himself on tape and sent it off to NBC. He caught Berg's attention when he bypassed the script and started talking off-the-cuff, directly to the camera.

"Hey, Pete, you looking for me, baby, you looking for me!" he called out. In that moment, the cocky, charismatic running back Brian "Smash" Williams was born.

Auditions for *Friday Night Lights* were a strange, topsy-turvy affair. "Pete knew that there wasn't going to be a lot of rehearsal. He knew that there was going to be an element of improv to it," Lowy told me. "So he wanted to make sure that all of the actors that we cast had the ability to be really flexible on the day of."

"Do this scene again and this time you're on heroin," Berg instructed one of the actors. Or he'd say: "Let's not even audition with the lines. Let's pretend that you're in Washington, D.C., and I'm the president." Sometimes he'd ask them to sing their dialogue.

Then, there was the great Coach debate. Lowy wanted Kyle Chandler for Coach Eric Taylor, the man tasked with bringing the Panthers to victory. She had seen him in a few mediocre movies that didn't feel worthy of his talent. He was the strong, silent type and there was just something so *appealing* about him, which she suspected might unlock a whole other set of viewers for *Friday Night Lights*. "The women that are watching this show—the women who are in their thirties and their late twenties and above that—are gonna want something. They can't lust over high schoolers. Give them the coach," she recalls thinking.

Lowy presented Berg with Chandler's reel, and he quickly dismissed it. "I don't know. I don't think so." Berg wanted Dwight Yoakam, a singer-songwriter from Kentucky, who had made a name for himself in country music. Lowy didn't think Yoakam was a good fit for Coach. Plus, she couldn't get Chandler out of her head.

So, instead, she decided to cast Chandler on *Grey's Anatomy* as a firefighter who would save the day but tragically die at the end of the episode. Audiences, she remembers, went "mental" over the actor. "Shonda had to bring him back from the dead. She literally did. The fans demanded it. We brought him back from the dead in a couple of dream sequences."

While Chandler was filming an episode of *Grey's*, Lowy arranged for him to meet with a begrudging Berg. Shooting was running behind that day, and Lowy got news that Chandler would be about an hour late. That was the last straw for Berg. "Linda, I told you. I do not like him. I do not want to see him. Cancel the meeting."

If a young casting director had been in that situation, Lowy told me, they probably would have pulled the plug immediately. But Lowy wasn't giving up. Also, she was kind of annoyed with Berg.

"Pete, I am not canceling this meeting," she said. "You will see him in one hour when he comes. And you will see him for five minutes if that's all you want to spend with him. But we're not canceling the meeting . . . we don't do stuff like that to actors."

Berg appreciated her chutzpah. "Ooh, I love when you get mad," he told Lowy. Just then, two of Berg's old colleagues from the show *Chicago Hope* walked in. "They were like puppies. Rolling around and hugging each other and the spirit was really high," Lowy remembers. She saw her chance. She needed to get Chandler in the room *immediately* while everyone was still in a good mood.

"Oh my God, is Kyle on the set yet?" she muttered, turning to someone who worked on *Grey's*. "Can we get him to get down here right now?"

"Let me quickly make a call," she was told.

Chandler was able to hustle to Lowy's office, where she gave the performance of a lifetime at his arrival. "Oh my God. Look! Kyle's here!" Lowy exclaimed as he walked in.

Chandler was exactly what she thought he'd be, a man of few words but so charming and with a real sense of strength. Within two seconds, Lowy said, Berg knew he was right for the role. In just one meeting—and with some strategic trickery—she had gotten them their Coach Taylor.

Berg wanted Connie Britton to reprise her role as the coach's wife. The answer came back as a hard no. Britton was done with wordlessly sitting in the stands. She had no interest in returning to the sidelines as a one-dimensional character or, as Berg later remembers her putting it: "'You think I'm going to spend ten years sitting on a hard-wood bleacher getting splinters in my ass and cheering on Kyle Chandler? You're out of your mind.'"

The director offered an impassioned pitch. The character, now renamed Tami, would be different, he said. She would be complex and layered. After some persuading, Britton was, if not full-heartedly, in. She was skeptical, because the pilot script didn't seem to have a whole lot for Tami, but she just had to trust that Berg was being honest. Britton wouldn't have to worry—Tami would turn out to be so many wonderful things, charming and warm, strong and smart, a loving but deeply frustrated parent. Berg stayed true to his word.

David Boyd was busy adding new walls to his house when his phone rang. It was his agent, reminding him that he had an interview for the job of cinematographer on *Friday Night Lights*. Boyd was sweaty, dirty, and needed to get the construction done before it started to rain. He had no interest in taking the meeting.

"No, no, you should go," his agent encouraged him. Boyd relented and, by the time he got there, was ready to say just about anything that would get him out of there and back to his house.

Then he met Berg. There was just *something* about Berg. "I quickly realized this guy is a pilot," he told me. "I looked at him down there, at the end of the table, and went, OK, wow. This guy's not interested in us landing. He's interested in something good. It was something fabulous which hadn't been done yet."

Suddenly, Boyd found himself saying all the things he had always wanted to say in interviews but knew it would cost him the job.

"Let's not put marks down. Let's not do rehearsals. Let's not put our hands all over it, like it's done all the time," he said. "Let's let actors know that we follow them. We don't tell them what to do. If, on take three, they want to go to the window, they can go to the window. Nothing has to be discussed. Just go. Do it. It's incumbent on the camera operators and all of us to let it happen."

He continued, "Why are we using these big cameras? Thirty-five-millimeter film cameras? Why aren't we shooting in sixteen millimeter? Why do we have to beg for two cameras, because I think three would be fantastic. Three cameras and three crews all the time."

In 2006, that was pretty much an impossible ask. In fact, you were out of your mind if you even tried. But the third camera, he insisted, was the secret sauce. It could move around fluidly throughout the scene, capturing dialogue, small moments, and tight, intimate shots. Directors were usually wary of the idea. They were so used to watching one monitor with all the action—how could they keep up with all three crews?

Boyd left the meeting positive he hadn't landed the job. Then, on the car ride back, not even halfway home, Berg called. "You're it," he said.

"Oh my God, this guy's going to do it," Boyd thought. "He might punch a few people along the way but he's going to come up with something that's really great."

In the beginning, it would prove difficult to convince the camera operators that they truly had the freedom to move and shoot as they pleased. That just wasn't the way they were trained. "You were petrified about making a pan or a tilt that the director didn't want or ask for," Boyd explained. "So I said, let's get rid of that right now. Everybody can do whatever they want anytime they want. Period. There's no repercussions."

During one of the first scenes they shot of the pilot, three cameras and the sound crew crowded into Tami Taylor's twelve-by-twelve office. They could barely move. The actors came in, started to do their scene, and then stopped. They looked around at all the people crammed into the room, and everybody broke into laughter. "It was just hilarious," Todd McMullen, the show's camera operator, and later cinematographer, recalls. "This is just ridiculous. How are we going to do this?"

McMullen still remembers shooting in the Saracen house for the first time. Camera on his shoulder, he clocked that Louanne Stephens, who played Matt's grandma Lorraine, was tapping her foot over and over. He didn't know if the actor was just nervous or if it was a character choice, but he lowered himself down to the floor and pointed his lens at her foot. That small moment would make it into the final cut.

No sets were built for *Friday Night Lights*. Everything was filmed on location, in or around the Austin area—from the Taylors' tidy, one-story home to the Dairy Queen that doubled as the Alamo Freeze, a popular after-school hangout. Berg wasn't interested in getting into the minutiae of location scouting. "Just go pick some places to shoot," he told Boyd.

A University of Texas football player owned the Riggins house. During shooting days, he moved out and the crew would move in, without touching the interiors. The whole place, Boyd said, was "deliciously scummy," down to the pool out back that was filled with algae. One day, someone opened up the refrigerator and discovered that it hadn't been turned on in weeks. The smell of sour milk cleared the room. And the cherry on top: every time they filmed there, the cast and crew kept getting mysterious, itchy bites. The place was fumigated multiple times before bugs were discovered living inside the Rigginses' couch.

Football scenes for the pilot were filmed at Pflugerville High School, just north of Austin, and shoots would go overnight, from late afternoon to early morning. The cinematographer, camera operators, and a separate group of NFL camera operators all descended on the field, where pro footballers and college players were on the scene, filling in as the stunt crew. Allan Graf, the show's football coordinator, set the plays and Boyd's team would need to capture wide and tight shots of the action, along with reactions from the sidelines. Then, they'd focus on the plays, zeroing in on all the big hits and touchdowns. It would get chilly at night and, as the hours wore on, cups of hot chocolate got passed around.

During the first game of the pilot, the crew had made it through two camera setups when Berg changed course. "You know what, let's do another scene," he said. He started walking away, toward the locker room, and Boyd followed him, delighted. "Yeah," he thought. "Screw that scene, let's do the locker room!"

There, Berg had Charles ad-lib a prayer as all the players knelt. "Don't act," Berg told Charles during the filming of that episode. "Just talk." There was something so comforting about the sentiment, especially to a young performer on his first television show. Charles took Berg's words to mean just show up and be honest.

A final version of the pilot was screened for a gaggle of NBC staff, from top executives to schedulers and publicists. As the episode drew to a close, cheers and applause filled the room. When lights came up, John Miller, the network's head of marketing, walked over to Angela Bromstad, the president of primetime entertainment.

"This is a really great pilot," he said. "But I really don't know how we're going to sell this."

Miller was right. They had a marketing problem on their hands. Ask any *Friday Night Lights* fan about the show and they'll say in knowing tones that it's not *really* about football. But how do you convince a mass audience, who might not have any interest in sports, to tune in?

The day after the pilot aired, Charles arrived at work to find people buried in their cell phones. "What's everybody doing?" he wondered. Within seconds, he found out. They were checking the ratings from the previous night. The episode was slotted against ABC's *Dancing with the Stars* and *American Idol*. *Friday Night Lights* got absolutely crushed by its competition.

After the pilot, Jason Katims, who had gotten his start as a writer on *My So-Called Life*, came on board as showrunner and quickly ran headfirst into the marketing quandary. While on a field trip to Sacramento with his child's class, one of the moms asked what he did for a living.

"I'm a writer," he replied, and started to tell them about this show he had just started working on, *Friday Night Lights*. As he watched their eyes glaze over with disinterest, he quickly tried to course-correct, explaining that it wasn't all about sports. "I think you would really like it!"

But he had already lost them.

The look on their faces, Katims later told me, read: "Oh, this poor writer trying to get us to watch this show that we would never watch."

Droves of fans might not have been tuning in, but critics could not have loved the pilot more. You'd be truly hard-pressed to find a television review more glowing than the one that the *New York Times* TV critic Virginia Heffernan wrote after the first episode aired.

"Lord, is 'Friday Night Lights' good," she began. "In fact, if the season is anything like the pilot, this new drama about high school football could be great—and not just television great, but great in the way of a poem or painting, great in the way of art with a single obsessive creator who doesn't have to consult with a committee and has months or years to go back and agonize over line breaks and the color red."

Friday Night Lights, she noted, didn't feel like television. "It could belong in a league with art that doesn't have to pause for commercials, or casually recap the post-commercial action, or sell viewers on the plot and characters in the first five minutes."

Earning such unabashed critical acclaim felt like both a blessing and a curse for Katims as the season wore on. "We'd joke about them in the writers' room," he said. "They'd be comparing us to a prose poem. They're comparing us to an opera. Just say it's sexy and raw! Say it's hot!"

But Heffernan was right in her praise. *Friday Night Lights* felt so different from the cut-and-dry television format we'd grown accustomed to, where the camera diligently went where it was supposed to go and the actors said the lines printed neatly on the page. Each location was so lived-in, the dialogue deeply natural, and the shots intimate. Even Coach's pump-up speeches, which could have easily veered into corny territory, transcended the usual sports-movie schmaltz. The character was rough, a little terrifying, and believed so fiercely in his team that he made believers out of us too.

In a way, *My So-Called Life* had left a small but important imprint on *Friday Night Lights*. Katims had learned about naturalism from Winnie Holzman all those years back when he was sitting in her office, late at night, watching her craft dialogue. Angela Chase and the teens of Liberty High didn't speak perfectly, so neither did the teens of Dillon High.

Much like Holzman, Katims would create an open line of communication between the actors and the writers. Charles remembers sitting down for lunch with Katims in a Los Angeles restaurant to discuss the character of Smash. Ever the prepared acting student, he arrived with a binder and little notebook in hand. "Hey, if you have a thought about your character just give me a call and let me know," Katims told him.

So, when Charles filmed a scene that featured Smash's mom catching him making out with one of the show's main characters, Tyra, he reached out to

Katims. "I just want to make sure we're going to find ways to keep Brian rounded and three-dimensional and we're not going down this teen-drama cliché kind of road," he told Katims.

The showrunner—Charles was delighted to discover—was actually receptive to his feedback. Smash would end up dating fellow high schooler Waverly, played by Aasha Davis, whom he tries to help as she struggles with bipolar disorder. We see a different side of Smash then, vulnerable and open with his pain, far from the guy we'd met in the show's pilot.

"Mental health hadn't really been featured very much on mainstream network television," Charles told me, particularly mental health from the African American perspective. "It's sort of hidden in plain sight, so to speak," he said.

Something new and wonderful was happening on-screen, Charles could just feel it. Early on, he remembers Chandler turning to the cast during a group dinner and saying: "You guys, this is a huge opportunity. This is not how things typically work. Take it, enjoy it, make the most of it, because you just don't get this kind of creative freedom and this opportunity to collaborate in this way very often."

Friday Night Lights collaboration went something like this, Allison Liddi-Brown, who came on board to direct in Season 1, recalled:

Say they were filming one of those breakfast scenes in the Taylor house. Liddi-Brown would ask the actors what they needed. Chandler might respond that he wanted some coffee because he was going to go over to the coffee maker. Liddi-Brown would alert the cinematographer, who would put a little LED light behind the appliance. The *Friday Night Lights* camera crew traveled light, using skinny, powerful lights in lieu of the standard bulky ones. If their equipment wasn't able to fit in a cube box, they weren't bringing it. They never took over streets while they were filming, and they didn't stop traffic with their trucks.

Dialogue was not sacred. It was always OK if actors spoke over one another—in fact, it was encouraged. One scene, Liddi-Brown remembers, involved Chandler in his office. Suddenly, the actor started fooling around with his chair, acting like it was broken. He summoned the other coach in. "Can you call that guy?" he asked.

"What guy?"

"The guy, I told you to call the guy about the chair," Chandler, as Coach, responded, irked.

Liddi-Brown nudged Aimee Teegarden, who played Julie, into the scene then. "Go in now!" Julie starts to try to talk to her dad, but he's still fooling around with the chair, annoyed. It was a small moment but felt gloriously real, Liddi-Brown later said.

"People [in the industry] are too afraid," she said. "[The] sound [crew] is afraid. Everybody's afraid. The audience might not understand, you might overlap! Uh-huh, human beings overlap."

Only later, Charles told me, did he come to understand the uniqueness of the experience. After *Friday Night Lights*, he'd go on to other shows. There were marks he needed to stand on. He couldn't ad-lib his lines.

In the show's third episode, "Wind Sprints," the Dillon Panthers are herded onto a school bus by Coach late at night. There's a rumble of thunder as they climb aboard, and it's pounding rain by the time they get off. "Wind sprints, let's go," Coach says, and the boys start running up and down a steep hill, sloshing through mud and massive puddles of water. "Champions don't give up!" Coach shouts over the downpour. "Champions don't complain! You're not champions until you earn it."

It's a captivating, cinematic scene, the camera carrying us dizzyingly up and down the hill, rain splashing everywhere, the young men brutally exhausted. As Charles ran through the water and muck, yelling, "Clear Eyes, Full Hearts, Can't Lose!" he felt like something special was happening. It was a moment in time that still stays with him, all these years later.

Jeffrey Reiner directed that episode. He remembers at one point looking over at Taylor Kitsch, who played Tim, standing in the pouring rain, and thinking, "That's a movie star." Tim Riggins wasn't just some hunky TV character. The person in front of the camera that day looked like a broken kid. Reiner made sure to get a great close-up of Riggins as Coach forces the teen to walk home instead of getting on the bus. He had shown up to practice drunk earlier, and this was his punishment.

As Tim trudges home, Lyla catches up with him. She's furious that he hasn't gone to visit her boyfriend—and Tim's best friend—Jason in the hospital. She starts hitting him over and over again. Then, she begins to cry and crumples into him. They kiss.

Reiner was skeptical, at first, about having this explosive moment between Lyla and Tim so early on. Shouldn't they draw the will they/won't they out? Liz Heldens, the episode's writer, stood firm. "Oh, you gotta push it," she told him. "You gotta."

Taylor Kitsch and Minka Kelly went straight into the intense emotion as soon as they started shooting, and Reiner quickly reined them in. "Don't play that up front," he said. "You can't play the end of the scene up front. Forget all that and let it come to you." It was an instruction he particularly liked to give to young actors.

So they did. Reiner watched as the two slowly worked their way up to that pivotal moment. "They were so brave in forgetting what they were supposed to be doing," he said. "They let it come to them organically—I felt so confident in those actors after that."

Back in Los Angeles, a group of writers crammed into Katims's office and tried to figure out where to take the teens of Dillon next. A big cork board sat at the front of the room, with all the characters' names running top to bottom, from Coach Taylor down to Buddy Garrity, the show's over-involved team booster. The group would figure out the central stories for the episode and then, writer John Zinman recalls, wordlessly walk to the board, note cards with scene descriptions in hand, and physically arrange each act.

Multiple writers had played competitive sports back in high school and they would reminisce about the athletes' clout and their sense of entitlement. They talked about the dynamics between the players and their parents, and the screwed-up hierarchy that put nonathletes at the bottom.

Despite the world having been designed entirely around a high school, Katims was startled when—seasons in—he heard someone refer to it as a teen show. "Oh! I never thought about it that way," he thought. Katims was following Holzman's blueprint: write about young characters with the same respect that you would give to adult characters.

And in many ways, they succeeded in avoiding the usual high school tropes. Landry was the smart kid in school who could have easily fallen into the nerdy stereotype. But he was in this pretty rocking Christian metal band called

Crucifictorious and earnestly confident in his approach to pursuing relationships with girls. *My* hot take is that Landry was actually quite cool.

Matt Saracen could have also been one-dimensional: shy, reserved, and cautious, a perpetual underdog. But he was given genuinely funny material, erred occasionally on the cocky side, and could be aggressive with his teammates. He was also in deep pain that he'd bottled up while balancing school, football, an afterschool job, and caring for his grandmother with dementia.

When Louanne Stephens landed the role of Matt's grandmother, Lorraine Saracen, she thought the character would just be filler. She showed up to set in glasses, slippers, hat, and gown and ate lunch at a table filled with twentysomethings in their tiny cheerleading outfits and football uniforms. The young actors would invite her out to the bars on Sixth Street in Austin, but it wasn't really her thing. She did get close to Zach Gilford, though. When I asked her what she remembers most about him, she responded that she has one funny story and one serious story.

The funny one happened when she was shooting a scene in which Mrs. Saracen gets out of a moving car and hits her head. Gilford, in character, runs over to help her up.

"You have to understand that Zach is the shyest, most gentlemanly young man," she told me. "Intellectual. If he ever did say a bad word, he said, 'Oh, Louanne, I'm sorry.'"

That day, Gilford accidentally grabbed her breast as he was trying to lift her. "I see his face is red. If I were nice, I would have just let it go. But in front of everybody, I say, 'Well Zach, you finally did it.'"

"'Louanne, you could have let that go,'" Gilford replied, mortified.

"'I know. I'm sorry. I could have. But you're just so nice. I had to embarrass you.'" These days, Stephens sends Gilford gifts for his daughter and has yet to let him live down the breast incident.

The serious moment came when Stephens had to lock herself in a closet and not emerge until her grandson sweetly crooned "Mr. Sandman" to her. "That is gonna be so dumb," Stephens remembers thinking. "That does not sound like it will work." Gilford, she remembers, also had his reservations.

Then, when they filmed the scene, Stephens almost started crying. She still feels like crying when she thinks about that moment today. "I think it's the relationship between the grandmother and the grandchild," she said. "It's one of the strongest bonds in the world and hardly ever mentioned." She still hears from grandkids who approach her in tears, asking her to sign something for a grandparent who has dementia.

While the show was airing, Stephens won an award from the L.A. Alzheimer's Association. NBC refused to pay for her plane ticket to attend the ceremony. "That's not right," Stephens remembers Katims saying. He made sure he got her there to accept her award. Stephens went to Neiman Marcus and bought a beautiful black silk coat and trousers to match. It was so fun; some people she met at the awards show were genuinely surprised to discover she was Grandma Saracen, she looked so elegant.

All the young actors made sure Stephens went up first to the stage. "The emcees were a woman with early onset Alzheimer's and her husband. . . . She was real young. Forties or fifties. She was very aware of what was coming. So it was also a rough night that way," Stephens said. "But they were very appreciative of the treatment of the person with dementia in *Friday Night Lights*. They felt like it was the best that had ever been as far as TV and movies were concerned."

The series was finding deeply emotional moments both on and off the field. When it came to creating those pivotal game-day moments, the work had to be pretty damn compelling—enough to keep non-football fans riveted and football fans convinced.

I really tried to get to the bottom of how *Friday Night Lights* made Panthers devotees out of non-football fans. As someone who knows little to nothing about the sport, I found myself gripping a large pillow on my couch during every game, muttering "Pass, pass!" under my breath with a ferocity that felt both deeply thrilling and very startling. After finishing the first season, I even asked my roommate if she might want to toss a football around with me in the nearby park (she politely declined).

How did they manage to make that happen? I asked Katims first.

"We realized there's only so many ways you're going to win a football game in the last three seconds. So we couldn't depend upon the excitement of the game alone," he explained. Instead, they focused on the character dramas. "Is Matt Saracen going to be able to step into QB1 when he's this third-string quarterback who hasn't started? What's it going to be like for Smash, getting recruited, and his success [riding on] his family and his family's future?"

The story was also in the stands, Boyd added. The plays weren't the focal point—it was Tami's reaction from the bleachers, Coach's intensity from the sidelines, Grandma Saracen watching her grandson fight to prove himself on the field. Boyd would shoot those crucial performances first and then send the crowd home. After that, for six or seven hours, it was just the camera crew and the football players.

One day, Reiner recalls, they had eight cameras at a football game—three in the stands, three on the sidelines, and three on the field. They were watching all the cameras behind the scenes and, he said, it made some people's heads explode. "Everyone had wired mics, so sometimes you'd have roughly nine people talking at the same time. We had a few sound guys quit on us very early on. I think a script supervisor might have had a slight nervous breakdown." He embraced the anarchy of it all.

During her first game in Season 1, Liddi-Brown stood on the field, three cameras whipping around the stadium, camera operators tripping over themselves to land a close-up shot. She didn't feel like she had to tell them where to go or when. They seemed to be following the story themselves, carefully watching the scene to find the moments that mattered for each character. "We would just chase the emotions," she said.

Liddi-Brown was one of two women who would direct *Friday Night Lights*. She had been up for a producer's role when the show first started, but Berg passed on her in favor of Reiner, who had grown up playing football. It was absolutely true that Liddi-Brown didn't know much about football, she told me, but she was willing to learn.

"I did a show called *Rise* with Jason Katims. It was all about theatre. I knew everything about that. That's exactly my world," she said. "But I don't think you'd look at my [episodes] of *Rise* and say, 'Oh, it's really far superior to the other people who didn't understand theatre.' You get in there and there's a whole world that's set up and you just make it as real as you can."

Friday Night Lights ended Season 1 the way it started—with disappointing ratings and an ongoing marketing struggle. Ads would showcase the whole group on bleachers, walking off the field, or sitting on the back of a pickup truck, letterman jackets in tow. It just wasn't drawing in the numbers that the network hoped for.

At the time, Reilly wondered if it was the show's overall structure that put off potential viewers.

"People talk and write to me to say they love it, but not enough people watch," he told *Entertainment Weekly*. "It's a sports show, but it's a relationship show; it's a soap, but it's got social issues. What makes it great makes it hard to market." The *Friday Night Lights* crew was dealing with the same problem *Freaks and Geeks* grappled with years before: it just didn't quite fit into a neat box.

Still, something was stirring. Liddi-Brown went over to direct an episode of *Grey's Anatomy* and overheard two of the show's writers in an all-out heated argument over *Friday Night Lights*.

"Where's my DVD?" one of them asked.

"What do you mean?"

"You said you were gonna give it to me."

"Well, my wife's still watching it."

"What do you mean your wife's still watching it? I need those back. My neighbor needs to watch it."

Come Season 2, the writers decided to up the ante. They concocted a buzzy story line that involved Landry murdering a man who had attacked Tyra. It was meant to grab an audience, David Hudgins, one of the show's writers, explained to me. He had just come off working on the WB teen drama *Everwood*, where story lines leaned more into melodrama than drama. *Friday Night Lights* was very much a drama, but *maybe*, Hudgins thought, a little melodrama wouldn't hurt. It was a big swing and felt like it was born out of the wrong genre.

It did, however, introduce us to Tyra and Landry, a pairing that—dare I say—had more spark than Tim/Lyla *or* Tim/Tyra. When the idea was pitched in the room, Hudgins was dubious. "Landry and Tyra, really?" he asked. It just didn't make sense. Liz and a few of the women writers responded: "Yes, that's the point!"

"Never in a million years would we have guessed that Landry and Tyra would have the chemistry they did," Hudgins said.

There wasn't much time to luxuriate in that new dynamic—or the rocky murder story line—before a writers' strike put the season on pause. When it ended, in February 2008, Katims approached the studio and the network. "We're ready to finish the season," he said.

"Oh, hold on one second," he was told. "You're not doing any more episodes this season." After a short stint on air, the show was seemingly all but canceled.

Then, a surprising Hail Mary.

While attending the Sundance Film Festival, Ben Silverman, then president of NBC, went out for Chinese food with Eric Shanks, the executive vice president of entertainment at DirecTV, a video programming distributor. He told Shanks about the *Friday Night Lights* dilemma, explaining that the show definitely had an audience that really loved it, but the numbers just weren't strong enough. Shanks listened, and by the end of the dinner they had cooked up a plan. NBC would partner with DirecTV and green-light one final season of the series.

For Berg, Katims, the writers, directors, and actors, this was a last chance to bid a proper goodbye to the town of Dillon. The murder story line was swiftly wrapped up and some other plot points hastily dropped, including an arc with Santiago, a Dillon Panther with a troubled past, who had moved in with Buddy Garrity.

"Not only did everybody hate that murder story and hold me personally responsible for it, but also the whole end of the season. We had already planned it out and written a lot of the scripts, and they weren't shot," Katims said. "So the show ended on a kind of weird episode that was not supposed to be the end of the season at all."

It was time to start fresh.

Season 3 would be the last time that characters like Jason Street, Tim Riggins, and Smash Williams were show regulars. One of the season's standout episodes featured a final goodbye to the first generation of Panthers, as Riggins and Street head to New York City to pursue a possible sports-agent job for Street.

True to *Friday Night Lights* form, the crew remained light-footed and efficient while shooting in the city. They filmed a scene in the subway without getting a permit, and the characters bought hot dogs from a real hot-dog vendor instead of a hired actor.

When they arrived in the city, there was a plan to shoot just an exterior scene in front of a fancy suit shop called Paul Stuart. But, after walking inside to use the bathroom, Reiner realized how much he liked the interiors for a scene. Reiner approached one of the salespeople. "Hey, we've got this TV show, I wonder if we could come up here and shoot for like a half hour?" Reiner asked.

"Oh, honey, I've been trying to get into SAG for twenty years," the clerk responded. "If you put me in it, I'll let you shoot there." So, they all hurried in, not bothering to light the location, and brought in Johnny the salesperson, whose name Reiner still remembers to this day.

That was one of the many, many times *Friday Night Lights* crew would, without reservation, cast nonactors in speaking roles. In one episode, Matt goes to a jewelry store to buy a present for Julie. A young woman had been hired to play the person behind the counter that day, but Reiner really liked the actual store owner, an older woman whom he met during the location scout. He put her in the scene instead and asked her to ad-lib her own lines.

Writer John Zinman would make his own cameo as a doctor after a somewhat confusing interaction with Reiner. "Jeff called me into one of the editing bays. [He said] let's read this scene," Zinman recalls. "Before I knew it, I was auditioning for this role. He said, 'You remind me of my wife's gynecologist.'"

Zinman landed the gig and, on the day of shooting, was greatly apologetic. "I don't know what I'm doing here," the writer told his scene partners. "Please forgive me."

The writers, convinced that Season 3 was their last, decided to wrap up the show by sending Coach over to East Dillon High to teach at a poorly funded school with a defunct football program. The final shot would be of Coach and Tami walking onto the run-down East Dillon field together, trying to absorb their uncertain future. Reiner never used a crane when he shot *Friday Night Lights*, but that day he did. It felt right as the show's final moment.

Little did they know, there were a few more chapters left to tell. Berg and Katims presented the network with one final pitch to save the show. By bringing the series to East Dillon, they explained, it would create a fresh new dynamic with a whole new cast of characters.

Moving the setting of the show "was like dangling a piece of meat in front of [the networks]," Kyle Chandler later said. "I always thought it made them say yes just for the hell of it, to find out what they were going to do next."

They got another season.

Katims was determined for *Friday Night Lights* not to be one of those high school shows where the teens are still hanging around the hallways years past graduation. The Dillon teens who needed to graduate would leave, leaving behind an enormous hole that would need to be filled.

It was, for Katims, terrifying. "Now, shit like that happens all the time in shows: main character dies, now we're going to see this [new] one. But at the time, this was . . . revolutionary. I was so nervous."

Zinman, meanwhile, was skeptical about the show's move to East Dillon. "I remember, in all honesty, I was opposed to it. I remember at first thinking this was a radical move. But I came around. My only concerns were that the audience was going to feel like they had just been dislocated. It was now a new school, new people, and it was a new show."

Linda Lowy's first memory of finding the new generation of Panthers zeroes right in on Michael B. Jordan. She had seen the twenty-one-year-old in *The Wire* and was impressed, bringing Jordan to try out for the role of Vince Howard, a troubled teen who joins the East Dillon football team. He did improv with Peter Berg, which revolved around a real-life incident that happened to Harvard history scholar Henry Louis Gates Jr., a Black man who was arrested under suspicion of trying to enter his own home.

"Obama heard about the incident and he invited them all to the White House to talk about it through an open forum," Lowy recalled. "He invited both parties to the White House to discuss the issue over a beer. So Michael B. Jordan's improv was that. I think he had Michael play the cop instead of Henry Louis Gates. Pete played the president."

Then Berg switched gears.

"He said, 'I'm the quarterback, you're the middle linebacker, now get into it, start talking shit,'" Jordan told *ESPN* in a 2012 interview. "'More, more!' I'm getting into it. He yells, 'Talk shit!' It got to the point where I ran over to him and I tackled him out of the chair. I couldn't help it. I dropped him. I thought to myself, 'I either got the job right there or I'm never working again in this town.'

"I ended up getting the job."

When Matt Lauria was tapped to audition for the *Friday Night Lights* generation of teens, he was in the process of looking for night security jobs. His acting career had come to a nerve-wracking standstill and he was living with his wife at her parents' house, almost an hour outside L.A.

One day, his manager, Mike Smith, sent over some DVDs of the show. Smith represented Gaius Charles and was so proud of the work he was doing. "You really gotta watch, it's so good," he told Lauria. Smith lent him the first three seasons and Lauria churned through them, transfixed. He was intoxicated by the fictional town of Dillon, Texas. Every shot seemed to be occurring at magic hour.

Lauria thought the series had been canceled. He turned to his wife, not long after the opening credits of the pilot, and said, "Damn, I should have been on this show."

They were halfway through watching Season 3 when Lauria got a call from Smith. The people over at *Friday Night Lights* wanted him to come in to audition for the role of a football player named Luke Cafferty. He freaked out. "What?!" Lauria exclaimed. "I thought it was off the air!"

He headed to meet Berg in an empty rehearsal space with linoleum floors and fluorescent lights. The director approached Lauria with a quizzical look. His audition scene revolved around Luke getting called out by Tami for using a fake address—2268 Oakdale Road—so he could qualify to play football at Dillon High, not East Dillon, the school he was zoned for.

"I want you to say the whole thing but only say 2268 Oakdale Road," Berg told him. "That's all you get to say. Just improvise the entire scene only using those words. I want you to beg her, I want you to threaten her, I want you to apologize, I want you to plead, I want you to do everything but with that one line and that's it."

Lauria did just that. No matter what line came at him, he responded, "2268 Oakdale Road." He flew into a rage at one point and broke down crying at another. Berg stood up silently and walked right over to Lauria. He was kind of a big dude, Lauria recalled. "You an athlete?" he asked. "Yes, sir," Lauria replied. "Don't lie to me," Berg said.

"No, no," Lauria responded. "I grew up sprinting, I was a sprinter."

"Don't lie to me," Berg said again.

"I'm one of the fastest you've ever seen!" Berg turned around and walked away. Lauria made it to the next round.

The last audition was a screen test for Katims and Lowy. It took place in a tiny back office, and when Lauria walked in, Kitsch was sitting inside. He was there to do readings with actors who were trying out for Becky, a new character with whom Tim Riggins develops a kind of brother-sister relationship.

Lauria didn't even try to hide his excitement. It was *Tim Riggins*. "Dude!" he exclaimed, and gave Kitsch an enormous high five. The two improvised together, just talking trash and posturing. It was such a magical experience getting to sit there with Kitsch, riffing with a character he had gotten to know so intimately on the screen.

Then came the waiting. "I hope I get it, I hope I get it," Lauria kept repeating to himself as the days stretched out. Something in him said he got it. He was mowing his father-in-law's lawn when the call came. Right away, he phoned his wife, who was babysitting at the time. When she heard the news, she screamed so loudly that the child started crying. Their lives, Lauria told me, had changed forever.

Dora Madison's life was about to change too. She had grown up near Austin, in the city of Round Rock, and had unsuccessfully auditioned for *Friday Night Lights* a couple of times. Then, just after graduating from high school, Madison got called in to read for Becky, first locally, and then she was flown out to Los Angeles for the next rounds.

It was all so surreal. She had never been to L.A., and there was a chauffeured car to bring her to the audition. Three other young women were in the room when she arrived. One was Lucy Hale, who had been featured in episodes of *Privileged* and *Wizards of Waverly Place*. It was terrifying competing for the same role as someone she had watched on TV.

Madison went in, did her reading, and headed back to the airport.

Then, she got a call.

"Hey, turn your car around," she was told. They wanted her to come back and improvise. Back in the audition room, Berg spun a scenario for her. She had gotten a ride from Riggins to school and, when they arrived, she spotted a teacher she'd had a relationship with, who had taken advantage of her. "I want you to get Tim to take you away," Berg told her.

"He's coming to the car! He's trying to open the door! Just get him to go away!" Berg called out as Madison went through the intense scene. Madison, as Becky, burst into tears. Then, suddenly, it was all over. She didn't know it at that moment, but she had landed the role.

"OK, that was great, thanks!" Berg said to her.

"Wait, what?" she remembers thinking. She wiped away her tears and asked her driver to take her to a KFC drive-through. Madison ate her chicken tenders in silence. She was assigned a new room at the Grafton Hotel on Sunset Boulevard that night and she stood on the balcony, looking out over all of Los Angeles.

It was a very movie moment, she told me. "I was like, 'I'm in Hollywood!'"

Madison bought a romper from Free People to wear to the first cast dinner before shooting. "You're a movie star, don't forget it," Berg told her, and she remembers feeling really good. That night, Berg had everyone go around the table and say, "No one pushes me around!"

Kyle Chandler sat at one end of the table and Connie Britton at the other. It all had the formality of a wedding rehearsal. The old cast and new cast were merging together to tell one final chapter about Dillon.

Chandler gave a toast that night. "Listen, you will never have a better job for the rest of your career. You will have great jobs and great experiences. But you will never have a job as good as this," Lauria remembers him saying. "Ever. Enjoy it. I hope you know what you're getting into and appreciate it."

His words had the weight of a Coach Taylor speech. Lauria didn't need to be told twice. He was already so serious about this.

Instead of being given series-regular roles, the new cast was billed as guest stars for the first five episodes with the option to get picked up as full cast members. Lauria and his wife stayed at the Marriott Residence Inn in downtown Austin. He became close with Michael B. Jordan, and the two would hang out in the city, driving around in a rental car and going grocery shopping together.

Jordan's first day on-set came before Lauria's, and Lauria called him afterward to pepper him with questions. "Dude, how was it? What happened? What was it like?" he asked.

"Dude, I just went for it."

"What do you mean?" Lauria asked, wanting more.

"I went for it hard-core. I was improvising."

Liddi-Brown directed that episode. The first scene she shot with Jordan was him, as Vince, waking up and going to get something to drink. He makes his way through a small, dark apartment, opens up a sparse refrigerator, and discovers that the milk has gone bad. He steps outside and sees his mom, strung out, lying on a ratty couch a few doors down.

"Michael looks at her and his face completely changes," Liddi-Brown remembers. "He's nothing but loving and compassionate." Liddi-Brown decided to send an extra to walk by, just as Vince is tenderly picking his mom up.

"His face completely changed. Like, *Oh. You look at my mother and judge her and I will take you down*. That's when I thought, 'He's a genius.' Right there. How he could quickly go to that place and then drop it and be back with his mother and caring for her and carrying her inside the house."

The strange, exciting *Friday Night Lights* format was all new for Lauria—he had never had to ad-lib for television before. His first big moment would take place on the Dillon football field, when Luke gets caught lying about his home address. Rain poured down that day as Lauria walked into the makeup trailer. Inside sat Brad Leland, who played Buddy Garrity. "Holy shit!" Lauria thought.

Lauria was given football gear, which he nervously fumbled with, trying to figure out how to get the pads and pants on. His wife snapped photos of him in his Panthers uniform and then he was out in the rain, ready for his scene. There were pro football players all over the place, filling in as background actors. "Oh God, please don't let me embarrass myself," Lauria recalls thinking.

Lauria was told that he'd need to run over to the end zone before Tami called him over. "You want me to go fast?" Lauria asked the football coordinator. "Do you want me to light it up?"

"Yeah, do that," the coordinator responded.

Lauria took off sprinting across the field. He had never run in football cleats and certainly never on Astroturf. He fell, smack down, on his face.

Mortifying tumble aside, Lauria would develop a warm affection for those days out on the field. He still remembers standing shoulder-to-shoulder in the freezing night air between scenes, wrapped in thermal coats and blankets. It bonded the group of young men. He really felt like they were part of a team.

Sitting in that locker room before a game or during half-time always felt real in its own way, crammed onto benches too small to fit all the cold, sweating, smelly bodies. There was nothing quite like seeing Kyle Chandler in action, delivering one of his speeches. The lines between the actor and Coach blurred; Lauria looked up to Chandler and wanted to have an appropriate decorum around him.

Chandler could nail anything he was given, and even managed to make awkward sponsored content work. Like, that time NBC inked a deal with Applebee's, which involved Coach eating at the chain and saying, "Damn, these ribs are good."

"This is bullshit," Jeffrey Reiner thought when he got wind that they'd have to do product placement. Then Chandler said the line. "Holy shit," Reiner thought. The actor had actually managed to sell it. It felt real. And, you know what, Coach probably *would* have been a fan of Applebee's.

Chandler directed one episode of the show, "Texas Whatever." Lauria remembers sitting at Luke Cafferty's family's ranch, filming a serious conversation opposite Madison, when Chandler approached him. "Don't move. Don't do anything. Don't look away, don't shift your weight, just stand there," he said. "Just let us see it. If you believe it, we'll believe it. If you see it, we'll see it."

That was the lesson the young actors were told over and over again. One day, director Patrick Norris (who had worked with Katims on *My So-Called Life*) spotted Madison's script, which was covered in scribbles and notes to herself. "What's this?" he asked. He took the papers away. "You don't need it. Just say the words."

Madison's character was initially introduced as a young woman with a big, painful crush on Riggins. She comes from a fractured family and, in the beginning, pursues the football star's affection. Madison got the sense that Kitsch wasn't crazy about the story line between the two of them. The actors were never particularly close, and Kitsch's way of bonding was "busting [her] balls." Sometimes, she remembers, people would tell him, "Hey, can you not pick on her so bad? She's still a kid."

Maybe it helped the dynamic? I asked her. Becky is constantly chasing Tim's affection and can never quite get it. In some small way, she was getting a taste of that same experience.

"For sure," she responded, adding with a laugh, "everyone always asks me when they stop me, what was it like kissing Taylor Kitsch? I'm like, 'It was fucking awful! It's like kissing someone that you know really doesn't want to kiss you. It's terrible.'"

Madison's story line evolved past the Riggins crush. In the middle of Season 4, Becky gets pregnant after losing her virginity to Luke. What follows is an unflinchingly honest look at the pain and inner turmoil a tenth-grade girl might experience—from talking through her options, deciding that she's not ready to carry a child, having horribly painful conversations with doctors, and going through with her decision to have an abortion.

After the episode aired, critics took notice. Teen pregnancy hadn't really been tackled from the perspective of a young woman who has an abortion. Usually, in the case of shows and movies of that era like *Juno*, *Gilmore Girls*, and *The Secret Life of the American Teenager*, the character goes through with the pregnancy. This time, it didn't go that way, and *New York Times* television critic Ginia Bellafante wrote—maybe the writers were angling for a larger message.

"Dillon is a difficult place where improperly-cared-for children materialize one after another, week after week. In a subplot to Friday's episode, Vince, another gridiron prodigy, is forced to scramble around for money to pay for his mother's rehabilitation in the aftermath of a drug overdose, which leaves him begging her to stop and pay attention to him," Bellafante recounted. "Again and again, *Friday Night Lights* seems to remind us, as if in klieg lights, of the consequences of parenthood pursued by accident or default."

On the day Madison shot the scene of her character going into the doctor's office, one of the women who worked on the show's production team walked over and held her hand.

"My big sister got an abortion pre-*Roe v. Wade*," she said.

That was all she needed to say. Madison knew something awful must have happened. She didn't quite grasp how important the episode was until that moment.

I asked Madison if she heard from any fans after her story arc aired. Not that one specifically, she said. But another moment jumped to mind. A year or two after the show ended, she visited her cousin in Mississippi. They met up with a lesbian couple, both of whom were in the military. One of them told Madison that she loved *Friday Night Lights* and Becky was her favorite character. "It was exactly how I felt growing up," the woman told her. "Like, 'Why don't my parents love me? Why aren't they like other parents? Why don't they care about me? Why do they just drink and leave all the time?'"

Madison still thinks about that exchange. "I was sitting across from someone who, on the surface, we couldn't be more different," she said. "She's gay, I'm straight. She was in the military and identified herself as more masculine and at the time I was very, very girly. But she related to Becky about something that was universal."

She added: "That's what's so cool about the show. That's why everyone is like, 'Oh, yeah that football show but it's about so much more than football.'"

As writing for the final season went into full swing, the room grappled with where to take Tami and Coach's relationship. The couple was so solid and, after five years, the writers wondered if they needed to throw a wrench into (arguably) television's most beloved marriage. When Britton and Chandler got wind that there was a possible cheating story line in the works, they went straight to Hudgins, who was running the show at the time, to shut it down.

"They were like, 'No. These two are solid. We're not interested in a story where the Coach cheats. Or where Tami cheats. Or where Coach turns to the drink. The core of this show is these two people.'"

Hudgins tried to explain his side of the argument. "You realize from a dramatic storytelling point of view the hardest thing to do is not change?" he asked.

They didn't care. The couple could be put through the wringer in many other ways, but they wouldn't cheat on each other and they would survive whatever challenges they came up against. "We gave them story lines where it was potentially a disaster for the marriage and they always made it through," Hudgins told me. "I'm glad we did it. It was hard, it was challenging, it's a lot easier to do episodes where there's tons of conflict. But they're like, 'No, this is who we feel like these characters are.' I respect them for that."

One story line did feel certain for Coach and Tami, and it had been sitting in Hudgins's head since he discussed it with Katims in the beginning of the final season. The couple was going to leave Dillon and start their story somewhere else.

He had this image of a football being thrown during an East Dillon game, spiraling through the air and landing in a different state.

Tami would get a big job in Philadelphia. Coach would want to stay put in Dillon. As a viewer, it's infuriating to watch. Tami sacrificed a lot for her husband's coaching career, and now, when given the opportunity, he's refusing to do the same for her. It took five seasons, but I suddenly disliked Coach with a deep passion. Were they just trying to give us a jolt of conflict for the last episode? Was Coach a selfish partner? *Or* were the writers offering us a nuanced take on the complexities and imperfections of human beings? I was too filled with rage to dissect any of it.

My fury quickly settled. Coach eventually decides to go with Tami to Philadelphia in the end. Hudgins liked the idea of the two moving on to a new place and both starting all over again, molding a whole new generation of teens. "You just knew: OK, wow. Next little town, they're lucky. They've got Coach and Tami."

Madison and Lauria's last scene would be the two of them at a bus stop, saying goodbye. Their characters had found their way to each other in the end, and he tenderly handed her his ring right before heading off to the military.

All of a sudden, out of nowhere, Madison found herself hyperventilating. She couldn't stop crying. It was all hitting her that the show was over. "I didn't really know what I was supposed to do after that. Everyone was like, 'You need to move to L.A. and you need to capitalize on this . . . ' I'm like, 'What am I gonna do next? Am I going to see these people again? Am I going to work again?'"

Madison had become close to Jordan. The two lived near each other, and they'd go over scripts together or hang out and play video games. "He tried to give me a lot of advice about immediately moving to L.A., and you need to do this and you need to do that and get incorporated and get an accountant and all this stuff," she remembers. "A lot of his advice I took and then some of it I didn't. Life happens and whatever."

In that final scene, she was also crying because she was thinking about Luke and Becky. Becky had finally found someone who really cared about her. "I loved their story line. I loved Becky's resistance to Matt. You're so desperate for someone to love you and then someone comes along and you're like, 'Wait, but not you,'" she says with a laugh. "Then they ended up having a very sweet relationship."

The camera hadn't started rolling when Madison broke down. Lauria spotted her face as he looked out the window of the bus and yelled out, "Oh my God, roll, roll camera! Get it, get it!" He had learned the ways of *Friday Night Lights*.

Hudgins and Katims always knew that Tim Riggins was going to be the one character who they'd keep firmly planted in the town. "He might go to prison, he might date his neighbor, but he's the kid who's never leaving Dillon," Hudgins said. "Every small town has that guy."

The very last scene shot of the series was Tim Riggins and his brother Billy building a house on land that Tim had bought. The crew intentionally filmed at five p.m., magic hour, for that beautiful, golden light. As the two brothers crack a beer, Billy looks over at Tim. The Riggins boys have been through it all—an absent father, not enough money, crooked schemes, and jail. Now, sitting on this piece of land that belonged firmly to them, there was a feeling that they were both finally free. "Texas forever," Billy says. "Texas forever," Tim echoes. The two clink bottles.

Scott Porter felt strongly that Jason Street should be in that scene, too, so he came back to Austin and they filmed an alternate take with all three characters. Everybody gathered to watch that last shot, huddling in a field that felt like the middle of nowhere. "Cut" was called. "Wow, that's it," Hudgins remembers thinking. "Five years."

The whole group went out to a honky-tonk bar that night. As the evening wore on, someone had the idea to go to the Panthers stadium one last time for a game of touch football. It was midnight when the *Friday Night Lights* crew descended on that well-worn turf. The show's line producer was pulling her hair out. "You're not supposed to be doing that!" she said. "Somebody can get hurt, we're not supposed to be here!"

Everybody threw on practice jerseys from the show's wardrobe, swiped flags, and ran around the field. It would be the last game played on the Panthers field.

Friday Night Lights, the show that wasn't really about football, redefined what teen television, and what television in general, could be. A network series about high schoolers was a leading contender in prestige TV and it had fought an ardent mission to push every envelope from cinematography to storytelling. That scrappy show, which was built on experimental filmmaking and an elegant cocktail of genres, managed to stay on air for five seasons.

We had almost reached the precipice of teen television being anything it wanted to be.

Almost.

There was still one show that would take a jackhammer to TV as we knew it, melding absurd comedy, absolutely wacky melodrama, riveting musical numbers, groundbreaking plot lines, and a crazy fake pregnancy story that remains a head scratcher to this day. Time to head over to William McKinley High. Glee club is in session.

Glee

(2009–2015)

Mr. Schuester, a Spanish teacher in Lima, Ohio, is minutes away from giving up on his dreams. He's been desperate to take the helm of the school's glee club, assembling a ragtag group of outsiders to bring music to William McKinley High, a school dominated by jocks who throw oversized Big Quench slushies at anyone who doesn't fit in.

Schuester has been browbeaten by a staff disinterested in the performing arts and students who look down on the very concept of glee club. When his wife announces that she's pregnant, Mr. Schue decides it's best to throw in the towel and apply for a job in accounting.

Then, as he heads out for the day, feeling utterly defeated, he hears it. That small group of students who joined his club had decided to practice on their own in the auditorium. The gentle but mighty opening notes to "Don't Stop Believing" echo from the stage. As he watches them up there, joyfully singing their hearts out, Mr. Schue decides he's not ready to give up on his dreams. Little did he know in that moment, he was in for an epic journey with those kids, filled with fierce devotion, much strife, bring-down-the-house performances, questionable rap numbers, and a whole lot of glee.

When *Glee* creator Ryan Murphy was a child, his mom and grandmother took him to see *Funny Girl*. The young boy left the theater with two thoughts: "I'm gay" and "I'm going into show business." Murphy was an early dreamer with a clear vision. He grew up in Indianapolis but decorated his childhood room to look like the glitzy New York City nightclub Studio 54, complete with shag carpeting and a mirrored ceiling. When his dad overheard Murphy reciting the girl parts from *Gone with the Wind* (they had better lines than the boys!), he gave him a backhanded slap. He'd get another slap when he stole a single red-heeled shoe from a department store.

"Why don't I see myself in you?" Murphy's father would ask him during one of the many nights he'd wake his son up, bring him into the kitchen, and try to get to the bottom of their fundamental differences.

Murphy sought solace in his grandma Myrtle, who instilled in him that his uniqueness was an asset, not a curse. He'd go over to her house down the street and sit on a stool as she did her makeup. "You're special," she told him. "Don't let them tell you you're not."

Murphy moved to Hollywood in 1989, with $55 in his pocket and a desire to tell stories about achievers, with big dreams and even bigger ambitions. His first show was the 1999 WB teen series *Popular*, which *The A.V. Club* would retroactively deem "the perfect teen dramedy," filled with snark and "off-kilter gems." Much to the network's dismay, it was nothing like their ratings darling *Dawson's Creek*. The series was canceled after two seasons.

A decade later, Murphy would get a second chance to tell the great American high school story—this time, on a scale network TV had never seen.

The idea fell serendipitously in his lap. Murphy was handed a film script about a high school glee club; a dark comedy penned by first-time screenwriter Ian Brennan, which had originally been envisioned as an indie movie. Murphy, along with his writing and producing partner Brad Falchuk, had other ideas. The root of the idea worked, but they wanted to turn the script into a TV pilot packed with chart-topping pop songs and iconic hits from years past.

There was a time when this behemoth of a show, which would need to seamlessly mix heavy-duty musical theatre numbers, comedy, and drama, would have been a tough sell. But Fox was interested. They had struck gold with *American Idol*, a singing-competition show, and thought *Glee* just might have the legs to reach a similar market of fans.

"The show is unconventional," Fox president Kevin Reilly told the Associated Press at the time. "It is a bit genre-defying. It's got music, but it's not a musical.

It's got comedy but it's not a comedy. . . . It's set in a high school but it's not a high school show. It's sweet and uplifting but it is not saccharine. It's got edge and attitude."

When casting director Robert Ulrich was tapped to find multi-hyphenate young performers who could effortlessly sing, dance, and act their way through an episode, he was excited. But he had some reservations about this ambitious pilot script. How, Ulrich wondered, could all this ever get done for a pilot, let alone week to week?

There wasn't much time to worry. He had a show to cast.

Murphy wanted the kids of the glee club, which Mr. Schuester would later dub New Directions, to feel real and unpolished. He wasn't interested in big names—an exciting prospect for Ulrich, who was usually tasked with finding marquee players. The main requirement was that they could sing and act. There wouldn't be dance auditions, so Ulrich had to hope that the actors could pull off the moves once they started shooting.

The heart of the show would be Finn Hudson, a popular football player who eschews his status to become the pillar of the glee club. A lot was demanded of that character. Murphy wanted him to feel believable as a cool athlete but also excel as a natural musical performer. As time ticked on, it would prove to be one of the hardest roles to cast.

At 2:30 a.m. one sleepless night, still at the office and rifling through audition footage, Ulrich's casting associate, Alex Newman, popped in a VHS tape of an unknown Canadian actor. "Robert, come look at this guy," she said, excitedly. "I love his face. He reminds me of Ben Affleck."

The guy was Cory Monteith, a twenty-seven-year-old who dropped out of school in the ninth grade and had worked as a roofer, Walmart greeter, and telemarketer. He didn't have professional acting or singing experience, but he'd had a few one-line parts in film projects around Vancouver and was playing drums in a local band. He filmed himself hammering away on Tupperware and wineglasses with pencils in his manager's office.

Ulrich called Monteith in for an audition. Fox wouldn't pay his airfare, so he hopped in his car and drove all the way from Vancouver to Los Angeles, blasting songs from *Rent* and teaching himself how to sing each one. He performed

"Honesty" by Billy Joel for his audition and beat out twenty-five other guys, who all had that cookie-cutter athlete look. Monteith didn't have the singing chops totally down, Ulrich remembers, but he had that je ne sais quoi: charming, funny, so enjoyable to watch.

Chris Colfer, eighteen, from Clovis, California, had even less experience than Monteith. He was fresh out of high school when his dad drove him roughly three and a half hours to his *Glee* audition. Colfer was trying out for the role of Artie, a student who doesn't fit into the social pyramid because he is in a wheelchair. The teen showed up wearing a black polo shirt, black Converse, and a messenger bag slung over his shoulder.

"Why do I have the feeling you've been Rolf in *The Sound of Music* before?" Murphy asked in his signature dry, deadpan way.

"I played Kurt," Colfer responded.

"Kurt! Close."

"Yeah," Colfer said with a sheepish grin. "I have Von Trapp written all over me." He sang "Mr. Cellophane" from *Chicago*, and Murphy was struck by his talent. He had never seen or heard anyone quite like him. Colfer didn't fit the role of Artie, or any of the characters written in the pilot script for that matter, but Murphy was intrigued.

So, he wrote a role especially for Colfer. Murphy named the character Kurt, a talented singer who could hit a high note like no other (while casually brushing the bangs from his forehead), had an eye for fashion, and was the target of bullies at William McKinley High. Kurt starts out the show in the closet and, if you can believe it, before Murphy met him, there hadn't been a gay character written into the *Glee* pilot.

For the rest of the cast, Ulrich assembled a whole group of triple-threat performers—and it's an extensive list, so buckle up. Amber Riley blew him away with her rendition of "And I Am Telling You I'm Not Going" from *Dreamgirls* and landed the role of the fiercely talented Mercedes Jones. Naya Rivera, who walked into Ulrich's office so confident and so beautiful, was cast as Santana Lopez, then a bit part for the pilot. Dianna Agron's sweet "Fly Me to the Moon" got her the role of cheerleader Quinn Fabray. Jenna Ushkowitz belted out "Waiting for Life to Begin" and won the part of goth outcast Tina Cohen-Chang. Kevin McHale got the role of Artie after his soulful "Let It Be" rendition. Heather Morris would play the small part of Brittany S. Pierce, who was later expanded into a central role. Mark Salling was cast as Noah Puckerman, the show's resident tough guy.

And Lea Michele, a Broadway veteran, landed the role of Rachel Berry, an ultra-ambitious teen with a tunnel vision for stardom. Ulrich still remembers meeting Michele for the first time. There was a scene in the pilot, which later got cut, that involved Rachel slapping Finn. In Michele's first audition, she walked over and slapped Ulrich, who was reading opposite her. She did it again for the network test.

The adult cast included Matthew Morrison as Mr. Schuester, Jane Lynch as the wicked, tracksuit-wearing cheerleading coach Sue Sylvester, and Jayma Mays as the kind if occasionally misguided guidance counselor Ms. Pillsbury.

William McKinley High School was filmed at three separate locations for the pilot: high schools in Long Beach and Burbank, and a junior college east of Pasadena. Later, production designer Mark Hutman would build replicas of those locations onto a Paramount sound stage. The choir room was loosely based on Murphy's memories of his own high school choir room, which he described in detail to Hutman. It would be the featured set of the show, though Murphy expressed early concern that using that space over and over again would get boring.

"Everything gets boring to him. It got boring to me too," Hutman told me. "That is why we had dance numbers in the auditorium, in the choir room, at a car wash, in people's bedrooms, in the gym. How do you keep anything fresh?"

Hutman later designed the choir room so that the wall with the whiteboard was built on rollers, allowing them to be pulled out and broaden the scope of the shots. On the other side of the choir room was Mr. Schuester's office, which had a window that looked out on the hallway, where extras walked back and forth. There were complaints because more extras meant more money. "Look," Hutman would respond, "I'm not here to break the bank but I am trying to provide the executive producer what he's asked for, which is something cinematic, something with depth, movement, people."

As the crew prepped for the pilot, Christopher Baffa, the show's cinematographer, still wasn't entirely sure he knew how they were going to make this whole musical format work. He turned to Murphy. "We're not gonna have people break into song, right?" he asked, concerned. "I don't know that people nowadays will understand that or appreciate it. It might be jarring."

"I don't think so," Murphy reassured him. "I think we'll always cut to somebody singing and then even if there's a full orchestra behind them, in the end it will be as if it was in their mind."

That all went out the window early on when Murphy directed Agron to burst directly into song. "You're gonna slam the locker, turn, and start singing," Murphy told her, and then looked over at Baffa with a boyish grin. It was kind of adorable, Baffa recalls, because his whole face playfully read: "Baffa's not gonna agree."

"Whoa," Baffa interjected. "What are we doing?" Again, reassurance. "Let's shoot it," Murphy said. "I think your assumption was accurate, but I'm curious."

Strangely, it worked. It felt like they were breaking the rules, but it worked.

Character development was happening on the fly as well. Jessalyn Gilsig, who was cast in the role of Terri Schuester, Will's wife and high school sweetheart, didn't have a real sense of who her character was ahead of shooting. As Gilsig walked from her trailer to set for her very first scene, Murphy stopped her. "Listen, I don't know who Terri is," he said.

Gilsig had about 200 feet to figure it out herself. "I basically made the decision that she was still seventeen, that she was still living in the mindset of a high school student," she told me. "I decided that right there and then and that's how I ended up with a higher voice. Then, that was it. I came up with Terri."

Murphy wasn't one to give notes, she remembers, but he did come over to her after one take. "Poor Terri," he said. "She's always right." That's how Gilsig felt too. On the surface, Terri was this manipulative, crazed partner who eventually fakes a pregnancy. But underneath, she was a wife who was watching her husband fall in love with the school's guidance counselor.

"I had always felt she's going insane because he's straying and she can feel it but he's denying it and the world is telling her it's not happening. But she's right. And it drives her mad."

The pilot's final, pivotal scene would have the kids belting out "Don't Stop Believing" in the auditorium. The group was originally going to wear color-coordinated, performance-ready bell bottoms, which the costume department had borrowed from an actual high school glee club. The day before they filmed, Murphy changed his mind.

"Hey," he told Lou Eyrich, the show's costume designer. "I want them to look more real. Let's have it more DIY." He chose red for the color of the T-shirts, which Eyrich cut up and styled for each character. The actors slipped into blue jeans and black Converse sneakers and they were ready to go.

Rewatching that performance is just as moving and arm-hair-raising as the first time it aired. The teens are so full of optimism. It's not corny, just powerfully sweet and hopeful. After being knocked around the whole episode, they've earned this wonderful moment, and so have we. The scene is the embodiment of that quote we see flashed on the screen earlier in the episode, credited to Mr. Schue's former choir teacher, Lillian Adler: "By its very definition, Glee is about opening yourself up to joy."

Baffa doesn't use the word "magical" lightly, but that's what it felt like watching the actors in the auditorium that day. "God, you've really done something here," Baffa said to Murphy. He wasn't alone in his assessment. Steve Perry, the lead singer of Journey, was on hand that day, and when Murphy introduced Baffa to him, the singer said, "I'm very grateful for *Glee.*"

Baffa was startled. "For what?"

"Now another generation is experiencing these songs," Perry said.

Fox went all out promoting their hot-ticket show. They scheduled the pilot after the finale of their juggernaut *American Idol* and released the pilot episode online, alongside behind-the-scenes footage and interactive singing competitions. All the stars aligned for this one. It was a great pilot, had a ton of backing from its network, and arrived in the television world at just the right time. *Glee* pulled in a whopping 9.62 million during its first airing. Fox had an immediate hit on its hands.

Glee's first season was a colorful hodgepodge of stories, all written by Murphy, Falchuk, and Brennan. Quinn gets pregnant after having sex with Puck but tells Finn that the baby is his, even though they never had sex (still a head-scratcher). Terri Schuester fakes a pregnancy to keep Will in her life. The teens take performance-enhancing Vitamin D. Amid a lot of wackiness, *Glee* was creating groundbreaking musical numbers, which required painstaking effort from every single production department. In one episode, "The Power of Madonna," the show would re-create, with incredible precision, frame by frame, outfit by outfit, the exact iconic music video for "Vogue," as performed by Sue Sylvester.

The young actors, Gilsig remembers, were doing so much of the heavy lifting. The adults got to sleep in for a few hours, but the kids were there constantly, dancing, singing, and acting. Monteith especially stood out to her. The two shared a scene where Terri moonlights as the school's nurse and Finn arrives, exhausted, just hoping to take a nap.

"That character was a real transformation. That's not who he was in my experience of him," she told me. "Oh my God, he's so good. He's so good in that scene."

After they were done shooting, Gilsig turned to Monteith. "How do you do it?" she asked. She wanted to know the secret behind the character of Finn.

"Oh, before the scene starts I empty my head," Monteith responded simply.

It was really something else watching those performers in action. Dot-Marie Jones, who played Coach Beiste, the school's football coach, remembers sitting on one of those stools in the choir room, getting a firsthand taste of their talent. New Directions sang a tender version of "Shake It Off," after Coach Beiste leaves her husband, who has been physically and verbally abusing her.

In that moment, Jones forgot that the camera was on her. She found herself tearing up. Their voices were just so beautiful. "I can still hear it and I can still see it and it still gives me . . . " She sighed, trailing off as she described it to me.

After that episode aired, Jones received letters from women and some men, telling her that the story line gave them the strength and the courage to get out of an abusive relationship. "Oh, honey," Jones would write back. "I'm so proud of you."

There was a real art to successfully filming the choir scenes. Every dirty look and baffled expression from the risers needed to be diligently captured. It was a complex, layered experience to shoot, Baffa remembers. So much of the scenes was about getting those looks for the camera, each building on the other to create a cohesive story. "Finn is reacting to something Rachel is doing, but then Quinn is noticing that Finn's reacting and then somebody who has a crush on Quinn is noticing her reacting to Finn reacting," Baffa said, adding: "It's heartbreaking that this person is looking at this other person with such love and it's unrequited."

By September 20, 2009, *Glee*'s version of "Don't Stop Believing," which retailed on iTunes for $1.99, had been downloaded 400,000 times. Five of *Glee*'s covers cracked the iTunes top 100, including Kanye West's "Gold Digger," Salt-N-Pepa's "Push It," and REO Speedwagon's "Can't Fight This Feeling." The Gleeks, as *Glee* fans affectionately called themselves, had arrived.

That summer, New Directions took their talents out of the classroom. *Glee Live* would be a seven-date tour, kicking off in Phoenix, Arizona, and ending at New York City's Radio City Music Hall, where it would be a three-night sold-out show. The cast sang staples from the first season's repertoire on a stage designed to look like the choir room.

The success of the first tour spurred a second round the following summer, which I—a self-identifying Gleek—attended, wearing a red floral dress from Urban Outfitters and a pink Nordstrom button-down sweater, both of which were identical matches to costume pieces Rachel Berry wore on the show (really earning my Gleek badge of honor here). It was a joyous experience watching the cast, in their matching red T-shirts, sing "Don't Stop Believing" live. The whole theater reverberated from applause when those first few "doo-doo-doo" notes drifted from the stage.

While writing this chapter, I connected with a friend of a friend, Michael—a fellow Gleek—to find out about his tour experience. "Glee Live was so fucking loud," he told me over the phone.

"When the show started, screams beyond belief—beyond belief!"

Merch stands sold big foam "loser" fingers and Michael purchased one, waving it in a sea of matching red *L*'s. He really loved *Glee*, even when he was eye-rolling and discussing episodes that jumped the shark.

"You mentioned you had a *Glee* poster—what other *Glee* merch did you have?" I asked.

"Did I say poster?" Michael quickly corrected himself. "I meant to make that plural. I had *posters*. Multiple posters. Some of them were signed by all of [the cast]. OK, are you ready for this?"

Michael had a set of *TV Guide Glee* covers, a *Glee* lanyard, *Glee* 3-D glasses, the *Glee Live* CD Special Edition, several calendars, a drawstring bag, "T-shirts up the wazoo," and *Glee*-themed Christmas ornaments. ("That's ornaments, plural.")

He was a freshman in high school when the show premiered, and watching that pilot felt "monumental." Michael found himself drawn into the relationship between Kurt and Blaine, a glee club member from Dalton Academy, a competing school. Blaine, played by Darren Criss, was confident, charismatic, and electric when he sang. He gave Kurt strength.

"I was one of the kids who didn't fit in with everyone else. I was still in the closet," Michael said. "Seeing Kurt and Blaine coming into their own and not caring about what the world has to say. Seeing two gay men encourage each other to be themselves at such a young age and having Blaine be the one who's keeping Kurt happy and confident. That's something I felt I needed at the time too."

Aside from his sexuality, Michael didn't relate to Kurt—he found him whiny and annoying—but he loved Rachel. She was always the target of ridicule, but she rose above it. "She kept going and everybody started to somewhat like her in the end," he said. "Her determination and drive was something that I connected with." He stuck a gold star next to his name on a school assignment, just like Rachel.

In Season 3, Murphy, Falchuk, and Brennan decided to alleviate their load and build out the writers' room. That's when Ross Maxwell, who would go on to write on teen hits like *Riverdale* and *Chilling Adventures of Sabrina*, came on board. He still remembers the awe he felt stepping through the grand iron gates of Paramount Studios for the first time. It was like he had entered some sort of dream factory. He walked by one sound stage and saw a person half-dressed as a robot. Plaques hung around the studio, detailing which legendary films and TV shows had been shot there. The building right across the way from where *Glee* filmed had been used for *Cheers*.

Then Maxwell stepped into a warehouse sound stage. Suddenly, there he was, inside a living, breathing Midwestern high school. There were several classrooms, two hallways that intersected, and a full-blown auditorium with lighting rigs. The theatre kid inside Maxwell felt his mind being blown.

Maxwell had studied for his first day in the writers' room. He watched every episode and, using a giant sketchpad, mapped out each of the central characters and how they related to one another. In his interview for the show, he had been asked about his favorite character, and he was savvy enough not to pick a starring one. ("They're not going to want to hear that you want to write for Rachel. They've got that covered.") Instead, he truthfully highlighted some of the supporting roles at the time who spoke to his sensibility—Artie, Brittany, and Emma Pillsbury.

Falchuk, Maxwell learned, loved the romantic stuff. He could nail a dramatic scene with Rachel and Finn. Anything that felt hard and had emotion to it—Falchuk was their guy. Murphy was the mastermind behind story structure. He also loved style and design and always wanted to make sure that an episode felt grand. "This isn't exciting enough," he'd say. "We need to go crazy with it."

As a junior writer, Maxwell was initially tasked with crafting scene directions for musical numbers. On one level, it was kind of frustrating, because he didn't get to write dialogue. But he invested in his assignments, carefully thinking through where the number would be set and which character would be singing which lyric. Stage directions could mean all the difference in a scene. In the fourth season, Marley Rose and Jake musically duel in a mash-up of Janet Jackson's "Nasty/Rhythm Nation." Maxwell had to figure out, with surgical precision, how to transition the characters from the school hallway to the perfectly re-created factory-like set from Jackson's original "Rhythm Nation" music video.

He settled on a moment when Bree, one of the cheerleaders, raises her hand to slap Jake. "You know my first name ain't baby. It's Janet. Ms. Jackson, if you're nasty," she says. Just as she's about to hit him, he grabs her wrist and we're smoothly transported into this alternate universe.

Often, Murphy would come into the writers' room and have an episode idea in mind. Usually it would be a theme, like love or tolerance, that could be neatly written by Mr. Schue on the white board in the beginning of the episode. No matter what strife went down for New Directions, there was almost always going to be a happy ending. Sure, every once in a while an episode ended on a bittersweet note, but more often you'd feel the warm glow of camaraderie in that auditorium, right before the signature "doo doo doo" of the final credits rolled. That was just inherent to the show's writing. It was an aspirational world.

"There were obviously bullying story lines because those are easy, go-to ways to express any sort of pain or hurt," Maxwell told me. "But ultimately, we triumphed. This was a world in which Kurt, little Kurt, had the backing of his friends."

Kurt's blue-collar dad, Burt, played by Mike O'Malley, was a mechanic who, in a different kind of show, might have been abusive or dismissive of his gay son. But Maxwell remembers it was important to Murphy that although Burt didn't quite understand his son at first, he never stopped showing how much he cared for him.

When Murphy came out to his dad as a teen, he was beaten with a belt until he was bloody. Many years later, Murphy would write his own version of that coming-out moment for Kurt. This time, he had the chance to rewrite history.

"I'm gay," Kurt tells his father, quietly, in the episode "Preggers."

Burt looks him square in the eye.

"I know," he says, not missing a beat.

"You do?"

"I've known since you were three. All you wanted for your birthday was a pair of sensible heels. I guess I'm not totally in love with the idea, but if that's who you are, there's nothing I can do about it. And I love you just as much. OK?"

As he watched behind the camera, Baffa was continuously struck by O'Malley's performance. The actor always pushed for his character to avoid being a cookie-cutter version of a father who completely understands his son. "Can I take a minute and take it in?" he'd ask Murphy while discussing an interaction with Kurt. "Or can I rub my eyes and then pull back?"

"Mike was so brilliant at physical acting," Baffa said. "Sometimes it would just be how he'd sit down and take his cap off in a way like, 'OK, I don't even know how to have this conversation but I know I have to have this conversation.'"

Murphy was shocked by the feedback after "Preggers" aired. Suddenly, he was getting messages like, "That episode made me talk to my dad" or "That episode showed me how to talk to my child."

Maybe the show could be preachy, Murphy said. But it was making an impact. It meant so much to him when he'd look out into the audience of those *Glee* tours and see teens in wheelchairs who had been driven by their parents across three states because they wanted to watch one of the show's stars, Artie, a character who looked like them, on the stage.

Few of the writers would get the kind of insight into Murphy, Falchuk, and Brennan's process that Jess Meyer had. Meyer got her start as a writers' assistant and would watch the trio sit around a table and go over everything that had been discussed in the writers' room that day. There, she got to know Murphy's inner workings. He was so confident in who he was, deeply opinionated and unquestioning of himself. He could be intimidating too. When she became a staff writer, she knew not to take it personally when Murphy had a big, negative reaction to one of her pitches. "Wow, he really didn't like that," she'd think, shrugging it off.

Growing up, Meyer found comfort in teen shows. She hated high school—it was a dark place where she never felt cool or accepted—and series like *Dawson's Creek* and *Gilmore Girls* were her safe haven, slipping away into the cozy fantasy worlds of Capeside and Stars Hollow. Getting a writing job on *Glee* was this rare opportunity to rewrite her own adolescent experience, with total and complete agency. "You can make fun of all the bullies and bullshit and the things that truly felt like they were world-ending," she told me. "You get to control what happens or who falls in love or how they get to fall in love."

Ali Adler, a TV writer who had come off Josh Schwartz's show *Chuck*, would quickly learn firsthand just how exhilarating and emotional it was to be a writer on *Glee*. The day of Adler's interview with Falchuk, she was reeling from a breakup, had just moved out of her girlfriend's house, and was crashing at a friend's guest home.

She walked into Falchuk's office, a renovated loft at Paramount Studios that Murphy had redone, and encountered her interviewer, who looked like a gorgeous jock straight out of a John Hughes film. Adler is a self-described buttoned-up type, but when Falchuk opened the conversation by asking her where she lived, she started to cry.

Much to her surprise, this beautiful man gently explained that he understood her pain. He, too, was going through a hard time in his relationship. The duo really got into it, discussing their intimate feelings and experiences. It was a *Glee*-like lesson, seeing this guy who she had assumed was one kind of person turn out to be someone so different.

Adler left the meeting thinking she had either "fucked up that job interview or fucking nailed that job interview." She fucking nailed it.

Later, Falchuk told Adler that he knew she was right for the show the second a tear fell from her eye. "The job is about relaying emotions," he explained. "I was just so excited to work with someone who had so much heart."

On Adler's second day of work, she was told to write a sequence around Beyoncé's song "Run the World (Girls)." She put her head down and dreamed up a complex scene that featured a flash mob starting in the hallways and ending in the auditorium, a frenetic performance of Brittany and the Cheerios tearing up the floor as the school band encircled them. The next day, Murphy told Adler to go to the set. There, she watched as her vision was brought to life, with 250 extras packed into that auditorium, Morris leading the charge, and a crane shot capturing it all.

"Every time I hear that song I think of that experience," Adler told me. "It was just so powerful to be a part of something so big."

Elodie Keene, who we last saw helming the series finale of *My So-Called Life*, would direct a total of seven episodes, including landmarks like "Bad Reputation" (featuring "Run Joey Run," which lives rent-free in every Gleek's head).

So much prep went into each of those episodes, Keene remembers, from pre-recording the music to setting the choreography, "That's never going to happen," she thought. "The scripts are going to start coming in late and all of a sudden everybody's going to start to scramble." Keene was right. That neat template lasted only a few episodes into the first season before things unraveled and everyone had to figure out how to keep up with this challenging new format.

The first year, she remembers, the actors were so excited to be there. Then, they were pushed very, very hard. Already exhausted from shooting, they were sent on that sweeping multistate tour.

"They were tired and they got stepped on by the powers that be, just like, 'Shut up and be grateful,'" she remembers. While the young actors were being run ragged, they were also being showered with excessive gifts and perks. One day, the Audi company showed up with some of their swankiest cars as a gift for the cast to drive for the week. "They're kids," Keene said. "They never had a pot to pee in and suddenly they're driving a $200,000 sports car."

Elodie Keene and Tate Donovan who, following *The O.C.*, had gotten deeper into the world of directing—described it as a singular experience of sorts.

Donovan's first episode for *Glee* was a sweet, memorable one, "Silly Love Songs." It's Valentine's Day and romance is on the brain for New Directioners. Kurt tells Blaine he has feelings for him and the episode is peppered with buoyant love songs, like "P.Y.T." and "When I Get You Alone."

"That was a hundred-and-eighty-degree difference [from] directing the teens in *The O.C.*," Donovan remembers. "[The *Glee*] kids were so hardworking and were just intensely into the show and into their characters. If they weren't shooting a scene, they were rehearsing a dance number or recording a song. It was like theatre camp. Twenty-four hours a day." Donovan felt like a teacher as he stood in front of the choir room, all the actors laughing, flirting, and goofing around.

There was an experimental feel to the whole thing. When Donovan was shooting the musical sequence for "P.Y.T.," a sound guy approached him.

"Hey, man, you should do it at high speed and it will look awesome," he suggested. "It will look like slow motion."

"Dude, do you think you can do that?" Donovan asked.

"Yeah," the sound guy replied. "I'll talk to somebody."

It ended up looking just as cool as they imagined it would, with Mike Chang gracefully dancing through the hallway in an almost dreamlike state, and Brittany and Tina waiting by the lockers, looking coquettish as Artie smoothly belts out the lyrics with his signature vocal swagger.

The second episode Donovan directed, "I Kissed a Girl," was a big one. Santana comes out to her grandmother. The scene was based on a conversation that Adler had with her own grandmother when she came out to her at eighteen. After she shared that part of herself, her grandmother never spoke to her again. "You make your choices and I make mine," she told Adler.

Adler pitched the idea in the writers' room. "What if she comes out to her abuela and her abuela just says no?" Adler suggested. "That's real for a lot of people. And it's not like there's a cute, happy ending and she sees the error in her ways." Adler wrote that scene, weaving in dialogue pulled directly from her own experience.

Santana is sitting in her grandmother's kitchen when it happens. At first, she stumbles as she tries to get the words out. "I've watched you my whole life," she begins. "And you've always been so strong. Done exactly what you believe, and never cared about what anyone else thought of you . . . "

"Tell me about your life, I know mine," her grandmother responds. So, Santana starts talking.

"Abuelita . . . I love girls the way that I'm supposed to feel about boys . . . I've tried so hard to push this feeling away, and keep it locked inside . . . but every day just feels like a war. I walk around so mad at the world, but I'm really just fighting with myself. I don't want to fight anymore. I'm just too tired. I have to just be me."

Her grandmother sits there silently.

"Say something, please," Santana begs.

"Everyone has secrets, Santana," she responds. "They're called secrets for a reason. I want you to leave this house. I don't ever want to see you again."

"Abuela, you . . . "

"Go."

"You don't . . . "

"Now."

As she watched the scene unfold from behind the monitor, Adler cried. Looking back now, it was cathartic. "I'm sorry that I missed out on my oma's life, I'm sorry she missed out on mine and my kids,'" she told me. "I'm glad that we got to show that because so many people have that experience too. They get to know that they're OK because it's happened to a lot of other people."

The script said that Rivera should be weeping when her grandmother rejects her. The actor diligently did just that. ("Naya could pop a tear like nobody's business," Donovan remembers.) But something told him that she shouldn't cry during that scene.

"I think save the tears; let *us* cry rather than you cry," Donovan told Rivera.

Later, Donovan found out that Murphy was angry that he didn't get the shot of Rivera crying. "So, that was a point against me," Donovan cheerfully recalls.

Santana does cry later in that episode. Finn sings a gentle, slow version of "Girls Just Want to Have Fun" to her in the choir room, and the tears slowly come. Donovan made sure that Monteith's performance felt stripped down and simple that day.

"We just kept trying to get him to not perform it," Donovan said. "He's a great singer and performer, and [we wanted] to have him let the song and the moment happen. The choreography was super simple. You run the risk of being boring.

But a really good script has hills and valleys, and this is a valley that I really wanted to have. That's one of my favorite moments that I had with those guys."

Baffa had his own memory of Rivera and her ability to nail those really emotional scenes. In one particularly heavy moment, Santana rushes off the stage and slaps Finn across the face when she thinks he's mocking her. The anger was on the page, Baffa remembers. But she brought another layer to it, this simmering, raw pain just underneath. Afterward, as Rivera was wiping away her tears, Baffa approached her.

"I just thought that was beautiful," he said.

"Thank you so much," she replied.

"You brought other levels than just anger, which made it so much more interesting and real and powerful."

It's hard to fit in every wonderful thing people told me about Naya Rivera. But I'll try, in their words.

Rivera died tragically in 2020 while boating with her four-year-old son, Josey, on Lake Piru, a reservoir in California's Los Padres National Forest. Josey, who was found asleep on the boat later that day, told authorities that he saw his mom disappear under the water after she boosted him into the boat. Ventura County Sheriff Bill Ayub suspected that in her final moments, she was saving her son. "She mustered enough energy to get her son back onto the boat, but not enough to save herself," Ayub said.

An autopsy determined that she had died from an accidental drowning.

"Naya could do it all. You could give her a meaty drama scene, she'd tear it up. You could give her a really challenging song, she'd do great. She could dance to anything and she was striking," Baffa said. "I think that one of the biggest tragedies is that she really could have been something remarkably huge, because there wasn't anything she couldn't do."

When I asked Jess Meyer about her proudest writing moments on *Glee*, she responded: "Any line of dialogue I got to write for Naya Rivera. She was a fucking star. She would show up and knock a monologue out on the first try. She lived and breathed that role. Getting to write for her was one of the best things I've ever gotten to do."

Later in our conversation, she mused on Santana: "That was a character who showed very few cracks in the veneer and boldly was determined to be herself and go after the things she wanted in this world."

Sometimes Meyer will go on YouTube and look up a commercial that was written for Santana's character, in which she hawks Yeast-I-Stat, a yeast-infection medication, all while cheesily running around with a floaty ribbon and beaming from a swing. So many actors would have refused to shoot a commercial like that, Meyer said. But Rivera was completely game.

"She came to set and brought it so hard," Meyer remembers. "That feels like a career high to me. That character will never stop living in my brain . . . for the rest of time."

After Rivera died, tributes poured in. Not just from people who knew her but from so many fans who had fallen in love with her performance as the fierce, funny teen with razor-sharp pride in who she was.

"As a lonely queer Chicana growing up central in Texas, it was monumental to see a character like Santana Lopez from *Glee* be unapologetically herself," Polly Anna Rocha wrote in an essay for *them*, following the death of Rivera. "When Santana confidently strutted down the fictional halls of McKinley High in her signature Cheerios uniform, millions of people were watching, including women and girls like me who had been waiting for a main character to represent both femme queerness and Latinidad on a major network television show."

Rivera knew how much Santana meant to struggling teens. In 2017, she penned a love letter to the LGBTQ+ community for *Billboard* in honor of Gay Pride Month.

Here's how she ended it:

"We are all put on this earth to be a service to others and I am grateful that for some, my Cheerios ponytail and sassy sashays may have given a little light to someone somewhere, who may have needed it."

Season 3 had the New Directions marching toward graduation. The writers of *Glee* began to grapple with the question that so many of their teen TV show predecessors had asked themselves. *How* in the world do we do this? Some methods were simple. Members of the glee club—like Blaine, Tina, and Sam—would be positioned as juniors, so the writers could keep parts of the show grounded at William McKinley High. Rachel would head to New York to attend the fictional performing arts school NYADA. Brittany, who by all accounts does not seem to be passing any of her classes, gets into the ultra-prestigious MIT (another time that the show gleefully leaned into the baffling).

In the midst of mapping out the characters' futures, the writers contemplated how to keep the New Directions the scrappy musical underdogs. It was an ongoing give-and-take. They would need to continuously give the kids an exciting win, like placing first at regionals, then knock them right back down again with a loss.

By that point, *Glee* had a finely tuned system for making those big final performances as dizzyingly exciting and can't-take-your-eyes-away compelling as possible. When it came time to shoot competitors, like Vocal Adrenaline, the camera operators would film wide shots from the audience, so the viewers wouldn't feel emotionally connected to the performers and, if anything, the rival groups should come off as one big faceless enemy.

It was a whole other story when New Directions performed. The cameras were up on the stage with them, capturing intimate, dynamic shots and tracking those crucial reaction shots like, as Baffa remembers, "Quinn's singing and dancing but she's looking at Finn and Finn's looking at her but then he's seeing Rachel seeing him look at her."

As Rachel, Kurt, Mercedes, and multiple others prepared to move on from the halls of William McKinley High, it was time to stack the cast with some new faces. And that's where *The Glee Project* comes in.

Samuel Larsen, a seventeen-year-old aspiring performer, was scrolling through MySpace one day when he saw a casting announcement for Season 2 of *Glee*. People were encouraged to send in videos with an introduction about themselves and a song. Larsen was really into the show when he discovered it in its first season. He liked the idea of all these different people coming together over their shared love of music.

Still, he didn't take the audition call seriously. "What's gonna come of that?" he said when he offhandedly mentioned it to his mom. The teen was about to go hang out with some of his friends, but his mom stopped him. "You're not allowed to go out and leave until you make that video," she told him. She handed him a camera and he obliged, retreating to his room to shoot some footage of himself singing "You Can't Always Get What You Want" by the Rolling Stones.

The deadline for when applicants were supposed to hear back came and went. "Told you," Larsen said to his mom.

Then he got a message in his Facebook inbox telling him to reach out to Robert Ulrich, the show's casting director. He wanted him to come in for the role of Sam Evans, a lovably goofy transfer student who would end up joining the New Directions and the school's football team, as well as romance several of the characters, including Quinn and Santana.

As Larsen went through the audition process for Sam, he remembers sticking out like a sore thumb. Larsen didn't look like most teens you saw on television. He had long dreadlocks, buttoned very few buttons on his shirt, and didn't tend to wear shoes. The six or seven guys who had made it to the last stages of the casting process looked the part of a typical jock.

"Can you button your shirt more for the callback?" Ulrich suggested, kindly. "Let's give you a fighting chance here."

The part ended up going to Chord Overstreet, a singer and actor from Nashville, and Larsen remembers how hard it was watching Overstreet on TV every week in the role he wanted so badly.

But Ulrich didn't forget about Larsen.

He reached back out with an unusual opportunity. *Glee* was getting a spin-off reality show of sorts called *The Glee Project*. Thousands of aspiring performers would compete to be on the program, which would be a week-by-week contest for the chance to win a role on the hit show. It was a grueling experience, where contestants would perform for guest judges, film music videos, and, if they landed in the dreaded bottom three, stand on a stage in front of Ryan Murphy and sing a song as a Hail Mary to stay for another episode.

"I was pissed off," Larsen told me with a laugh. "Thousands of kids. I was like, 'What? I was down to six people, you want to throw me in with a thousand people? This sucks.' So I kind of ignored it and they emailed me again and were like, 'Hey, we know you must be upset. We're not gonna throw you in the very beginning, we'll throw you in when there's like 250 people.'"

Larsen had already been on *American Idol*, where he made it to the top forty-eight. If he was going to brave another reality TV show, he decided he needed to go in with a strategy. When he arrived, everyone was singing their highest high notes and dancing their hardest. "I remember thinking, 'You guys are gonna be stuck. [The producers] are going to be like 'More of that!' . . . and you're like, 'That's literally all I have.'" Larsen decided to hold back in the beginning. He would carefully do *just* enough to get by without standing out as bad or good.

Talking to Larsen, it's no surprise that he would eventually walk away as the show's winner. He personified the grit and scrappiness that Kurt, Rachel, Mercedes, and so many of the New Directions members displayed in their unabashed quest to make it. The motto, he explained to me, was: "Let's go get the job."

Damian McGinty, a member of Celtic Thunder, a popular Irish singing group, would tie with Larsen for first place that season. At first, he felt out of place. His competitors were so theatrical and over-the-top. McGinty wasn't really built that way. And then, he remembers, there was the dreaded Vulnerability Week when each contestant had to write their darkest insecurity on a sandwich board. He turned to his friend Cameron, who was also competing on the show, and the two exchanged looks. "God, I just—I don't have a card to play at all," he thought.

As time went on, McGinty became more comfortable in this strange new reality TV setting. It felt as if he was going through a *Glee* boot camp of sorts. One evening, they filmed a music video for a medley of the songs "Ice Ice Baby" and "Under Pressure." The shoot took place in a high school, ending in the wee hours of the morning, and McGinty experienced his very first slushie in the face.

"How bad was it?" I asked.

"So bad," he said. "It is so bad." That would turn out to be one of his favorite videos they filmed, but man, did everyone get butchered.

Larsen was very, very nervous on his first day of shooting *Glee*. When he watched his first appearance after it aired, he cried. "I thought I was so bad," he said. He could tell how terrified he was on-screen. Later, he'd learn to loosen up, and he gives Monteith a lot of credit for that.

Don't take this too seriously, Monteith would urge the performer. Sometimes he would joke: "This is ridiculous, isn't it? You're a TV star now. Let's have some fun."

McGinty was given that same kindness. The first song he performed was a wistful version of "Bein' Green." The cast gathered to watch him perform, and he couldn't help but feel judged. It was nothing personal but he knew they didn't like the whole concept of *The Glee Project*. "Am I good enough?" he wondered. "Am I worthy of this spot on the show?"

Relief came in the form of Monteith. McGinty's first acting scenes were with the show's quarterback and, when they were done shooting, the two walked back to their trailers together. "Soak it in," he remembers Monteith telling him. "It's going to be crazy, but be present and enjoy it as much as possible."

As McGinty was changing out of his costume, he saw that Monteith had tweeted: "Great scene tonight with @damianmcginty . . . season three is lookin gooooood. . . . . :)" The name-check meant so much to McGinty. In that moment, he felt like he had earned his right to be there.

As Larsen's character arc unfolded, he had to learn to stop judging himself. It was so hard to get a note from a director about his performance and not spiral out of control. "Oh my God, they hate me," he'd think. But then he started to notice that all the big-name actors had those moments. "I think that really helped," he said. "I was like, 'Darren just messed up. Wait, Mark just messed up. People are messing it up and it's OK. They're just laughing it off.'"

Vanessa Lengies, an actor and singer who had appeared on the drama series *American Dreams*, made her debut in the third season alongside Larsen and McGinty. She played Sugar Motta, a sassy, spoiled high schooler with a wealthy father who owns a piano business.

Before Sugar joins New Directions, she becomes a part of a smaller all-girl singing group called the Troubletones, alongside Santana, Brittany, and Mercedes. There, Lengies got a front-row seat of the trio in action.

Whenever Amber Riley sang, Lengies felt like she should be paying to be there. On the days of her solo performances, cast and crew buzzed with excitement. "It was so fun to be there, at an Amber Riley concert," Lengies told me.

Riley, she added, was a "truth teller. Like she's no-bullshit, always said what she thinks, and would call things out." Lengies felt safe around her. Heather Morris was the best dancer Lengies had ever seen, and her comic timing was bar none. Naya Rivera put her heart and soul into Santana, Lengies said, and she was so funny and mesmerizing. "Her laugh, like, you would try so hard to get her to laugh because it was such a gift."

As the Troubletones performed onstage together, whipping through epic mash-ups like "Rumor Has It/Someone Like You," Lengies noticed that Rivera and Morris would make eye contact. When she was onstage, they'd catch her eye too. It wasn't in the stage directions . . . it was just something they did, creating a moment of connection. Lengies remembers how good it felt when those glances would come her way. She felt accepted.

In high school, Lengies didn't fit in with the cool kids. She felt anxious, in the closet, and was hiding who she really was. Her experience on *Glee* was the opposite. She felt like she could be whoever she wanted to be. A part of her teen self healed and became whole on the show. She ended up coming out as genderfluid afterward.

By the time Lengies arrived, the show had become a well-oiled machine. They would go from rehearsal to the studio, then back to dance practice, then to the set to film a choir scene. Lengies was thrown into the deep end—quite literally—in one of her early episodes, when she was part of an elaborate musical performance featuring New Directions in the swimming pool, doing a synchronized dance to Rihanna's "We Found Love." The group practiced the choreography in the rehearsal room, pretending they were in water, following along as they were instructed: "And now you splash the water, splash the water. Now spin around, spin around."

A bunch of the actors were drunk during the filming of that dance sequence, Lengies remembers, and she shared a floatie with Lea Michele. "That was the day I think I was having the most fun with Lea Michele that I've ever had with her. She and I were getting along really well that day . . . She was really warm and open and friendly." Lengies allowed for a pause. "In that moment."

Years after *Glee* ended, stories about Michele's bad behavior on-set came tumbling out. It all started when the actor tweeted about the murder of George

Floyd, a Black man who was killed by a police officer in Minneapolis. "George Floyd did not deserve this. This was not an isolated incident and it must end," Michele tweeted, alongside the hashtag #BlackLivesMatter.

Her former *Glee* costar, actor Samantha Marie Ware, who played Jane Hayward in Season 6, tweeted in response: "Remember when you made my first television gig a living hell?!?! Cause I'll never forget. I believe you told everyone that if you had the opportunity you would 's— in my wig!' amongst other traumatic microaggressions that made me question a career in Hollywood."

Everything blew up after that. People who had worked with Michele began opening up about her actions. Some of *Glee*'s stars spoke up about their own memories of working with Michele, like Heather Morris, who called her "unpleasant." "It was something that was very hush-hush on-set," Morris said during an episode of the "Everything Iconic with Danny Pellegrino" podcast. "We absolutely could have stepped up and gone to the Fox execs and said how we felt about the situation, but no one did."

Michele offered an apology on Instagram following Ware's tweet. "Whether it was my privileged position and perspective that caused me to be perceived as insensitive or inappropriate at times or whether it was just my immaturity and me just being unnecessarily difficult, I apologize for my behavior and for any pain which I have caused. We all can grow and change and I have definitely used these past several months to reflect [on] my own shortcomings."

Later, Ware gave an interview with *Variety*, where she detailed her experience with Michele. A longtime fan of the show, Ware had been so excited to get a role on *Glee* for its final season.

"I knew from day one when I attempted to introduce myself. There was nothing gradual about it. As soon as she decided that she didn't like me, it was very evident," Ware recalled. "It was after I did my first performance, that's when it started—the silent treatment, the stare-downs, the looks, the comments under her breath, the weird passive aggressiveness."

One day on-set, Ware was goofing around off-camera during a group auditorium scene. After shooting was done, Ware recalls Michele stopping in the middle of the stage and doing a "come here" gesture to her. Ware told *Variety* that Michele said, "You need to come here right now." When Ware refused, Michele allegedly threatened to call Ryan Murphy and get Ware fired. After that exchange, Ware had a conversation with Michele.

"When I tried to speak up for myself, she told me to shut my mouth. She said I don't deserve to have that job," Ware recalled. "She talked about how she has reign."

I asked Jess Meyer about the allegations when we spoke on the phone. "Listen, I absolutely experienced it," she said. "No one's lying about what Lea did or who Lea continues to be. She was like that before *Glee*, she'll be like that after *Glee*."

Lengies also witnessed a lot of what people reported and was on the receiving end of some of it as well. In her words: "This is what I tell people about Lea Michele: if she said that the wall was purple and you looked at the wall and saw that it wasn't, she'd say it again and you would look and it would be purple. She was so powerful in her conviction of things, which I think made her as that character so electric to watch."

Michele had a "shadow side" to her, Lengies said, and being on the negative end of someone with that much conviction was not pleasant. Maybe it came from a place of narcissism or unconscious insecurity—probably a mix of both, Lengies added.

"I want to come to her defense in a little way. She was being rewarded constantly for that behavior. She was encouraged and propped up and given kudos for the personality that later people admitted was hurtful and abusive."

Lengies didn't say it, but as I listened to her talk about the blurring between real life and *Glee* life, it sounded like Rachel Berry was a version of Lea Michele. Perhaps, by making Rachel's hurtful, diva-like behavior OK (and even sometimes charming!) on the show, it was making Michele's behavior OK, too.

"I feel a lot of the time the producers or creatives were pulling from people's personalities and turning the volume up on things that they already saw in people, and that was what made the characters so rich and so great," Lengies said. "[But] I think that looking back, there's some danger and some shadow to doing it that way."

For all *Glee*'s lessons of kindness and acceptance, there could be an ugly edge, particularly when it came to the dialogue, which readily poked fun at people's race, religion, or weight and voiced deeply specific criticisms of the actors' physical appearances. That uncomfortable malice has been a thread through Murphy's shows, and I was struck by a 2017 article by Alison Herman for *The Ringer* looking back on *Popular*, which pointed out some of the same sharpness in Murphy's early work.

"[The show's mean girl] Nicole is also an outlet for one of Murphy's more questionable instincts: writing belittlement a little *too* well, giving himself cover for truly nasty or reprehensible sentiments (racism, fatphobia) by putting them in the mouths of ostensible villains," Herman noted.

Sometimes it all got way too personal. In an interview for the podcast *Showmance*, Naya Rivera recalled being handed a whole monologue where her character brutally destroys every inch of Kurt, including his mouth, which she compares to a "cat's ass" and his smile, which she says looks like he had removed his top row of dentures. "It was so mean. It blurred the lines too much and I remember [Colfer] being upset about it, and me just having to do it over and over and over again," Rivera said. "I was like, 'I'm sorry. I didn't write it.'"

The show's third season would give New Directions their biggest victory yet. They win Nationals, and the moment happens in slow motion onstage, red and blue confetti flying through the air as we watch the glee club members embrace one another. They arrive back at school, trophy in hand, to a silent hallway, filled with rows of students staring at them. Two members of the hockey team approach, slushie cups in hands. As the members of New Directions squeeze their eyes shut in anticipation, confetti rains out of those cups and they realize, with delight, that for once, they've earned their classmates' favor. The song "Tongue Tied" plays. Tina and Mike kiss. Brittany and Santana kiss. A jock hugs a startled Kurt. It's the perfect happily-ever-after for the seniors of William McKinley High.

Finn says goodbye to Rachel when he drops her off at a train station in Lima, Ohio. They were supposed to get married, but he changes his mind, telling her that he's going to set her free. She needs to go to New York to try her luck at Broadway and he needs to follow in his dad's footsteps and join the army. That day, Falchuk told Baffa that they would need to capture both Michele and Monteith's reactions in real time.

It was an unusual request. "OK," Baffa responded. "Can I ask why?"

The response was that Monteith and Michele, who were dating in real life, were at a point in their relationship where things were a little bumpy and the producers were expecting the scene to be particularly charged between them. They wanted to get all that emotion on camera.

"Absolutely," Baffa agreed, strategically placing a camera in both car windows. It was a tight squeeze—if someone panned a quarter of an inch, they'd catch the other camera. Go back to rewatch that scene and you'll see the pain of those intimate shots. It's suffocating, as we're stuck in this cramped car with them, unable to look away when Rachel cries. It's heartbreak and pleading and stubbornness, capturing all the raw emotion in a breakup.

Maxwell was excited to venture into the college years. He loved the idea of Rachel going to New York to attend NYADA, which would allow the writers to craft their own version of *Fame*. There were the big challenges, too, like tearing apart some of the show's central relationships, instigating a wave of breakups, and navigating long-distance romances. And they needed to introduce some more characters to William McKinley High, including the shy, talented Marley, and bad-boy-turned-good, Jacob.

"It was just tricky to re-create the magic," Maxwell explained. They wanted to build characters who didn't feel like duplicates of their predecessors. How, for instance, do you make Marley, with her leading-role status, not remotely like Rachel Berry?

As soon as Season 3 ended, Hutman hopped on a plane and went on vacation to Mexico. He let Murphy's producing partner know where to reach him and, promptly after landing, they called. Hutman needed to cut his trip short to fly back to Los Angeles ASAP and build Kurt and Rachel's Brooklyn loft. Murphy told him the space would be in Bushwick, which hopefully might make it believable that the duo could afford such an expansive apartment. Fake bricks added texture to the walls, and Hutman made the loft look like it was chock-a-block full of thrift-store finds. In the end, he was pleased with the results, which looked like Kurt and Rachel had cobbled together their apartment in a "weird and tasteful way."

There was also the dance studio, where Rachel would meet Cassandra, a tough-talking instructor played by Kate Hudson, who pushes Rachel to her emotional limits. Hutman designed that space like a dance studio from a Degas painting, all streaming lights and big windows.

As the show found its footing in this strange new terrain, a mix of the college years, the high school years, adulthood, and adolescence, tragedy hit. In July 2013, the cast and crew of *Glee* lost their quarterback. Cory Monteith was discovered in his hotel room at Fairmont Pacific Rim in downtown Vancouver, dead from a drug overdose.

Three months later, New Directions said goodbye to Monteith—and to Finn Hudson—in an episode titled "The Quarterback." It opens onstage, each character dressed in black, belting out "Seasons of Love," with emotion that was all too real. They ended the song by turning together, as a group, and looking up at a projected image of Monteith, on the football field, wearing his McKinley High shirt. The music cuts out and the screen fades to black, with the *Glee* title card appearing, the *l* in the word replaced by a silhouette of Monteith, raising one arm in the air.

Murphy made the decision not to tell viewers how Finn, in the *Glee* universe, passed away. Kurt briefly mentions it at the beginning of the episode, saying, in voiceover, "Everyone wants to talk about how he died, too, but who cares? One moment in his whole life. I care more about how he lived."

At first, Maxwell found that choice an odd one. Maybe, he thought, it could have been a teachable moment of some kind? "Not to be crass and blur the lines between Monteith's real life and the character, obviously no one wanted to disrespect his family in real life, but considering that there was drugs involved it was sort of like, 'OK, do we say that maybe it was a binge drinking thing at college?'"

He was concerned the audience would flip out once they saw how that moment was written. In retrospect, Maxwell told me, it was actually a really powerful choice to make. He liked how Kurt's narrative told the audience everything they needed to know. "The episode was going to be how everyone feels about it," he said.

Filming that episode was nothing short of painful. Scenes had to be shot in one take because it was so difficult for the cast and crew to get through them.

Offscreen, a memorial was held for Monteith on the auditorium set. They sat in the audience as the cast got up and performed or talked about Monteith. People were breaking down. In that moment, Maxwell remembers, it really felt like they were a family.

"The truth is, Cory was Finn," he said. "He was just a good kid. He was a golden retriever of a person. He bounded with positive energy." In the early days, Maxwell added, when the kids were making the transition from relative obscurity to mega fame, Monteith was the leader they needed.

Much like with Naya Rivera, it's hard to fit in all the wonderful things people said about Cory Monteith. Lengies told me he reminded her of a big oak tree. He was gracious and wise. The two of them would get wrapped up in conversations about the planet and space and why we're all here. Elodie Keene, who directed the last episode of *Glee* that Monteith was in, remembers the actor as kind and talented. "I just loved him."

Monteith used to go over to Baffa between takes and ask questions about the camera. He was interested in directing and was so curious about the decisions that Baffa was making behind the scenes. "We're going to push into you," Baffa explained, letting the actor know that the camera would be coming close.

"What are you trying to get from that?" Monteith asked.

"We're trying to get in your character's head," Baffa said. "Imagine somebody who's stepping closer to be able to see more details in your face. That's kind of what the camera's doing."

"God, I miss him," Dot-Marie Jones told me. "We talked a lot about his childhood. He was a little hellion. I used to work juvenile probation before I started acting. So we would laugh about that, if, like, I had to be his PO probation officer when he was a minor."

Jones doesn't really like that cliché about someone lighting up a room but, she said, that's exactly what Monteith did. He'd come in with swagger and that smile and Jones just wanted to hug him.

She still thinks back to a scene she filmed alongside Mark Salling, while shooting "The Quarterback" episode. Coach Beiste and Puckerman are planting a tree in honor of Finn, just outside the football field. They have a plaque installed that reads "Finn Hudson 1994–2013," and Puckerman kneels down and puts his finger on the dash.

"You know what's tripping me out is this line between the years," he says. "It's his whole life. Everything that happened is in that line."

"What are you gonna do with your line now, Puckerman?" Coach Beiste asks.

That moment meant something to Jones. "I think about it often," she told me. "The line between the day you're born and the day you die. It's what you do with that line."

The moment feels even heavier now. Years later, in 2018, *Glee* lost another cast member: Salling died by suicide after being charged in a federal indictment for receiving and possessing child pornography. A search warrant discovered more than 50,000 images on his computer and thumb drive. Few cast members have addressed his death, facing an uncomfortable balance of mourning their friend and grappling with the painful conversation around his pedophilia.

But *Glee* found its way back after "The Quarterback" episode, returning to its usual optimistic self, all while keeping Finn's memory alive through song and references. Ratings had begun to dip for the onetime juggernaut of a show, with the last episode of the fifth season hitting a series low, falling to just 1.92 million viewers. Fans were tuning out and Murphy was finding himself pulling away from the halls of William McKinley. In 2011, he co-created the anthology series *American Horror Story*, alongside Falchuk, a dark show about killers, cults, and violent ghosts. It was a direct response to his time on *Glee*.

"I was like, 'I can't write any more nice speeches for these *Glee* kids about love and tolerance and togetherness. I'll kill myself," the showrunner said. "I'm going to write a show about anal sex and mass murders."

A sixth and final season was ordered, with a truncated thirteen episodes. Landmark moments mark that last hurrah, like Brittany and Santana getting married in a ceremony bursting with joyful songs and cheery, bright costumes in a rustic barn (it's where Brittany's mom, played by Jennifer Coolidge, gave birth). The New Directions kids decorate the space with string lights and gauzy material and, in inexplicable *Glee* fashion, Kurt and Blaine get married, impromptu, as well. That day, Lengies returned to set after a hiatus from the show and donned a fringed sunshine-yellow dress.

It kind of felt like they were there dancing and singing for Rivera and Morris, along with Brittany and Santana, that day. "The wonderful thing about it was that Naya and Heather had so much chemistry off-screen too," Lengies said. "You were celebrating two people that you loved together."

The last episode of *Glee* would take us five years into the future. Aptly titled "Dreams Come True," it's an unabashedly sunny and sentimental one. Sue Sylvester stands up on the stage and christens the Finn Hudson Auditorium. She used to think that the glee club was filled with a bunch of "cowardly losers" who went to the choir room to sing their troubles away. But not anymore.

"It takes a lot of bravery to look around at the world and see it not as it is but as it should be," Sue tells the group. "A world where the quarterback becomes best friends with the gay kid and the girl with the big nose ends up on Broadway. Glee is about finding a world like that and finding the courage to open up your heart and sing about it."

And so, in those very last moments, that's exactly what the *Glee* cast did. Almost all the generations of New Directions gathered to belt out the wonderfully bright OneRepublic song "I Lived," filled with a message of hope and tenacity. Emotions were high that day. There was grief in the room because of Monteith ("He should be here, dammit," Jones remembers thinking), and there was something else going on too. Here's how Lengies remembers it.

"I feel like so much wasn't being said and there was a lot of tension . . . coming into that last number, I was just like, 'It doesn't feel great in here.' I would love to say it was this wonderful *Glee* last moment, but it was so much more complicated than that."

It was a surreal experience for Samuel Larsen, who returned for the final number. He didn't feel like he quite fit into that moment. He wanted to give all those original cast members the space to celebrate, mourn, and feel all the feelings that came along with saying goodbye to a show that they built from the ground up.

"It was weird; I was part of the cast and part of the fan club," he said. "I wanted a picture with everyone in a different way than they wanted a picture with each other."

We say goodbye to New Directions just as they're singing the last notes of "I Lived." They gather on the risers together and tuck their heads down for one final bow, as the auditorium lights dim.

The ending shot of *Glee* brings us to a plaque hanging just outside. Under the words Finn Hudson Auditorium, there was that quote again: "See the world not as it is, but as it *should* be."

Glee got to be everything it wanted to be. For six years, it split network television wide open, releasing an array of colorful, messy, weird, ambitious content on a weekly basis. Behind it was an eager network, willing to stake its name and reputation on a show that was raging hard against the usual machine.

We got antiheroes for protagonists, marginalized characters turned into stars, and a potentially alienating genre—musical theatre—that reached a broad, committed audience. I never really got into *The Rocky Horror Picture Show* but *boy* did I rewatch *Glee*'s version of "Time Warp" a crazy number of times.

A teen show was finally allowed to be its whole self.

For so long, teen TV existed in a box. There was such a narrow idea of what a show could be, perhaps in no small part because there was a narrow idea of who audiences could be. For every painfully bleak moment on *Freaks and Geeks* that made one viewer shudder and turn off the TV, another viewer was sitting in a living room somewhere, feeling a little less alone in their own struggles with adolescent awkwardness, lack of kissing experience, and getting picked third to last during gym class (editorializing over here).

Greg Berlanti would fight hard for a split-second kiss between Jack and Ethan on *Dawson's Creek* so that boys who liked boys felt less alone, and maybe even saw a glimmer of hope in their future. Ed Zwick, Marshall Herskovitz, and Winnie Holzman duked it out to the bitter end on behalf of teen girls everywhere who needed a realistic depiction of their intimate lives—small, emotionally confusing moments and all. *Glee* received its share of eyebrow raising for trying so aggressively to check off as many boxes as possible, but still, for every underrepresented character who was given significant story lines, romantic relationships, and allowed to be just as complicated, relatable, and occasionally irksome as the rest of the New Directions . . . that was a victory.

Many of these shows elegantly and sneakily used the Trojan Horse concept to their advantage, inheriting a scrappy mentality of telling the stories they wanted to tell within the rigid confines of network television. *The Fresh Prince of Bel-Air* found moments of truth and reality sandwiched within a heavily polished, laugh-a-minute sitcom structure. *The O.C.* proved that a prettily packaged concept could also be hilarious, kooky, and dotted with realism. And as crazy as it might sound, let's put *Dawson's Creek* in that same category. The writers managed to turn a show about teens who spoke with a confusing amount of poetic eloquence into a mainstream hit. They diligently captured the intrigue and soapiness that teen TV had come to be associated with, all while holding tight to the pilot's pure and unabashed sense of romance and optimism.

Other shows, meanwhile, refused to even remotely conform. And for that, they're to be greatly admired too. Paul Feig and Judd Apatow's total refusal to give their characters stereotypical victories paved the way for other shows to do the same. I always think of the vein that runs directly between *Freaks and Geeks* and *The Office*, both of which were frequently helmed by Feig and Ken Kwapis. *The Office*, after some initial viewership struggle, was able to be fully appreciated in its time. Part of the show's magic was just what Feig was trying to do so many years before, creating small, realistic moments and sprinkling in bite-size victories, like the simple act of Jim's crush, Pam, resting her head on his shoulder or, after a particularly brutal breakup, a pretty waitress at Benihana laughing at Michael Scott's joke.

And *Friday Night Lights*, from start to finish, pounded that very same path. The whole cast, crew, and writers gleefully lit a fire to every television rulebook, determined to do anything for the sake of creating deeply true television. Artifice was never acceptable, and the show that wasn't *really* about football remains a shining example of TV that genuinely, and without effort, feels like an actual slice of life. Any arguments to the contrary, I direct you back to that New York City episode. I think it might help prove my point, and it's also just really, really great TV.

I didn't really know what to expect when I sat down to rewatch these shows. Most had been collecting dust in a time capsule in my brain. Would they still hold the same power? Would the kisses feel as thrilling and the drama as poignant? Much to my relief, they did. I still felt very intense feelings when Pacey tells Joey, "I remember everything." The final scene of the *Freaks and Geeks* pilot is just as moving now as it was then.

Still, I didn't quite appreciate the significance of revisiting all this nostalgia until a few months before I sat down to write this. My friend invited a group to her bachelorette-party weekend in Palm Springs. Not all of us had spent time together, and I was a little nervous about what the social dynamic might be. One late night, we settled into the living room, pajamas on, blankets and pillows strewn about, trying to figure out what to watch on TV. Someone suggested *The O.C.*, and it was a quick, unanimous yes. We switched on Hulu and were transported back to the well-worn world of Newport Beach, settling comfortably into the Cohen house. I watched, delighted, as the show became a uniting force. Everybody had opinions. Everybody sang the theme song. Everybody hated Oliver. In that moment (and several days after—we really tore through the first season), we were brought together by a piece of pop culture history that had defined our teen years. For a wonderful stretch of time, it felt like we were back to the best parts of high school, sitting in someone's parents' living room, deep in a sleeping bag, watching TV, and talking late into the night. The magic was alive and well.

REFERENCES

THE FRESH PRINCE OF BEL-AIR

Andrews-Dyer, Helena. "The Story Behind Will Smith's Iconic 'Hug' Scene in 'The Fresh Prince of Bel-Air.'" *Washington Post*, September 11, 2020. https://www.washingtonpost.com/arts-entertainment/2020/09/11/fresh-prince-bel-air-hug-father-scene/.

Betancourt, Bianca. "Karyn Parsons and Coco Jones on the Art of Being Hilary Banks." *Harper's Bazaar*, February 22, 2022. https://www.harpersbazaar.com/culture/film-tv/a39133303/karyn-parsons-coco-jones-hilary-banks-conversation/.

Bookman, Sandra. "Janet Hubert, Aunt Viv on 'Fresh Prince,' on Why She Left Show—and Will Smith's Apology." WABC, December 13, 2020. https://abc7ny.com/janet-hubert-will-smith-aunt-viv-original/8744089/.

Braxton, Greg. "Television's New Theme: L.A. Riots." *Los Angeles Times*, August 27, 1992. https://www.latimes.com/archives/la-xpm-1992-08-27-ca-6928-story.html.

Cerone, Daniel. "A Breath of Fresh Prince." *Los Angeles Times*, July 1, 1990. https://www.latimes.com/archives/la-xpm-1990-07-01-tv-1133-story.html.

Cramer, Maria, and Allyson Waller. "What the 'Fresh Prince' of the '90s Tells Us About Race Now." *New York Times*, November 17, 2020. https://www.nytimes.com/2020/11/17/arts/television/fresh-prince-reunion-hbo.html.

Gross, Terry. "'Orange' Creator Jenji Kohan: 'Piper Was My Trojan Horse.'" *Fresh Air*, August 13, 2013. https://www.npr.org/transcripts/211639989.

HBOMax. "*The Fresh Prince of Bel-Air* Reunion." November 2020.

Hume, Ashley. "Will Smith Sings and Dances with His Mother Caroline Bright as They Celebrate Her 85th Birthday: 'Let's Dance Our Way to 100.'" *Daily Mail*, January 17, 2022. https://www.dailymail.co.uk/tvshowbiz/article-10412507/Will.

James, Caryn. "Take Action and Blood; Sprinkle with Laughs." *New York Times*, April 7, 1995. https://www.nytimes.com/1995/04/07/movies/film-review-take-action-and-blood-sprinkle-with-laughs.html.

Kiefer, Halle. "Will Smith Unpacks Feud with Janet Hubert on Red Table Talk." *Vulture*, November 20, 2020. https://www.vulture.com/2020/11 /will-smith-unpacks-feud-with-janet-hubert-on-red-table-talk.html.

The Lazy Journalist. "1990–91 Ratings History," The TV Ratings Guide. http:// www.thetvratingsguide.com/1991/08/written-torn-between-cosbys -simpsons-by.html.

———. "1992–93 Ratings History," The TV Ratings Guide. http://www .thetvratingsguide.com/2020/03/1992-93-ratings-history.html?m=1.

Klady, Leonard. "Six Degrees of Separation." *Variety*, November 30, 1993. https://variety.com/1993/film/reviews/six-degrees-of -separation-3-1200435017/.

Maslin, Janet. "Review/Film: 'Six Degrees of Separation.'" *New York Times*, December 8, 1993. https://www.nytimes.com/1993/12/08/movies/review -film-six-degrees-separation-john-guare-s-six-degrees-art-life-stories.html.

Nanu, Maighna. "Now This Is a Story . . . How the Fresh Prince of Bel-Air Redefined the Nineties Sitcom." *Independent*, July 4, 2020. https://www .independent.co.uk/arts-entertainment/tv/features/fresh-prince-bel-air -anniversary-will-smith-karyn-parsons-hillary-banks-sitcom-a9599861 .html.

New York Film Academy. "New York Film Academy Guest Speakers: James Avery Biography." NYFA. https://www.nyfa.edu/nyfa-news/guest -speakers/james-avery/.

Nussbaum, Emily. "Jenji Kohan's Hot Provocations." *The New Yorker*, August 28, 2017. https://www.newyorker.com/magazine/2017/09/04/jenji-kohans- hot-provocations.

Penfold, Phil. "Joseph Marcell: From Fresh Prince of Bel-Air to a Yorkshire Stage." *Yorkshire Post*, March 13, 2020. https://www.yorkshirepost.co.uk/ whats-on/things-to-do/joseph-marcell-fresh-prince-bel-air-yorkshire -stage-2449400.

Randolph, Laura B. "The Real-Life Fresh Prince of Bel-Air." *Ebony*, April 1991. https://books.google.com/books?id=0MsDAAAAMBAJ&lpg =PA33&dq=Rozzell%20Sykes&pg=PA30#v=onepage&q=Rozzell%20 Sykes&f=false.

Respers France, Lisa. "James Avery, Star of 'The Fresh Prince of Bel-Air,' Dies at 68." CNN, January 1, 2014. https://www.cnn.com/2014/01/01/showbiz /celebrity-news-gossip/james-avery-obit.

Rimer, Sara. "Obscenity or Art? Trial on Rap Lyrics Opens." *New York Times*, October 17, 1990. https://www.nytimes.com/1990/10/17/us/obscenity-or -art-trial-on-rap-lyrics-opens.html.

Rohter, Larry. "'Fresh Prince of Bel Air' Puts Rap in Mainstream." *New York Times*, September 17, 1990. https://www.nytimes.com/1990/09/17/arts /fresh-prince-of-bel-air-puts-rap-in-mainstream.html.

Rossen, Jake. "Out of This World: An Oral History of ALF." *Mental Floss*, September 22, 2016. https://www.mentalfloss.com/article/86458/out -world-oral-history-alf.

Schladebeck, Jessica. "Will Smith's Father Willard Carroll Smith Sr. Dies." *Daily News*, November 8, 2016. https://web.archive.org/ web/20161215184305/http://www.nydailynews.com/entertainment/smith -father-willard-carroll-smith-sr-dies-article-1.2864074.

Smith, Will. "How I Became the Fresh Prince of Bel-Air." May 10, 2018. https://www.youtube.com/watch?v=y_WoOYybCro.

———. *Will* (New York: Penguin Random House, 2021).

THR Staff, "The Fresh Prince of Bel-Air Review" (Reprint), *The Hollywood Reporter*, September 25, 2014.

Tucker, Ken. "'The Fresh Prince of Bel-Air': EW Review," *Entertainment Weekly*, September 7, 1990. https://ew.com/article/1990/09/07/fresh -prince-bel-air-2/.

Vibe Staff. "Will Smith Celebrates 25th Anniversary of 'Bad Boys.'" *VIBE*, April 8, 2020. https://www.vibe.com/news/movies-tv/will-smith -celebrates-25th-anniversary-bad-boys-678981/.

VladTV. "Karyn Parsons on Auditioning for Hilary Banks Role on Fresh Prince of Bel-Air." November 20, 2020. https://www.youtube.com /watch?v=_Mdzqa63bJI.

Young, Danielle. "Janet Hubert Spills the Tea About That Infamous Pink-Leotard Dance Episode of *The Fresh Prince of Bel-Air*." *The Root*, May 1,

2018. https://www.theroot.com/janet-hubert-spills-the-tea-about-that
-infamous-pink-le-1825574938.

MY SO-CALLED LIFE

Braxton, Greg. "'My So-Called Life' Gets a Second Life on MTV." *Los Angeles Times*, April 3, 1995. https://www.latimes.com/archives/la-xpm-1995-04
-03-ca-50415-story.html.

Fitzpatrick, Molly. "A Matter of 'My-So Called Life' or Death." *MEL Magazine.*
https://melmagazine.com/en-us/story/a-matter-of-my-so-called-life-or
-death.

Goldstein, Jessica. "*My So-Called Life*'s Wilson Cruz on Rickie Fans, LBGT
Awareness, and '90s Fashion." *Vulture*, September 5, 2014. https://www
.vulture.com/2014/09/wilson-cruz-my-so-called-life-1994-1995.html.

Mann, Judy. "A TV Show Worth Saving." *Washington Post*, January 13, 1995.
https://www.washingtonpost.com/archive/local/1995/01/13/a-tv-show
-worth-saving/8128fea7-e77a-4c24-b9e3-63dbc73e0ece/.

Taylor, Jonathan. "My So-Called Life." *Variety*, August 23, 1994. https://
variety.com/1994/tv/reviews/my-so-called-life-1200438164/.

Watkins, Gwynne. "The Agony and the Angst: An Oral History of 'My So-
Called Life.'" *Elle*, November 16, 2016. https://www.elle.com/culture
/movies-tv/a40594/my-so-called-life-cast-interviews/.

Weber, Bruce. "The So-Called World of an Adolescent Girl, As Interpreted by
One." *New York Times*, August 25, 1994. https://www.nytimes
.com/1994/08/25/arts/television-review-so-called-world-adolescent-girl
-interpreted-one.html.

Zoller Seitz, Matt. "Why 'Euphoria' Feels So Real, Even When It Isn't
Realistic." *Vulture*, August 14, 2019. https://www.vulture.com/2019/08
/euphoria-sam-levinson-filmmaking-influences.html.

DAWSON'S CREEK

ABC News. "GLAAD Heralds Dawson's Kiss." ABC News, April 30, 2001.
https://abcnews.go.com/Entertainment/story?id=105904&page=1.

Artavia, David. "Greg Berlanti Shares the Backstory of 'Dawson's Creek' Gay Storyline." *Advocate*, June 22, 2020. https://www.advocate.com/television/2020/6/22/greg-berlanti-shares-backstory-behind-dawsons-creek-gay-kiss.

Daniels, Susanne, and Cynthia Littlejohn. *Season Finale: The Unexpected Rise and Fall of the WB and UPN* (New York: HarperCollins, 2007).

James, Caryn. "Young, Handsome and Clueless in Peyton Place." *New York Times*, January 20, 1998. https://www.nytimes.com/1998/01/20/arts/television-review-young-handsome-and-clueless-in-peyton-place.html.

Rice, Lynette. "How the WB Broke New Ground by Promoting *Dawson's Creek* in Movie Theaters." *Entertainment Weekly*, March 31, 2018. https://ew.com/tv/2018/03/31/the-wb-dawsons-creek-movie-theater-promotion/.

Richmond, Ray. "Dawson's Creek." *Variety*, January 19, 1998. https://variety.com/1998/tv/reviews/dawson-s-creek-2-1117436782/.

Stack, Tim. "*Dawson's Creek* Cast Reunites for Its 20th Anniversary on This Week's EW Cover." *Entertainment Weekly*, March 28, 2018. https://ew.com/tv/2018/03/28/dawsons-creek-reunion-ew-cover/.

FREAKS AND GEEKS

Archival author interview with Allison Jones, 2018.

Hodge, Brent (director). "Freaks and Geeks: The Documentary." *Cultureshock*, Season 1, Episode 4, original air date July 16, 2018.

Jacobs, A. J. "*Freaks and Geeks*: Unhappy Days." *Entertainment Weekly*, September 10, 1999. https://ew.com/article/1999/09/10/freaks-and-geeks-unhappy-days/.

Kaufman, Amy, and Daniel Miller. "Five Women Accuse Actor James Franco of Inappropriate or Sexually Exploitative Behavior." *Los Angeles Times*, January 11, 2018. https://www.latimes.com/business/hollywood/la-fi-ct-james-franco-allegations-20180111-htmlstory.html.

Lloyd, Robert. "2 Good 2 Be 4Gotten: An Oral History of *Freaks and Geeks*." *Vanity Fair*, December 6, 2012. https://www.vanityfair.com/hollywood/2013/01/freaks-and-geeks-oral-history.

Philipps, Busy. *This Will Only Hurt a Little* (New York: Gallery Books, 2018).

Richmond, Ray. "Freaks and Geeks." *Variety*, September 20, 1999. https://variety.com/1999/film/reviews/freaks-and-geeks-2-1200459037/.

Schmuckler, Eric. "Low Times at McKinley High." *New York Times*, January 9, 2000, https://www.nytimes.com/2000/01/09/arts/television-radio-low-times-at-mckinley-high.html.

THE O.C.

All Things the OC with McG (podcast). "Welcome to the O.C., Bitches!" August 31, 2021. No longer available online.

Baila, Morgan. "Olivia Wilde Almost Played Marissa on *The O.C.* (& 8 More Trivia Tidbits)." Refinery29, June 13, 2016. https://www.refinery29.com/en-us/2016/06/113730/the-oc-creator-josh-schwartz-secrets.

Barton, Mischa. "The Grim Truth About Growing Up in the Public Eye." *Harper's Bazaar*, June 11, 2021. https://www.harpersbazaar.com/uk/culture/a36660824/mischa-barton-harassment-the-oc-comment/.

Bricker, Tierney. "Mischa Barton Is Finally Ready to Tell the Real Story Behind Her Exit from *The O.C.*" *E! News*, May 18, 2021. https://www.eonline.com/news/1270301/mischa-barton-is-finally-ready-to-tell-the-real-story-behind-her-exit-from-the-o-c.

de Moraes, Lisa. "The Beautiful People of O.C. Deliver Some Ugly Numbers." *Washington Post,* August 7, 2003. https://www.washingtonpost.com/archive/lifestyle/2003/08/07/the-beautiful-people-of-oc-deliver-some-ugly-numbers/59185479-ed4f-4cc6-8e15-8d9495665eb4/.

Etkin, Jaimie. "'The O.C.' 10th Anniversary: Creator Josh Schwartz on Mistakes, Mischa Barton's Exit, Chrismukkah & More." *Huffington Post*, August 5, 2013. https://huffpost.netblogpro.com/entry/the-oc-10th-anniversary-josh-schwartz_n_3705457.

Fox News. "'The O.C.' Cancelled Due to Poor Ratings." January 13, 2015. https://www.foxnews.com/story/the-o-c-cancelled-due-to-poor-ratings.

Freeman, Hadley. "The Making of a Golden Boy." *Guardian*, January 22, 2005. https://www.theguardian.com/media/2005/jan/22/broadcasting.fashion.

Gopalan, Nisha. "Josh Schwartz on *The O.C.*, Casting George Lucas, and the Onslaught of Emo." *Vulture*, August 5, 2013. https://www.vulture .com/2013/08/josh-schwartz-the-oc-anniversary-interview.html.

Highfill, Samantha. "Secrets of *The O.C.* Pilot, Straight from the Creator." *Entertainment Weekly*, August 5, 2018. https://ew.com/tv/the-o-c-creator -looks-back-at-the-pilot-15-years-later/?slide=5974755#5974755.

Marsh, Ann. "Gallagher's Golden Moments." *Tufts Magazine*, 2005. https:// news.tufts.edu/magazine/fall2005/features/cover.html.

Posner, Ari. "No Experience Required." *New York Times*, March 21, 2004. https://www.nytimes.com/2004/03/21/arts/no-experience-required.html.

Ryan, Suzanne C. "OCcupational Hazard." *Boston Globe*, October 29, 2006. http://archive.boston.com/news/globe/living/articles/2006/10/29 /occupational_hazard/.

Sepinwall, Alan. "'The O.C.,' 10 Years Later: Josh Schwartz Looks Back." Uproxx, February 22, 2017. https://uproxx.com/sepinwall/the-oc-10-years -later-josh-schwartz-looks-back-part-1/.

Shales, Tom. "'The O.C.': Land of the Brooding Teen." *Washington Post*, August 5, 2003. https://www.washingtonpost.com/archive/lifestyle/2003/08/05 /the-oc-land-of-the-brooding-teen/c7c18c5c-b01c-4d76-9d6d-b808d133ae6c/.

FRIDAY NIGHT LIGHTS

Bellafante, Ginia. "Abortion in the Eyes of a Girl from Dillon." *New York Times*, July 9, 2010. https://www.nytimes.com/2010/07/10/arts /television/10lights.html.

Gold, Jon. "Michael B. Jordan Talks Shop." ESPN, February 8, 2012. http:// www.espn.com/espn/page2/story/_/id/7537758/michael-b-jordan -discusses-friday-night-lights-wire-chronicle-career-page-2.

Heffernan, Virginia. "On the Field and Off, Losing Isn't an Option." *New York Times*, October 3, 2006. https://www.nytimes.com/2006/10/03/arts /television/03heff.html.

Mays, Robert. "Clear Eyes, Full Hearts, Couldn't Lose." *Grantland*, July 28, 2011. https://grantland.com/features/clear-eyes-full-hearts-lose/.

Tucker, Ken. "It's Fourth and Long for 'Friday Night Lights.'" *Entertainment Weekly*, January 23, 2007. https://ew.com/article/2007/01/23/its-fourth -and-long-friday-night-lights/.

GLEE

Albiniak, Paige. "Can't Stop the Music." *New York Post*, September 20, 2009. https://nypost.com/2009/09/20/cant-stop-the-music/.

BBC. "Cory Monteith: Glee Star Died from Alcohol and Heroin." July 17, 2013. https://www.bbc.com/news/world-us-canada-23338486.

Carlson, Erin. "Fox 'Glee'-ful about New Series." Associated Press, May 10, 2009. https://www.berkshireeagle.com/news/local/fox-glee-ful-about -new-series/article_f0250c03-f1a6-56ba-abc2-13cdb5d9133e.html.

CBC Arts. "Glee's Song and Dance All New for Cory Monteith." November 18, 2009. https://www.cbc.ca/news/entertainment/glee-s-song-and-dance-all -new-for-cory-monteith-1.783848.

Chitwood, Adam. "Tuesday TV Ratings." *Collider*, May 14, 2014. https:// collider.com/tv-ratings-agents-of-shield-glee/.

Ferguson, LaToya. "Before *Glee*, Ryan Murphy Perfected the Teen Dramedy with *Popular*." *The A.V. Club*, January 17, 2017. https://www.avclub.com /before-glee-ryan-murphy-perfected-the-teen-dramedy-wit-1798256351.

Finke, Nikki. "EMMYS Q&A: Ryan Murphy About 'Glee.'" *Deadline*, August 5, 2011. https://deadline.com/2011/08/emmys-qa-with-ryan-murphy-about -glee-153242/.

Herman, Allison. "How 'Popular' Predicted 'Feud'—and the Rest of Ryan Murphy's Career." *The Ringer*, March 3, 2017. https://www.theringer .com/2017/3/3/16044634/how-a-little-known-high-school-show-explains -ryan-murphy-43f7a02a595a.

Koblin, John. "Ryan Murphy Heads to Netflix in Deal Said to Be Worth Up to $300 Million." *New York Times*, February 13, 2018. https://www.nytimes .com/2018/02/13/business/media/netflix-ryan-murphy.html.

Moore, Matt. "Ryan Murphy Reveals That His Father Beat Him 'Bloody with a Belt' When He Came Out." *Gay Times*. https://www.gaytimes.co.uk /culture/ryan-murphy-reveals-father-beat-bloody-belt-came/.

Nussbaum, Emily. "How Ryan Murphy Became the Most Powerful Man in TV." *The New Yorker*, May 7, 2018. https://www.newyorker.com /magazine/2018/05/14/how-ryan-murphy-became-the-most-powerful -man-in-tv.

Pellegrino, Danny. "RHONY Ratzville Recap + Heather Morris." *Everything Iconic with Danny Pellegrino* [podcast], May 26, 2021.

Rivera, Naya. "Love Letter to the LGBTQ Community." *Billboard*, June 1, 2017. https://www.billboard.com/culture/pride/naya-rivera-gay-pride-month -love-letter-7809682/.

Roberts, Julia. "Ryan Murphy." *Interview Magazine*, January 7, 2012. https:// www.interviewmagazine.com/culture/ryan-murphy.

Rocha, Polly Anna. "I Was a Queer, Trans Latina Growing Up in Texas. Santana Lopez Gave Me Hope." *them*, July 17, 2020. https://www.them.us /story/naya-rivera-santana-lopez-essay.

St. James, Emily. "Ian Brennan, Co-Creator of *Glee*." *The A.V. Club*, February 4, 2011. https://www.avclub.com/ian-brennan-co-creator-of -glee-1798223997.

"*Glee*: Casting Sessions." *Glee* Season 1, Blu-Ray DVD, Release Date September 14, 2010.

Steller, Brian. "A Long Wait Stirs Enthusiasm for Fox Show 'Glee.'" *New York Times*, September 1, 2009. https://www.nytimes.com/2009/09/02 /business/media/02adco.html.

Stone, Natalie. "Naya Rivera 'Mustered Enough Energy' to Get Son on Boat but 'Not Enough to Save Herself': Police." *People*, July 13, 2020. https:// people.com/tv/naya-rivera-mustered-enough-energy-to-get-son-on-boat -but-not-enough-to-save-herself-sheriff/.

Ushkowitz, Jenna, and Kevin McHale, "Showmance or No-mance: Glee Edition." *Showmance* [podcast], June 7, 2019.

Wagmeister, Elizabeth. "'Glee' Actor Samantha Ware on Why She Called Out Lea Michele." *Variety*, June 11, 2020. https://variety.com/2020 /tv/news/samantha-ware-glee-lea-michele-interview-black-actress -hollywood-1234631015/.

West, Kelly. "*Glee Live in Concert* Tickets Go on Sale This Friday."
Cinemablend, March 1, 2010. https://www.cinemablend.com/television
/Glee-Live-Concert-Tickets-Go-Sale-Friday-23190.html.

ACKNOWLEDGMENTS

L inda Konner, my agent, took a chance on my proposal and went about selling it with such a commitment, a can-do attitude, and an incredible eye on the prize. I'm so grateful to have her as my agent and equally grateful for her friendship, which has been a warm, enduring fixture in my life.

Shannon Kelly was an absolute joy to work with. She was such a thoughtful, accessible, smart editor. It was a real pleasure getting to do this with her. Thank you for encouraging me to find my own voice.

Thank you so much to the Running Press team for believing in this idea. Jess Riordan and Kara Thornton, I was incredibly excited about the prospect of working with you both from that very first Zoom meeting when we dove headfirst into *Gilmore Girls* and Chad Michael Murray.

So many people took the time to speak to me for this book. They so kindly and gamely walked down memory lane, riffled through their archives to find mementos, generously opened up their rolodexes, patiently answered obscure questions, and took the time to rewatch their episodes just so they could offer even more helpful insights. I appreciate each of them so much.

Thank you to: Andy Borowitz, Susan Borowitz, David Steven Simon, Shelley Jensen, David Pitlik, Ed Zwick, Marshall Herskovitz, Winnie Holzman, Scott Winant, Devon Gummersall, Devon Odessa, Charlie Lieberman, Patrick Norris, Jason Katims, Elodie Keene, Senta Moses, Paul Stupin, Marcia Shulman, Alan Hook, Garth Ancier, David Semel, Kerr Smith, Dylan O'Neal, Tom Kapinos, Gina Fattore, Maggie Friedman, Mark Matkevich, Rina Mimoun, Paul Feig, Samm Levine, Becky Ann Baker, Joe Flaherty, Natasha Melnick, Jefferson Sage, Debra McGuire, Jeff Judah, Gabe Sachs, Patty Lin, Bob Nickman, J. Elvis Weinstein, Ken Kwapis, Steve Bannos, Sarah Hagan, Josh Schwartz, Stephanie Savage, Patrick Rush, Tate Donovan, Loucas George, Norman Buckley, Sanford Bookstaver, J. J. Philbin, Lev L. Spiro, Michael Cassidy, Michael Lange, Linda Lowy, Gaius Charles, David Boyd, Todd McMullen, Allison Liddi-Brown, Jeffrey Reiner, John Zinman, Louanne Stephens, David Hudgins, Matt Lauria, Dora Madison, Robert J. Ulrich, Mark Hutman, Chris Baffa, Andrew Glover, Jessalyn Gilsig, Lou Eyrich,

ACKNOWLEDGMENTS

Dot-Marie Jones, Ross Maxwell, Jess Meyer, Russel Friend, Ali Adler, Samuel Larsen, Damian McGinty, Vanessa Lengies, and Patrick Gallagher.

I want to give an extra-big thanks to Paul Feig, Tom Kapinos, Gina Fattore, Ken Kwapis, and Paul Stupin, who have taken the time to speak to me multiple times over the years. I've loved hearing your stories. Ross Maxwell, Tate Donovan, Samm Levine, Marshall Herskovitz, Elizabeth Olsen, Brenna Kouf, and Ed Zwick were so kind to reach out to friends and colleagues on my behalf.

Michael Filardo, thank you so much for hopping on the phone and talking to me about all things *Glee*. Alex, thank you for sharing your Marissa death episode experience, for being such an amazing friend, and for your enduring love of Seth Cohen.

Carrie, I'm so grateful for your kindness, helpfulness, and getting to talk "Sabrina" with you.

I really cannot express my appreciation enough to Veronica Baker, who was so incredibly kind and generous with her time and energy. You were completely invaluable to this project and I'm so grateful. Julia was the transcriber for much of the book and she was always super efficient, fun to work with, and made life over this past year much easier. To the many friends who have been so wonderful and supportive throughout all this: Lillie, Cara, Violet, Polly, Em, Madeline, Molly, Caleigh, Sofije, Olivia, Abigail, Britta, Jessica, and Amy.

Rebecca, you once drove us roughly twelve hours to get to Wilmington, North Carolina, so we could eat at Pacey's restaurant—forever grateful for the Capeside trip that will live in infamy, your friendship, and for doing very eccentric things with me. Rima, my eternal roommate, I pitched this book to you in our living room and you were so wonderfully supportive, thoughtful, and filled with great ideas, as you always are. Emily, thank you for being the best reader I could ever ask for, all while tucked in your Paris bed. Ben, you've made this year so very special. I love you, the Coach T of my heart.

I came to Jennifer Armstrong with the early stages of this idea and she helped shape it with such clarity and guidance. She also happens to be one of my favorite writers, so that's an added joy. I'm so appreciative to the ITA crew, Erin Carlson, Saul Austerliz, and Kirthana Ramisetti, who have been there for every panicked email, offering guidance, comfort, and support.